OPERA

OPERA

Edited by Rudolf Hartmann

Translated by Arnold J. Pomerans

William Morrow & Company, Inc. New York 1977

Library of Congress Catalog Card Number: 77-303

ISBN 0-688-03212-5.

Contents

Introduction

Rudolf Hartmann

When Wolfgang Haefeli and Franz Stadelmann first suggested opera production and stage design as the subject for a book, they launched this present volume on its way to publication.

As they themselves have explained, personal impressions gathered at Salzburg and the illustrated brochure *50 Jahre Salzburger Festspiele,* published by the Salzburg Festival Committee, persuaded them of the need for a book absent from the otherwise comprehensive mass of literature devoted to the theatre. There are numerous works on stage designing, most of them autobiographical accounts by designers themselves; there are notes by prominent opera producers on their preparation and presentation of specific operas, but the collaboration of the two, the actual fusion of their ideas, has never been the subject of a special publication.

It redounds greatly to the credit of the two initiators of this book that they have helped to remedy a deficiency that has been troubling specialists no less than interested laymen for a very long time.

When the curtain rises in an opera-house, the audience confronts a finished product, the result of months of preparation, including heart-searching questions about the best approach and laborious efforts to achieve the required effects, the quest, the striving and the discovery, and growing involvement in the opera itself.

How is an operatic stage conception born? This question is often put by those opera lovers who do not attend just to listen to the music but who also want to absorb the full spectacle in the greatest possible harmony. They cannot help but wonder about something that remains concealed from them behind the curtain.

More precisely, they wonder about a rebirth, the quickening of an established work entrusted to the re-creative genius of a stage interpreter. By 'entrusted' I mean that the guidelines drawn up by the actual creators of the opera—the composer and the librettist—cannot be altered at will, let alone ignored. I mentioned the composer first, since operas, of course, revolve about their music. Music is the immutable foundation on which all opera productions have to take their stand. The libretto, generally written by another, provides the composer with a spur to endow his melodic inspirations with precise meaning. This is true, at least, of the libretto and the music of the older operas, but does not apply to Wagner's music drama, and his passionate insistence on 'total art'. Wagner wrote his own libretti, making words resonate and writing tone poems to achieve unprecedented concentration and intensity on the opera stage. The 'new' school made its triumphant entry, and its radiance has remained undimmed to this day.

Wagner's great ideal, convincingly re-echoed amongst others by Richard Strauss, Hugo von Hofmannsthal and Hans Pfitzner, made the highest scenic demands and hence raised the greatest expectations. And, indeed, stage designers and producers working in close collaboration have heeded the call, infusing scenography with new life, and turning it into a new art form.

While little has changed in the performance of the purely musical part of opera since its first emergence—conductor, orchestra and singers have always had precisely defined tasks—the theatrical side has had to cope with a flood of new challenges. They have set the

producer and his principal collaborator, the stage designer, a host of fresh problems, and will continue to do so in response to a continuous flux of fashion and style.

In much the same way as the conductor is responsible for the musical interpretation, the producer bears general responsibility for everything that happens on stage, for the actors no less than for their surroundings—that is, for all the visible elements. It is as true that he needs a large number of assistants as it goes without saying that the conductor must be able to call on a representative orchestra under a competent leader or concertmaster. The 'instruments' of the complicated stage apparatus are the various studios, the technical machinery, the lighting equipment and so on, all needing expert direction and artistic leadership. This is the task of the stage designer, and seen in this light he is a 'scenic concertmaster', a position of paramount importance and one whose creative scope is the greater the earlier and closer his contacts with the producer. The producer develops an original idea, expresses wishes, looks for the best way of realizing his conceptions and in the exchange of views with his scenographic partner discovers new paths that are often remote from his original itinerary. Nothing less than a marriage of the two arts is demanded of both participants, and it is natural that differences in temperament will cause the occasional storm in the ebb and flow of ideas before a mature understanding is reached. All that matters is that the final result is homogeneous, that no trace of destructive duality is allowed to spoil the common effort.

To portray the co-operation of two artistic personalities is an important object of this book. Following the basic plan suggested by Wolfgang Haefeli and Franz Stadelmann, it begins with a historical section devoted to the origins and development of what we generally lump together under the title of 'stage design'. The account leads from the 'dancing floor' of the Greeks to the contemporary stage; the baroque theatre with its master designers (the forerunners of such famous nineteenth-century theatrical families as the Quaglios, Janks, and Brückners) is discussed and so are the beginnings of modern stage design (Gordon Craig, Adolphe Appia *et al.*) and the new and independent profession to which it eventually gave rise.

The next section is devoted to a detailed examination of the work of stage designers. It follows them through workshops and studios, from mock-ups to the final sets, and also looks at traditional and modern aids, and especially at the latest lighting and projection techniques.

Closely connected is the discussion of 'opera production'. It starts with the producer's original 'commission' to the stage designer, and also examines the crucial link between the performance and the vital element of the opera, its music. Here we meet the conductor in his capacity of musical 'guardian' and examine his relationship to the producer, who must send out sensitive feelers in two directions—the musical and the scenographic—an aspect of his work that is not always as simple as it might be.

The presence of this triad of 're-creators' is not always thought the ideal answer. Combining the roles of producer and stage designer may prove a happier solution—provided there is enough talent—and this has, in fact, been attempted. Unfortunately, the combination of the two functions has a number of disadvantages. To begin with, the daily round becomes an unbearable burden and the supervision of so many detailed tasks encourages excessive delegation to assistants, and hence leads to less direct personal involvement in the work. Moreover, and this is a crucial factor, there are no fruitful discussions with a fellow artist and hence no spur for critical self-examination. In short, the combination of the roles of producer and stage designer cannot be recommended as a rule, though it may prove beneficial in individual cases.

Much the same is true of the producing conductor. What leads him to adopt this double role is often dismay that a rank 'outsider' with no feeling for the music should have the effrontery to produce an opera, and sometimes an exaggerated view of his own powers. The interpretation of great music demands complete concentration on the conductor's part, and the presentation of an opera cannot possibly be enhanced when the leading musician beats time with his right hand while using his left to prompt the actors. Something must surely give when that happens.

The structure of the book is such that it also allows prominent producers and stage designers to present their own views of various productions in which they have collaborated. Their different approaches to specific operas are extremely instructive, and the text is graphically amplified by specially selected illustrations.

The carefully chosen operas include, apart from usual repertory works, two of Richard Wagner's controversial contributions, currently in the limelight.

Each of the operas discussed has a special introduction reflecting the editor's fifty-odd years' experience as a producer. These introductions give his personal views, a point that should be remembered if some of them may seem to clash with the detailed accounts that follow. They were, however, specifically intended to satisfy the main objective of this book: to allow the reader to form his own opinions, to help the opera-going public to recover a healthy attitude to modern stage presentations lest they betray a lack of critical acumen by their thoughtless approbation of cheap and ephemeral sensations.

For at the beginning is the work. The inescapable task of the interpreter must be to serve it, to make use of every real step forward that presents itself in order to enhance it. Self-serving productions and cheap publicity stunts must be shunned, both because they come dangerously close to unscrupulous attempts to take in a gullible public, and above all because they are bound to confuse the young who have nothing with which to compare their first impressions.

If this book should help opera lovers to arrive at valid judgements of their own, and also provoke further self-examination among the professionals, then it will have fulfilled its purpose.

Stage Design in the History of the European Theatre

Heinz Bruno Gallée

An Approach

In the cycle of our lives, imitation is as powerful a drive as hunger and love. It presides over the enrichment and dissemination of culture. Imitation is an art from which few mortals can escape; its liberating rhythms make acting an inexhaustible source of life, and together with the imagination the mainspring of all creative activity. Thanks to it the theatre, with all its offshoots, flourishes, and illusion and fantasy have room to grow. It is to the stage that the Aristotelian call for the unity of place, time and action seems to apply with particular force, to the set, that abstract simile of the world in which the action takes place. Scenic art is art for the moment, something by which nature must be interpreted, not imitated. Scenic space should be 'felt' rather than 'filled'. Here, on the 'play islands of fantasy' (Sellner), the stylized, elemental and symbolic become transformed into dramatic reality and spiritual enchantment. This effect cannot be achieved with a doctrinaire approach. Its charm lies in variety, and it is subject to the same laws as also govern the unfolding of man's highest creative powers and constitute the ground of his spontaneity.

When examining the development of scenic art we must look at aesthetic as well as historical forms. Here we shall try to treat them in unison. History can be a rather uncertain business, and theatrical history is probably the most uncertain of all. True, fairly accurate texts have come down to us, and we also know something about the architecture of the theatres in which they were staged, but what of the scenery, the costumes and the stage properties? All were designed for the day, and hence quickly forgotten.

Great demands have always been made on stage design—the term is misleading and should perhaps be replaced by 'space design'. To form a fitting complement to the poetry and music, the set should not be a mere frame or background for the play, neither an architectural skeleton, a life-like environment nor abstract symbolic space. Rather it must translate the direct impact of the poetry and music into a space-framed, pictorial language that carries the spectator along, not least by providing him with clues and by inviting his direct participation. This involves the visual presentation of traditional ways of thinking and looking. For the image came before the word.

It has always been a question of taste where to draw the line between clarity and over-precision. Take the choice of symbols, for instance. From the menhir to the phallus, it has undergone many changes over the centuries. The more conscientious the choice, the sooner the magic begins to cast its spell.

While some have relied on historical accuracy others have employed artefacts or abstract forms. But at all times the harmonious fusion of the elements has served to establish a symbolic representation of the world in which the action was set.

Like all human activities, even revolutions draw their sap from the roots of tradition. That is why, in retracing the history of stage design, it would be idle to turn one's back on the past and consider the future alone. Those who think they can ignore the past are suffering from a dangerous delusion. The future brings us nothing; what we must do is to assimilate the treasures we have inherited, the better to transform them with our creative spirit. The vague realms of the future overlap, and the past must endow them with form. This is especially true of the theatre, and of the scenic world in particular.

Play-Space and Space-Play

The space in which the dramatic action is set is comparable to a magnetic field of force. Where its lines intersect lie the actions of men whose path is marked with figurative signs. Basically, it suffices to fix distances and to introduce a few elements against which the actors can be set off. Wherever elementary distances are spanned, space is created. These distances are made manifest by actions in the fixed points, by words, sounds and movements. All of them delimit the intellectual space that writer and composer have striven to create.

Scenery only becomes stylistic space-art when its structural elements are used to establish an arena that is not a copy of real space but, with the help of a few aids or stylistic characters, provides pointers to place, time and action.

Empty stages of 'lurking stillness' can only be filled by human movements and corporeality. Slight indications, lines, surfaces and signs close the tensional arc. Between markings (Heidegger called them *Orte,* places) differentiated space can emerge.

Each space and its boundaries are swept by the spectator's eye in search of directions and perspectives. The eye looks for symmetrical and asymmetrical accents and tries to link them with man and human actions as the measure of all things. As a result, the scene is transformed into living space, whose attributes must be harmonized, and hence re-created, time and again during the performance.

The upright vertical of the moving figure stands out automatically from the horizontal plane of the stage. Fixed optical points of the choreogram define the scene—it is of secondary importance whether the space mantle is historical or abstract. The modern isolation of the players from the spectators, cloistered in their boxes or seats in the circle, tends to break the spatial unity and has been doing so for close to three hundred years.

It was the emergence of the baroque stage that first afforded man a glimpse into the visionary depths of simulated space. Painted infinity helped to transform dreams into space. Thanks to the often confusing possibilities provided by the machine theatre and, since the nineteenth century, by lighting and other new stage techniques it has even become feasible to represent cosmic space. Man's longing for infinity tempts him to try to re-create the wide open spaces of the Greeks in the solid structure of the modern theatre. The successful fusion of the two—illusion and cosmic reality—has never been achieved, despite countless attempts in our own century, except, perhaps, on the arena stage.

Max Reinhardt in particular endeavoured to point the theatre back to its origins by projecting the stage into the arena, into the midst of the spectators. According to him it is playground, dance floor, space for crowd scenes and for pageants all rolled into one. This approach helped to restore the freedom of symbolic space—to resurrect the play island over which figures have moved ever since the days of the *mimos*. And this very freedom has always been reflected in the spatial unity of stage and auditorium as we know it from the great pinnacles of dramatic art: the ritual plays of the Greeks, the mediaeval mystery plays and the Shakespearean stage.

Man has always been fascinated and disturbed by the perplexing and obscure phenomenon of space, which, though it can be confined, is essentially boundless and intangible. A similar relationship exists between fantasy and reality, between conceptual (mental) and perceptual (visual) images.

Man is capable of assimilating space with his senses: he can see it, hear it, smell it, touch it, and move through it. This enables him to compare real space (life-space and constructed space) with apparent space (illusional or magical space) and to distinguish its manifold forms, e.g. central space (the dome), processional space (the aisle of the basilica), static space, dynamically flowing space, light space and colour space, and finally energetic space, the dimension of space and time.

All this may sound highly theoretical, but it has to be said if only to trace the experience of theatrical space back to its origins, the better to elucidate its subsequent development.

'As long as we live we are moving in space', said the great stage designer, Caspar Neher. We are placed into a small space—a crib—as soon as we are born, and into an equally narrow space when we die. Between the spaces of life's beginning and its end the fantastic and near boundless space of the theatre can become a decisive experience.

The Magic of the Circle as the Origin of the Stage

Long before the *skene* there was the *kyklos,* the circle. In it man's primordial urge to objectify magical and religious experience in play could be given free rein. What few indications have come down to us suggest that this space was an emblem of the supersensory, the transcendent and the numinous. The circle was held to be sacred and divine and to be the basis of all human movements. Within the circle it was possible to give symbolic expression to a heightened sense of vitality. In ritual, man had his first experience of a united community surrounding and closing the scene in the form of a chorus. Here rhythmically repeated words and phrases, reflecting inner tensions, gave rise to external movements; here hunts, battles and victories were celebrated or re-enacted with ecstatic fervour;

here the favours of mysterious nature demons could be invoked, or shared funeral and other rites give visual expression to the meaning of life.

The mystery cults of classical antiquity have something in common with the ritual dances of primitive races: in both cases an anointed initiate or a man in a trance steps into the magical circle as spokesman of the gods or of the assembled community. He is witch, doctor, priest, poet or actor, and as such holds the centre of the stage. He either plays the part of intermediary, engaging in a dialogue with the divinity on behalf of the community, or else he admonishes the latter as an agent of the former. His relationship to the community will differ from case to case to suit the external circumstances. Movements and speech quicken. The undirected circle received an axis in the form of a processional path, as we know from accounts of the Dionysus festivals, the 'goat songs' and the Eleusinian mysteries of ancient Greece.

Pindar, too, mentions the fact that the chorus gave expression to the thoughts and feelings of the poet, through dances and concentric movements.

The visual, aural and tactile exploration of the simple circle stamped out of clay has always been accomplished by the imagination, creator of the world of images and emotions. Creative fantasy inspires the senses and helps man to give formal expression to inner and outer appearances. In the development of the theatre over the millennia, direct inspection together with mystical ecstasy were always needed to reveal and unfold the deeper realms of the human psyche. To that end the theatre was plunged into an ocean of contradictions and contrasts (life and death; celebration and mourning; man and woman; black and white).

It may be that the circular shape of our pupils causes us to experience the circle as the original symbol of 'nothing' and 'all'. In the *kyklos* of the circular Greek *orchestra* we find the highest form of the play island, a form we have been unable to abandon and, indeed, have good reason to preserve. It is the simplest, all-embracing form in which man can find or lose himself—in the darkness of the cave or the light of the sun. Here alone the *metanoeite,* the 'change yourselves' of classical antiquity, the tangible transformation of human fate, encounters the oriental Tao, the absolute in an empty circle expressing eternal recurrence. This 'great encounter' is reflected plastically in the bright-obscure polarity of the Yin-Yang symbol, in the I-Thou, heaven-earth relationship.

The acquisition of space is man's first conscious expression. In the dark we turn and stretch with extended arms in all directions, to experience space with all our senses. We procure palpable space before we surround ourselves with a magic circle of our own. We consider the circle a natural element and make it the most important factor of human ornamentation. Outside this sphere of the visible, the palpable, the odorous and the audible, lies the alien, the uncanny, the numinous. Deeply stirred, we execute our movements in silence. The pantomime is born. Only the word, language, can create sound space. The call enters the darkness, penetrates the mystery. We await the echo, the message, with heads bent eagerly

 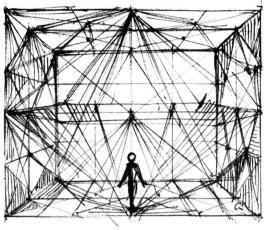 

Space is filled with dynamic tension by man alone. It must be sensed and experienced with the whole body. O. Schlemmer was the first to point to measurable lines of force in the Bauhaus.

Even static, genuine space derives all its relations from man. It is interior and exterior at once and has something of the formal regularity of a crystal. This form is shaped by the viewpoint of every individual.

Apparent space combines statics with dynamics. It turns symmetry and asymmetry into a play between nearness and farness, stillness and movement.

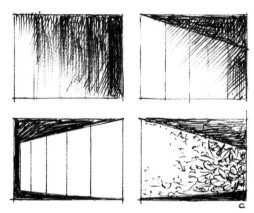  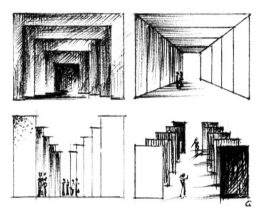

Depth can be achieved with shade and colour, foreshortening and other perspective devices, and with graphic effects.

The tiring effect of strict symmetry can be tempered with the deliberate grouping of men in stepped series, with surface structures and with colours.

The picture-frame form and the creation of walls by the staggering of equal masses allow quick entrances and scene changes. Depth is achieved by the displacement of surfaces or by reduction.

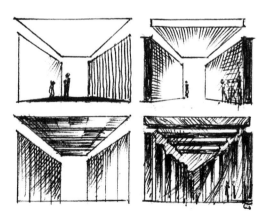 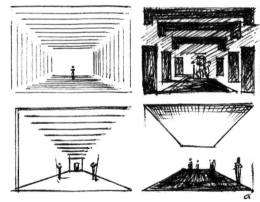 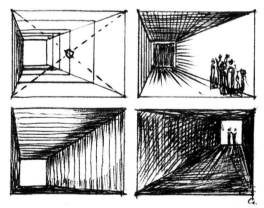

Slanting surfaces and a low horizon intensify depth. Sculpted wall sections increase the force of the spatial element. The height effect depends on the colour and brightness of walls and ceilings.

The 'picture-frame' is created with ceilings, beams and floors. Uniform elements decrease the effect; the contrasting elements—wooden beams, stone floors—enhance it.

Greater depth can be achieved by shifting the centre. Downward displacement increases, and upward displacement decreases, the depth. Graphic techniques heighten the three-dimensional effect.

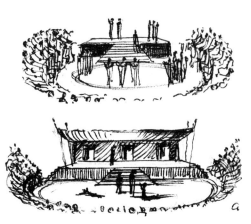

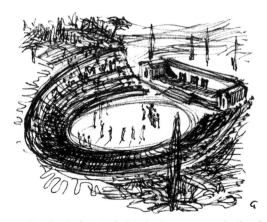

The circle has been treated as a magic realm since time immemorial. The sacrificial stone, the priest, the leaders of the chorus and dance, are its midpoint. A platform in the centre was the stage in the Greek orchestra.

A raised structure was added to the periphery of the circle and joined to the acting area by a flight of stairs.

In the classical period Greek theatres were built of stone. The changing-booth had made way for the skene. The auditorium formed a three-quarter circle, within which the actors moved freely.

In the Roman theatre the circular orchestra of the Greeks made way for a semicircle, which held the tribunalia, seats of honour, of senators and other distinguished spectators. The stage was long and narrow and lavishly equipped.

Auditorium and stage constituted a solid whole. The rear wall, or *scena frons,* was an architectural showpiece, and the actors were confined to the area immediately in front of it.

Roman mock façades were painted and had depth. Illusory rooms or landscapes painted on backcloths or panels could be changed at will.

In the early mediaeval English mystery playhouse the various locations were arranged in a circle. The scenery was sparse: heaven and hell alone were provided with roofs.

Central European mystery plays were staged in church interiors. They involved quick changes and spacious movements that drew the assembled spectators and believers into the action. Sacral space had turned into living scenery.

The individual stations of the mediaeval mystery play were built side by side in a simultaneous setting, or else drawn past the improvised spectators' platforms on wagons.

forward. We convey it to our partner, and the dialogue can begin. Desire and fear, plea and plaint lead others to this place. They surround my protective circle. It becomes the magical arena of the encounter in which I repeat the action, for all. The rhythm of my movements, the sound of my speech resolves the rigidity of the others, the spell is broken, the dance round the centre begins. Thus the arena, the *thing,* the playing circle was born.

Another type of stepped-out dance geometry also developed, like the growth of ice crystals or of crystalline micro-organisms, from the centre towards the periphery. The point occupied at any one time is always the origin. From here one axis runs to the left and to the right, another forward and backward, a third rises upward. Thus human movement gives rise to a co-ordinate system of scenic space in the theatre. The human figure moving in circles, spirals, straight lines or diagonals projects its inner relationship from the planimetry of the surface into the stereometry of three-dimensional space. In the portrayal of space every passage, every external movement is a reflection of an invisible interior. This is precisely why so many religions treat the centre of the circle as the 'gate' or 'cave' of redemption, as the primitive symbol of the uterus or of the sun, as a perceptible constant. Here, in the assumed seat of the divinity, physical movement and speech are triggered off by concentration. A stone cast into the ocean of consciousness causes the waves of concentration to spread out in circles that reach the deeply moved, receptive audience, the community. Poets in all ages have known how to describe this process. Thus Rilke wrote: 'I live my life in growing circles...' and T.S. Eliot spoke of the 'still point of the turning world... neither from nor towards'.

The magic and protective power of the circle is reflected in the Sanskrit *mandala,* that traditional circular figure filled with patterns of rays, polygons and crosses, resembling a dance notation. The ground plans of many ritual buildings, too, are based on circular forms. Aztec sun priests, like mediaeval magicians, officiated in the centre of a circle drawn on the ground, and in Babylon it was the custom to pour a ring of flour round the sick and the possessed.

Greece

For millennia Greek rituals were enacted in the orchestra, a dancing floor stamped out of clay. Sowing and birth, harvest and death were their main themes. Rhythm, dances and speech reflected sacrifice, prayer, joy and fear, sorrow and desire. Gods, spirits and demons were conjured up in the wordless language of the pantomime. Before the emergence of the *theatron* a thin line used to separate profane from sacral space. In early Greece the spectators would stand round the edge of the circle, separating the inner from the outer. The centre of the festive space was invariably marked by a sacrificial stone, an altar or a pillar, from which the actors could address the assembly.

The theatre, the *skene* infused with life, arose out of the encounter of human with extra-human forces, out of magical and unusual situations. In the fifth century B.C., after numerous changes, it gave rise to the chorus, to tragedy and to comedy. The spectator, always included, was part of the scene; he constituted the backcloth at the other side of the circle, and formed an indivisible whole with the chorus and the actors. The focalization of the action along one axis was a later refinement. As a result, the actor inside the circle, previously seen by all as a plastic figure moving freely in space, was forced to adopt new behaviour patterns. It was in the circle that the 'transitory' work of art, in Lessing's sense, was enacted before a receptive audience.

As early as the ninth century B.C. the magical invocation ceremonial with its mythological inspiration gave rise not only to goat songs or *tragodias,* but also to *comodias* or 'revel songs', cheerful plays constructed with the simplest dramatic means. They were entirely artless, resembled the improvisations of a later age, were made up of brief farcical scenes and dispensed with all stage effects. They originated chiefly among the Dorians, but in the seventh and sixth centuries B.C. they spread to the rest of Greece, to reach their apogee in the third century. They dealt with episodes from the lives of the heroes and gods, and the lack of scenery was made good with descriptive comments. The actors were called mimes, and later, to mark the striking character of their representations, biologists, that is, interpreters of life with great dramatic skills and a sharp eye for topical events. They needed no other set than a small podium in a circle staked off on the street, in market-places and courtyards. Their personal equipment, a vestige of the archaic ritual, reduced to a large strapped-on phallus, a false paunch and grotesque buttocks. These 'phallophores' began by performing their comedies and acrobatic interludes before simple villagers and townsmen, and it was not until later that the upper classes came to take pleasure in their bawdy jokes with their deeper allusions. Until the Alexandrian period the stage was reserved for classical tragedians and barred to comedians—strolling players had no privileges. Even Plato said of them: 'Crown them with garlands but chase them across the borders.' It was only the Peripatetics who paid greater attention to comedies: their realism accorded fully with the Aristotelian demand for verisimilitude. The 'new' comedy which emerged after 300 B.C., however, was sadly lacking in Aristophanic vigour and caustic wit.

It was in honour of Dionysus Eleuthereus, the Thracian god and renewer of life, the lord of death and the herald of fertility, that the Greeks held their greatest festivals. To the accompaniment of orgiastic revels, dithyrambs and choruses, the great quickener of life with his enraptured Satyrs, Bacchantes, Maenads and Sileni would make his ecstatic entry during the Attic spring celebrations. And it was also in his honour, during the great Dionysus and Lenaea festivals, that, particularly in Athens, *agone* contests were held, in which poets and actors vied with one another before an enthusiastic public. The prize-winning tetralogies, chosen by jury, would then be repeated for more critical audiences in large theatres. In early times the statue of the god was carried in festive procession to the centre of the orchestra where he presided over the play. Later, when the circle was given a special orientation by the addition of a tangential booth or tent, and the spectators in their improvised seats focused all their attention on the scene unfolded directly before them, the statue of Dionysus was left in his temple. It was only then that the audience could wholly surrender to the magnetism of the great classical tragedies of Aeschylus, Sophocles or Euripides. The stage became a framed picture, the actor moved against a background, was seen 'in relief' and no longer in unconfined space. The tent became a permanent structure with three doors, the *skene. Parodoi,* or wings, connected the *kerkides* or circular segments of the auditorium, its tiers hugging the mountain slope. The best extant example of this type of construction is the theatre at Epidaurus on the coast of Peloponnesus.

A three-quarter circle of marble steps extended round the structure, first built of wood and later of stone, and forming a single-storeyed palatial façade adorned with pillars. It was provided with steps and a podium and, on a platform above the doors, carried the *theologeion,* a crane for simulating the flight and descent of the *deus ex machina*—god or hero. In the fifth century B.C. painted 'wheel-outs', for showing interior scenes, were placed in the doorways. The lowering of actors or clouds and the rotations of the prism-shaped *periaktoi* marked the beginnings of stage machinery and scene-shifting. Their development reflected the inventiveness and imaginative power of the 'all-impelling' Greek spirit. Here, an illusionist set attempted to recapture the real world behind the play, fulfilling the Aristotelian demand for unity of place, time and action. Costume and mask provided an elegant complement to the actors' performance and declamation. Wearing cothurni, thick-soled boots, and dressed in flowing and costly robes and masks, their voices amplified by megaphones, they proclaimed the message of the god or hero to their far-flung audiences.

The chorus, which usually had twelve members, stood aside from the main action of the play, commenting upon it and accompanying the entry and exit of the hero with song. It also executed dances and other graceful movements. Flutes, cymbals and tambourines strongly emphasized the message of the parabases. Before and with Aeschylus, the chorus played a prominent part, providing a scenic element of great importance, but it began to wane with Euripides and finally lost its significance altogether. It was always the wreathed messenger of the gods and supplied the link between tragedy and crude realism.

Roman Theatre

To the Romans such concepts as state, order and security were much more important than the creation and enjoyment of beauty. Artistic talent attracted them far less than the ability to recognize and develop other faculties. That is why the Roman theatre lacked the Dionysiac power to mobilize ecstatic responses. Moreover, it was the preserve of an *élite* of officials and jurists—*polis* and *res publica* were fundamentally different entities. Romans at large loved lighter diversions of every kind: spectacular displays, circus acts, comedies, gladiatorial contests, pantomimes, fireworks, horse-races and setting animals to fight one another. Gala performances in the Colosseum, in provincial amphitheatres and in the Circus Maximus served largely to express dreams of empire. Juvenal coined the phrase *panem et circenses.* Pomp and circumstance can, in part, still be detected in the extant ruins of Rome. Power and glory were extolled everywhere and the *ludi romani* often involved bestial displays of realism. The people clamoured for human blood and corpses, and it was to satisfy these demands that poetry was paralysed and art became dishonoured.

We know much more about the playhouses of the Romans than we know about those of the Greeks. In particular we can consult the writings of Vitruvius, whose famous ten books on architecture are a mine of useful information. We are also indebted to him for a host of details on the Greek theatre, which he was wont to use for purposes of comparison. The popular *Atellanae* originated in Southern Italy and Sicily. At first, the Romans' puritanical outlook led them to scorn all decorative effects: their earliest plays were performed on a light wooden structure placed on a low platform.

The great stone theatres built by Pompey, Marcellus and Augustus, holding from ten to twenty thousand spectators, developed from these improvised wooden structures during the course of three centuries. Here the tiers of the semicircular auditorium were ranged round a two- or three-storey scenic wall that had developed from the wooden booth and became increasingly resplendent. The circular area of the Greek orchestra made way for a semicircle which held the *tribunalia,* seats of honour, of senators and other distinguished spectators. There was no longer any direct access from the auditorium to the elongated stage; the tiers were supported by masonry through which passages led from the outside. Where they adjoined the stage they made way for elaborate boxes. The new theatres were built in the most elegant city thoroughfares and were free-standing, no longer built against a hillside hollow, as had been the Greek custom. Moreover, the audience was often protected from the sun by awnings sprayed with cold water. The stage itself became ever larger and more profusely equipped, not least with trap-doors and cranes for the performance of crowd scenes and processions. The *scena frons* was the chief architectural showpiece. Built in the resplendent style of a Roman palace, it was divided by colonnades and embellished with statues and paintings. But even the most luxurious of these theatres, graced by more than three hundred columns and one thousand statues, could not disguise the shallowness of its spectacles. All that was left of the simple *skene* of the Greeks was the system of three doors through which the actors made their entrances: the *porta regia* in the centre and the two *portae hospitales* at the sides. The use of painted scenery remains a controversial question. It seems obvious to me that the Romans employed it. The mock façades of private dwellings excavated in Pompeii suggest that Vitruvius was right when he stated that the Romans made excellent use of perspective to cover the lower part of the *scena frons* with painted screens.

Similar evidence can be found in Pliny and Virgil. Other writers, however, hold that the Romans made do with the permanent architectural background of marble and vitreous, gilded or silvered columns. But the discovery of pivots on either side of the proscenium suggests that scenery must have been shifted across the stage. Virgil, in particular, has left us several indications to that effect. He not only mentions such *scena ductilis,* but also refers to *tabulae pictae,* three tableaux used respectively as backcloths for comedies, tragedies and interludes. It seems reasonable to suppose that they were pulled up or flown on the stage from the storeys below or above. Although the Romans had no curtain in our sense of the word, they were capable of producing astonishing changes of scenery, chiefly with the aid of *periaktoi,* the mighty prism-shaped revolving screens they took over from the Greeks.

The amphitheatres staged the most spectacular performances, including particularly the so-called *naumachia,* mimic sea battles of great splendour which supplied a grateful public with all the dead and wounded they desired. The populace would also use such gala occasions to applaud or deride the rulers and procurators present, who would acknowledge these demonstrations with a good-natured and shrewd show of tolerance. The Emperor Hadrian staged spectacles more splendid than any of his predecessors, and was a past master at supplying his people with bread and circuses, if only cruelly to inflame them against one another.

Mediaeval Mystery Plays

There is no record of passion plays in the West before the tenth century. When they were first performed they, too, were pantomimes invested with sacred and symbolical meanings—a sequence of allegorical scenes that served to embellish parts of the text of the Mass in the form of tropes. The Dionysian spring festival having made way for Byzantine Easter celebrations, the church with its spectacular dome became the chosen site for the proclamation of Christ's message of salvation. Here jubilee hymns (sequences) were chanted in praise of the new Lord Jesus Christ at Easter and Christmas, and no longer to the Roman *sol invictus,* the invincible sun god.

The theatrical instinct could now flourish to the full. Immense scenarios offered vast possibilities for the performance of pantomimes, dramas and often of farces. Elsewhere, the basilica with its elongated approach to the altar, its aisles, arches, piers, columns and arcades invited players and congregation alike to embrace the mystery in all its poignancy. A few stage properties and costumes sufficed to interpret most biblical passages. As in antiquity the actor-priest moved freely across the stage, while the spectator became

directly involved, often rubbing shoulders with the chief characters of the play and joining in the action with his laughter or tears. Mass hysteria was not uncommon, the more so as the constantly moving scene greatly enhanced the dramatic tension. If we compare such spectacles with those performed in the radially symmetrical interior of the Byzantine church, then we come face to face with the contrast between West and East. Against the background of the iconostasis and the golden glow of the Byzantine mosaics, the static heralds of the divine message—the priest and deacons—seemed to transcend the ritual of the actions they performed.

'The believer dissolves in the sanctuary, as if he had entered heaven itself', as one Byzantine put it. Their halting in still space extinguished the will of the congregation and afforded them a passive experience.

Not so in the West and the North. Here the answer lay hidden in the dark vaults of the elongated church, and here the congregation was swayed by active forces. The spatial axis was cut time and again by the changing scenes and the attention of the faithful was guided to the central point, the altar, by detours—intersections and contrasts of light and shade. It was here alone that a mobile, decentralized spectacle, one that disappears into the dark and must find its way to the light, could emerge. Salvation is the path, blessedness the evanescent goal, and the miracle prevails over death. In this atmosphere deep resignation alternated with fanatic faith. Nothing mattered except total absorption of the consciousness in the drama of the play. The mere witnessing of such active dramatic processes had a lasting effect on the subsequent development of the Western theatre. Rushing through the church from one spot to the next while watching the entrances and exits of the actors, the spectators participated in exciting changes of scenery on a vast set. Language, mimicry, gesture, costume and music all combined to turn the sacral site into a fabulous, formless and ever-changing concourse.

Open-Air Theatre

The story of the mediaeval open-air theatre is quickly told. Once the church could no longer accommodate the vast crowds that kept flocking to the mystery plays, the spectators began to spill out into the porches, squares, markets and streets. Here they would wend their way in procession past a host of improvised platforms, milling round the actors or sitting on special stands. Having stopped to watch the set pantomimes, they would move on again with the *tableaux vivants.*

Only when a stage was erected on the largest square, where all the individual scenes could be combined into one great spectacle, was it possible once again to present dramatic actions, often with grandiloquent and long-winded texts set to music. The simultaneous setting, made up of numerous small mansions or *loca,* usually offered a medley more reminiscent of the fairground or puppet theatre than of the passion play. For all that, it stimulated a great many mediaeval artists to design and construct elaborate scenery. For where else was it possible to combine so many disparate biblical scenes, to present the 'mouth of Hell' side by side with the gates of Heaven? Many of their inventions continue to inspire modern stage design, for it was their tremendous achievement to represent on a single stage, some sixty yards long, ten to twenty such different places as the Temple, Golgotha, Paradise, the house of Herod or Caiaphas, and others. We have evidence of this development in the form of stage directions and designs that have come down to us from fifteenth- and sixteenth-century Valenciennes, Lucerne, Cologne and Vienna. And, indeed, in countless representations ranging from Gothic tableaux to late Renaissance, and even to baroque, paintings, we discover this simultaneity, this association of scenes in the work of the great masters.

In the popular theatre, too, mediaeval customs continued to live on, though the deeper content of the passion was blunted by attempts to achieve spectacular but hollow external effects—the passion became a carnival, allegory a farce and the morality play a burlesque show. No doubt this change was also responsible for the separation of the stage from the audience. The faithful made way for the mob. Like the Romans, they preferred crude jokes, brawls, obscenities, duels, hell and the devil, to saintly figures in exaggerated and pious poses. At the beginning of the Renaissance the increasingly self-confident bourgeoisie, finding that the church refused to stage secular scenes in its hallowed precincts, turned market squares and streets into festival sites, all the guilds vying with one another to produce the best amateur actors, to acquire the most effective stage properties and the most luxurious wardrobes. Dramatic societies and writers of occasional verse combed the Bible for striking scenes, many of which had to be put on in 'shifts' so as to contain the inflated text, as witness particularly the productions of the mastersingers. The wagon stage, perfected in England, introduced a new dimension: the passage of a sequence of elaborate pictures, supported by structures up to two storeys high, presented the stage designer and painters of scenery with a number of novel creative challenges.

The Renaissance

A complete change of style in stage design occurred in Italy during the age of discovery and invention, when the simultaneous setting gradually made way for the 'perspective stage'. To begin with, there was a return to the framed picture of the Roman *scena frons*. The nobility and the academics took charge of the theatre, and introduced the hierarchical principle: plays were once again performed behind closed doors, especially at princely courts and in the universities, where the revival of classical motifs called for a radical change of theatrical conventions. The classical *De architectura* of Vitruvius

became the new gospel of theatre-builders, Leo Battista Alberti and other Renaissance theorists referring expressly to Vitruvius' views and the new stage decorations and style they entailed.

The new interpretation of classical texts and ideas was often confused, with the result that the conceptual world of the classical theatre tended to degenerate into a jumble of traditions and mistranslations. For the rest, the late Greco-Roman love of decoration fell on fertile ground among princes and patrons of the art. Once again it was possible, under the cloak of the classical heritage, to stage majestic spectacles. To that end the noble amateurs, the comedians and strolling players had first to be provided with special architectural platforms in palaces, courts and parks.

Scenic development led to the emergence of the picture-frame stage, and, thanks once again to the influence of Vitruvius, the prism-shaped *periaktoi* were brought back. Sebastiano Serlio, in particular, developed this idea when he introduced two-sided and carefully foreshortened sets receding at right angles from the stage, the so-called *telari*. The result was a series of columnar buildings, streets and squares constructed in accordance with the latest laws of perspective drawing. His banqueting halls, in particular, achieved a convincing illusion of depth. Andrea Palladio, the teacher of an entire generation of architects, and renowned even outside Europe, used the traditional palace façade as a stage background, placing foreshortened streets into the three obligatory doorways. His Teatro Olimpico at Vicenza with its semicircular auditorium became the model of sixteenth- and seventeenth-century European theatre architects. Here proportion and elegance, symmetry and harmonious articulation, together with skilful optical illusions, were fused into a fascinating architectural scene. Giambattista Aleotti, by his extension of the central *porta regia,* provided the stage with its first complete system of 'wings' in the Teatro Farnese, Parma. Other resplendent theatrical buildings rose up in Rome, Venice, Florence, Genoa, Urbino and Ferrara. They reflected a new aristocratic-humanistic life style, one that the Germany of the Reformation tried to adopt soon afterwards. Meanwhile, the invention of book-printing having made literature more widely available than before, worldly and sensual life increasingly gained the upper hand over the mediaeval, other-worldly and transcendent style. A new picture of humanity was being fashioned, chiefly by art. Symbolic, mystical love made way for the worship of woman as the new ideal. The nude had returned to the world of art.

The wagon stage made it possible to enact triumphal processions, at first of saints and martyrs. This was the origin of the *trionfi,* masques and popular entertainments in which the masses could once again participate. Great theatre halls and gardens once more teemed with mythological figures and landscapes. Nymphs, satyrs and masked dancers invaded caves, rocks, palaces and rural idylls. Ariosto, Torquato Tasso and Machiavelli wrote plays for them, while Raphael, Bramante and Leonardo designed scenery and costumes as well as cranes for gods and spirits alike.

Thanks to the introduction of wings, the theatre was given a new lease of life. The curtain closed off the fourth wall, shutting out the

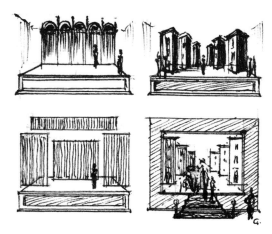

Renaissance theatres were built in accordance with rediscovered ancient designs, and marked a return to the framed picture of the Roman *scena frons*. Stylization and the simplification of perspectives helped to convert the stage into a three-dimensional area with classical features.

Sebastiano Serlio's sets were two-sided and carefully foreshortened. By skilful use of rotating prisms Serlio also introduced quick set changes.

Andrea Palladio's Teatro Olimpico in Vicenza revived the resplendent palace façade of the ancient Roman theatre. Behind each of the three arches he built a street of houses diminished in perspective.

Giambattista Aleotti is credited with the invention of wings. In the Teatro Farnese, Parma, he built the central opening of the first picture-frame stage.

The baroque indoor and garden theatre deployed highly developed stage machinery for coping with the many painted and built theatrical effects. In the dreamlike and intoxicating baroque scene, theatrical painting rose to unprecedented heights.

Galli da Bibiena, the most famous theatre architect of his day, was the creator of fantastic settings. During the Absolutist period, the axis of the stage ran from the seat of the reigning couple to the vanishing point of the painted set.

At the end of the Baroque period the scenic axis was rotated and the set ceased to be parallel to the spectator.

Nineteenth-century bourgeois theatre tended to lose itself in idealistic landscapes and exaggerated naturalism, which it mistook for 'historical accuracy'.

It was not until men like E. Gordon Craig and Adolphe Appia dusted down the stage at the turn of the century that light, shade and colour became the new creative elements which have retained their pride of place to this day. Man rediscovered his relationship with space.

Epidaurus: Theatre designed by Polycletus the Younger.

spectator. The three great masters—Palladio, Serlio and Aleotti—and their countless pupils, amongst them the architects and painters Scamozzi, Peruzzi, Sangallo, Lancia, Pellegrino, Buontalenti and Parigi—helped greatly to develop the Italian Renaissance theatre and were its first stage designers. They succeeded in transforming the simple platform into a panoramic stage and, relying on perspective illusion, endowed the set with a spatial autonomy of its own. Italian stage technique was copied in Germany in the early seventeenth century, Joseph Furttenbach designing in Ulm the first theatre with a full set of wings. In England, Inigo Jones took over the mantle of Palladio and enriched his style with the help of revolving screens and mobile scenery.

The Baroque Stage

The full magic of the theatre did not make itself felt until the Baroque period, when the leadership of the theatre architect was challenged by the scenographer, whose art was fostered by entire families. Quick scenic changes demanded advanced techniques and lightly built sets. Here the painting genius of the Galli da Bibiena family, the Burnacinis and later of the Quaglios could come into its own, so much so that their mechanical and artistic perfection has never been rivalled. Here an overbrimming wealth of imagination went hand in hand with a mastery of perspective. As a result, scenic painting came to hold pride of place among the arts in the seventeenth and eighteenth centuries, often becoming an end in itself rather than an aid to presentation. The painter set the scene, choosing Greece, Egypt or Rome at his whim. The music for the resulting opera or ballet was generally contributed by the court composer. The scenery, like the wardrobe, had to be beautiful; the characterization was of secondary importance. Even the blackest dungeon often resembled a state-room. There was a plethora of optical effects, which served to subordinate the actor to the limitations of the set. Wherever such masters as Ludovico Burnacini or Giuseppe Galli da Bibiena worked, they evoked tremendous enthusiasm and unreserved admiration, particularly at the great festivals staged in princely courts north of the Alps. The Vitruvian demand for unlimited illusion was met unreservedly by the baroque scene, its architectural fantasies exceeding all bounds and spilling over into the auditorium. During the absolutist period the axis of the stage would usually run from the seat of the reigning couple to the vanishing point of the painted set: castles, avenues and parks.

The baroque theatre was a combined festival hall for staging plays, operas, ballets, concerts and masked balls, and for holding receptions. Actors, singers and dancers were confined between surfaces, lines, light and colour. During the later period it became possible to reveal rooms of varying depth by rotating the scenic axis. As a result, the stage ceased to be parallel to the auditorium and the spectator's eye was free to roam through arches and colonnades into changing landscapes, gardens or woods. A special effect was

introduced by the architect and engraver Piranesi with his *carceri,* or dungeons. Here the palatial façade made way for monumental buildings composed of symbolic units, the whole conjuring up the cruelty, grotesque romanticism and deathly hush of Roman ruins.

In these rooms the visions and intoxication of the baroque were combined with deep emotions, sometimes tinged with fanaticism. 'Once again the European intellect produced a great synthesis of life, art and philosophy' (Frey).

Romanticism and Naturalism

After the French Revolution nineteenth-century romanticism began to make itself felt increasingly in scenic art. The classicistic, antiquating architectural stage had anticipated this development. Scenic art now became large-scale, historical painting. The Romantic poet, painter and musician E.T.A. Hoffmann summed it all up when he wrote:

We are spoilt children. Paradise is lost, but we cannot go back. We need scenery as we need costume. And yet our stage must not resemble a peep-show. The true aim of scenery is generally forgotten. Nothing is more ridiculous than the attempt to persuade the spectator that he need not make any imaginative effort to believe in the reality of the painted palaces, trees and rocks, however improbable their size or height. It is all the more ridiculous when the illusion supposedly wrought in this way is shattered at one stroke. I could mention hundreds of such cases, but to take just one, may I remind you of those misbegotten 'practicable' doors and windows placed between the wings, which inexorably destroy the artificial perspective of the architecture. Trying to copy nature with true magnitudes and thus to deceive the spectator is a childish and pointless game, but one that is being played everywhere with sets, battle scenes, processions, etc. The audience, far from being taken in, remains on its guard, like someone anxious to catch a pickpocket at his tricks the better to expose him.

Another nineteenth-century critic, the painter Anselm Feuerbach, deriding the attempt to 'render these rooms and forests true to nature', exclaimed:

...I hate the modern theatre, because I have sharp eyes and cannot see beyond the cardboard and the make-up. I hate this scenic flim-flam and all that goes with it from the bottom of my heart. It spoils the public, kills the last remains of artistic sensibility and fosters a barbaric taste.

With equally caustic derision many satirists, including Nestroy and Raimund in Vienna, mocked at baroque theatre machinery and at magic operas, though with philistine disingenuousness they were only too glad to take advantage of these devices whenever they could. Friedrich Schinkel alone set his face resolutely against the *maniera italiana,* creating exquisite scenery of classical beauty for Mozart's *Magic Flute.*

Working against the background of props, wings, mobile panoramas, trees, painted forests, idyllic views and plush, Richard Wagner combined the appeal of the romantic peep-show with that of the classical and ritual amphitheatre, and developed his own style in Bayreuth. The result was treated with reverence for decades, to be dusted down in the end by his grandchildren and thus brought into harmony with its musical essence.

By the turn of the century the Swiss scenic artist Adolphe Appia had already tried to lay bare the basic structures of the Wagnerian musical theatre with the help of lighting and special effects. But the times were not yet ripe for dispensing with all but stylized decorations, colours and visual symbols.

As the last in this series of scenic artists I must mention E. Gordon Craig, who ushered in a veritable scenic revolution in the twentieth century, and in whose hands, light, set and man became one artistic whole. He pioneered a new sense of space based on that of classical antiquity. Craig knew that man's visual sense reacts more quickly and more critically than all his other senses. He called for the restoration of spatial order and insisted that the set must develop from the ground plan and prove itself in the elevation. He once again turned space and man into co-actors, and has provided a great impetus to producers and stage designers over the past seventy years.

Clearly, it has been impossible to mention all periods and phases of development in so brief a survey. Thus I have had to omit such important elements as Shakespeare's theatre in Elizabethan England and modern stage design. But precisely in these two elements the parable of eternal recurrence is made manifest with particular force—the attempt to infuse new life into the old. What I have been chiefly concerned with has been to examine the origins of theatrical scenery and its links with the human body in space.

The Set Builder

One of the strangest creatures to settle on the theatrical shore emerged several decades ago, just when the last vestiges of the old styles and traditions were in danger of vanishing. The stage designer, or 'set builder' as Brecht prefers to call him, was born as painter, sculptor, craftsman and architect all rolled into one. With him a new art form—scenic design—saw the light of day, and in his creative hands it became infused with theatrical instincts and dramatic spirit. The stage designer's job is to compose pictures out of spaces, people, surfaces, colours and light, and ever since his appearance he has been on a par with that other new arrival on the stage: the theatrical producer. Not for him the easy life of the studio painter, of whom Wolfgang Liebeneiner said, 'He thinks of a picture. He has time to let it mature and completes it with his own brush and pallet.' The scenic artist, by contrast, works to a tight schedule as a member of a theatrical collective. Of his evanescent art little more than a few

sketches and photographs survive, and odd fragments of this and that. And if that were not bad enough, he has also to prune his budget, which means dispensing with scenic flourishes. Still, bareness is no longer equated with lack of imagination; on the contrary, if the composer of scenic space relies on a small number of great, interrelated motifs, we admire his authenticity and self-restraint all the more. He can, of course, also rely on optical aids to highlight important elements of the plot and of individual scenes, but this 'creative freedom' is restricted by the specific interrelationship of the actors and their behaviour in space and time. He is expected to be familiar with the social and historical background of the play and to present the fruits of his imagination not only pictorially but also with technical expertise. As Brecht put it: 'The set builder must think in order to produce art.' In other words, he must not only depict reality, but also make it explicit.

The expressive force of the stage designer is reflected in his ability to step back modestly and to provide the actor with an appropriate and well-designed environment rooted in poetry and music.

To hide in the shadows and yet to be fully present remains his greatest distinction, that and to ensure that the attentive spectator, in tune with the atmosphere, responds to his pictorial signals. For before the word came the image, no matter whether ritual, visionary or starkly realistic. A return to simpler means might well spell an advance to richer content.

Adalbert Stifter's comment on the Viennese Prater has been applied to the scenic picture and the stage designer:

What exactly is scenic design?
A spatial structure? NO!
A decorative effect? NO!
A painting? NO!
Perhaps a sculptural creation? HARDLY!
A craftsman's job? NO! NO!
A technical and mechanical product? NO!
The co-ordination of costumes? NEVER!
Well, then what is it?
All these factors taken together!

Future Outlook

A permanent revolution has been proceeding hand in hand with a conservative trend over the past fifty years. Some claim that no new stimuli have reached the theatre since the days of Oskar Schlemmer and the Bauhaus. Worse still, there is said to be a lack of critical consumers. Others hold that the modern stage wards off the natural shocks that flesh is heir to by comfortable and conformist presentations. The modern theatre with its tricks and experiments is said to impair the stage designer's flights of fancy, no less than do stage hands working to strict rules and the scarcity of true craftsmen. Or else his work is said to reduce to decorative flourishes, stale conventions, and macabre make-believe effects. A radicalism born of prosperity is taking its toll, as new ideas are too quickly and hence badly digested—as if all that mattered was playing Hamlet in tails, or painting abstract pictures or tableaux on the stage. A surfeit of kinetic phenomena moving with the precision of mathematical sets cannot but lead to a deadly cyberno-aesthetic schematism. The upshot is art for a minority, for the elect or for a refurbished consumers' society. At the opposite pole lies the leaden weight of the traditional bourgeois theatre, that is, classicism side by side with the mechanical workings of the computer.

Abstract art, born in 1910, has encroached upon the theatre, what with optical art, kinetic art, pop, and informal art being transformed into 'environment', 'happening' or the 'theatre of the absurd'. The 'void' has been rendered visible and with it the order it has replaced. As in science, all that is static, fixed and irreplaceable has been banished or at least displaced, transformed into 'virtual movement' with fluid boundaries. Naturally all these experiments, in which the spectator's credulity is strained to the limits and chaos reigns supreme, are of a piece with the infernal world of neon lights, advertisements and of air and sound pollution.

The poor citizen must apparently be shaken into awareness of the 'absurdity of the absurd and the horribility of horrific scenes' (Vostell). And, in all truth, there is no shortage of shocking effects. But why cannot light and colour suffice as formative space factors, and sound and kinetic effects as extensions of physical space? And why not capture the world of dreams by filming unconscious processes and projecting them on the stage? Constantly changing social structures keep introducing new elements into our more and more obtrusive technical media, while star billings and the festival cult tend to foster hypertrophy and contempt for the public. The new multiplicity of currents and forms, as we saw, addresses itself exclusively to a small stratum of intellectual cognoscenti, to an exclusive audience, so that despite its very high level and great technical perfection the effects of the modern theatre have remained insignificant. At the other end of the spectrum, superficiality is fostered by too many popularizations. Amateur dramatic societies try with varying degrees of success to carry works written for professionals to even the most out-of-the-way places. No doubt they can make a powerful impact. But cheap formalistic performances destroy the unity of the theatrical or musical stage. On the other hand anxiety, agitation and despair merely serve to bring home the pointlessness of human existence without showing the way out of crisis and misery.

In short, if we should try to meet all the positive or disparate wishes, demands, currents and forces then we should be condemning the theatre to the same tragic end as befell the mime, the singer or even the works they performed. For that reason the archetypal nucleus of the theatre must be laid bare once again, even at the cost of routine avant-gardism.

Only a return to decorative simplicity in the form of apparently effortless representations, not of exaggerated virtuosity, can elicit the spectator's full response to the stage portrayal of joy and tragedy, of shock and of dreams. Only then will he follow us through fire and water, into the pits of hell and the light of heaven and ultimately forget space and time, while surrendering himself to the set builder's illusionary effects.

Max Reinhardt has claimed that a dream without reality means as little in the theatre as reality without a dream. And is it not the task of every true scenic artist to transform reality into dreams and *vice versa?*

I shall conclude with a quotation from Hugo von Hofmannsthal: 'The stage is as nothing and worse than nothing if it is not marvellous. It must be the dream of dreams or else it is a wooden pillory in which the imagination of the poet is foully prostituted.'

From Commission to Première

Günther Schneider-Siemssen
Pantelis Dessyllas
Heinrich Wendel
Jean-Pierre Ponnelle
Günther Uecker

Chapter 1   From Drawing-Board to Workshop

BY PROFESSOR GÜNTHER SCHNEIDER-SIEMSSEN

This account was written chiefly for those interested in how a set is created and by whom; and in whether the stage designer is an agent who carries out the orders of someone higher up in the hierarchy, like a soldier. He is, in fact, more like the field-marshal of his profession. He has to be architect, painter, illustrator, sculptor, art historian, costume designer, stage technician, light designer, inventor—even psychologist; in short, master of a whole range of professions. He must also have a highly developed musical sense; he must be well-versed in theatrical methods and theories and be familiar with the humanities in general. Some leading stage designers have even become highly successful producers.

A whole series of paths leads from the drawing-board to the finished work seen on the first night. I can only describe the road I myself have taken, along which I have met three characteristic situations:

In the first, the producer presents the stage designer with a fairly clear-cut plan; he has a particular set already in mind, at least in outline. If he has not, he is nevertheless clear about certain details of the presentation. The stage designer, persuaded by the producer's arguments, will make a few rough sketches at once, starting the process of translating the producer's ideas into practice.

Sometimes the stage designer has a clear dramatic concept and, if it agrees with the producer's own ideas, then the producer will follow his lead in presenting the concept on the stage.

There are also occasions when producer and stage designer have no more than vague, rudimentary ideas about the presentation. They start a game of ping-pong, a give and take that is as fruitful as it is intense. At the end it is usually impossible to tell what ideas were contributed by whom.

In this connection I should like to explain why I do not try my hand at opera production. First of all, I have much too much respect for the producer's vocation and his artistic achievements to try. Secondly, there are many stage designers who have, without turning producer, nevertheless had a profound influence on style and who have set new theatrical standards. Nor can I spare the time for additional duties; I am fully stretched by my work as it is. No assistant can relieve me of the burden of painting from 150 to 200 slides, each bearing my individual signature. Thirdly, I am already a kind of 'outside producer', who sits in frequently with the producer, joins in his thoughts, helps along and supplies useful hints and suggestions. The battle is won where the essence of the work is given concrete form, and here the producer is happy to have an ally at his side.

Let us return to the exchange of ideas between producer and stage designer, when style, history or literary sources are first discussed. This process sends the stage designer to the art books and the libraries. It depends on the nature of the opera to be performed, whether he comes up first with sketches of details or with the ground plan. He will have to use different approaches in designing architectural, fantastic, or starkly dramatic sets.

Even at this early stage a first crisis may loom up in the choice of theatre. For this reason many ideas are buried even before they are born. We may hear bitter—often justified— complaints about the auditorium or the stage, about all sorts of annoying frustrations, about the architect who has left some vital ingredient out of his calculations, or failed to consult his clients and left them to cope with the result for the rest of their lives. An ill-conceived set is soon forgotten; an ill-conceived theatre is not.

The composer and librettist may also come in for their share of criticism during this first round of discussions. Often the analyses and diagnoses lead to such sharp differences of opinion that one feels like withdrawing from the whole enterprise. But when all the creases have been ironed out at long last, a new start can be made. One comes to terms with the work and the tasks it poses, it having been agreed whether the presentation is intended for a repertory opera, a festival theatre, a small stage or a touring company—for all have different requirements.

On the basis of sketches and ground plans, a new round of discussions with the producer is begun. Often, for the sake of clarity, a small model on a scale of $1:50$ is produced at this point, enabling the producer and stage designer to reconsider their ideas and make changes if necessary. One thing is very important to me at this stage: I must be given enough time to discard any sketches I do not like and produce more satisfactory substitutes.

During this period of planning and preparation, artistic and financial considerations are of very great importance: the stage designer must know just how large his budget is, especially as he is generally set very strict limits when working in medium-size or small theatres. Realistic sets are often more expensive than symbolic or stylized sets, or effects based on light and projection.

After several discussions with the producer, a technical *rehearsal* must be arranged at the earliest possible opportunity.

On the basis of the ground plans and with the help of available rostra, stairs and walls, the sight lines of the set are examined from various angles—from the first row of the stalls to the upper circles and the boxes. With a surveyor's pole the necessary corrections are made on stage and entered in the ground plan by the stage-manager. At the same time the lighting design and all special technical equipment are tested.

Badly marked-out technical rehearsals are pointless: instead of clarifying problems, they merely complicate them. If there is no technical rehearsal—and this is not uncommon—the most important issues have to be settled with the help of the model. This once happened with Otto Schenk who told me spontaneously at the first stage rehearsal, 'What a splendid ground plan! Please, no technical rehearsals ever again!'

After this point, all the stage designer's sketches will be in colour and based, *inter alia,* on the lighting plot. As soon as working drawings, ground plan and coloured sketches are done, various spatial and acoustic questions have to be settled at a preliminary discussion between the conductor, the producer and the stage designer. In operas involving a large chorus, contact must also be made with the chorus master and the precise grouping of the members determined.

Time and again stage designs fail to do justice to the musical character of an opera, even violating it. I am referring to unpleasant acoustic results. The musical theatre is still crucially dependent on the conductor and the singers: I have often seen an indifferent production with an indifferent set turn into a great theatrical experience thanks to a first-class conductor and a first-rate cast—but the reverse is never the case. On the opera stage acoustics are an important factor, and the scenic picture is the only one in all the plastic arts that can *sound* good or bad. The stage designer must therefore know precisely what materials and substances have an injurious acoustic effect and which lend the voices positive support. The addition of wooden platforms, ceilings and closed rooms or even of a piece of rock or a shell can make tremendous extra demands on the voice.

The 'gauze' known to every theatre-goer, a curtain that has a distracting effect even if it is not painted—when it makes the spectator feel that he is watching a murky aquarium—is sometimes an unnecessary object of dispute between Italian singers on the one hand and the producer or the stage designer on the other. For quite a few singers of the Italian school the stage ends behind the safety curtain, which is precisely where it begins for others; an excellent reason for singing this aria or that at the extreme front edge of the stage. With the rather spurious claim that the curtain absorbs the tone, these singers refuse to acknowledge its advantages, and no amount of scientific measurement can make them change their minds. As far as I am concerned, in all such cases, vanity must make way for truth, and the gauze cloth, which has been in existence for decades, must stay where it was designed to be.

On the basis of the colour sketches, the stage and costume designers now create the costumes; detailed discussions between them and the producer about the characterization of the roles form the basis of the 'vocabulary of the language of costume'.

Recently it has proved very useful to subject samples of special materials to preliminary light tests. Stage and costume designers can then see their true effect from a distance, since nothing looks the same in the house as it does in the workshops by daylight. Unpleasant surprises are avoided and so is the waste of money entailed in hours of making good any mistakes.

At about this stage in the work the stage designer and his assistants will make architectural drawings—on a scale of 1:20 or 1:25—of all pieces to be built and add detailed notes for their construction. The drawings must already take into account the eventual separations or folding of the scenery so that it can be transported and stored. The most curious mistakes sometimes happen at this point: a number of pillars and walls may be made ten centimetres too high and have to be cut down to size before they can be carried through the door. To be safe from such surprises, particularly during tours and guest performances, it is best not only to know the sizes of the various stages but also the measurements of the various passages and gateways.

Once the architectural drawings have been completed—along with the drawings of the furniture and the props—the assistant begins the construction of the stage model. He does this on the same reduced scale from a large variety of materials—balsa wood, wire, fabric, plastics, modelling clay—and he may spend up to three months on the work. At the same time the stage designer has to make up his mind what materials and colours he will use for the final set. These are, it is true, different from those used on the 1:25 scale model, but there is nevertheless a connection between the two. The finished scale model is painted by the stage designer himself, using a variety of techniques.

With the help of the model and of figures to scale, the entire play is examined with the producer, whose wishes can be taken into consideration at this point and the model changed accordingly.

Once there is complete agreement between producer and stage designer, discussions can be held with the technical director and the lighting designer during which—once again on the basis of the model—all construction and electrical problems can be reviewed. In the subsequent discussions between the stage-manager, the technical director and the heads of the painting, carpentry, metalwork, sculpture, upholstery and other workshops, all outstanding architectural, artistic and technical details are discussed, as is the purchase of materials, the costs and time schedules.

The ordeal of the stage designer and of his hard-pressed workshops now begins in earnest. Although he has cleared the first great hurdle, he cannot rest: he must supervise every step in the manufacture of the scenery he has designed. This can be hard enough even if he has daily access to all his workshops, for unexpected problems keep arising and changes must be made. It becomes much more difficult and strenuous when his tours of inspection are done by air from country to country, or from continent to continent. Questions surface all the time, and revisions are inevitable.

Chapter 2   In the Workshop

BY PANTELIS DESSYLLAS

Asked about my profession, I say 'stage designer' or simply 'designer', whereupon my interlocutors usually start gushing about the glorious business of creating a fantasy world, a world of dreams and reality, of beauty and emotion.

Well, that may be how my profession looks in theory; in practice unforeseeable difficulties dog the designer's footsteps from the moment he produces his finished designs. To begin with he cannot ignore such factors as time and money, for many a beautiful idea has had to be abandoned for lack of either. No doubt, even during the heyday of scene-painting in the seventeenth century many a Burnacini, Bibiena, Juvara, and Piranesi had the same problem, if on a more generous scale.

Over the years there has been a crucial change not only in the financial approach to scene construction but also to the time set aside for any one production. The size of the individual sets and the choice of materials is a pressing subject of discussions not only in the workshops but also in the administrative offices, and the phrase, 'That's all we can spare,' is heard with increasing frequency. It is not hard to accept the idea that a particular set is too large and that it exceeds the budget by, say, £2,500; it is much more difficult to prune the finished concept by that amount and to retain one's best ideas at the expense of costly materials. Paring down is often the cause of time-consuming discussions in the workshop.

Luckily the imagination and inventiveness of the many anonymous experts in the workshops can work wonders. Their suggestions, their models, their variations on the 'genuine article', their make-believe materials, and so on, may eventually enable the designer to keep within his budget.

Hardly has this problem been disposed of, when a sword of Damocles begins to threaten the whole production, faintly at first and then palpably so. That sword is time. All one's calculations, all one's estimates, have come to nothing with the discovery that there is only half the labour force needed to do the work as it was originally planned. For the rest, working hours, industrial regulations, failure to discover alternative methods—all these force one to make compromises. Early on in my career these compromises used not to be too painful: the management generally made up the shortage of time with money. A great deal of the work was farmed out. This escape route is, however, being blocked by the general financial crisis; at best it remains open for the larger opera-houses.

It also happens quite often that finished designs, though technically solved, remain in the drawer while awaiting financial approval. It may then be claimed that there was not time enough to 'implement' them. Behind that failure there often hides the bitter truth that the designer has ignored money or time. He has designed a scenic picture—for a wall but not for the stage.

One way of coping with this problem is to finish the drafts in particularly good time—in a major opera, up to eight months before the first night. A designer does this not for filing purposes, but to allow the workshops to start work, or for the hiring out to be arranged. If this is left until too late there is a very real danger of not finding a reliable supplier or of exceeding the budget through overtime and other emergency measures. Even if the sketches are made in good time it may happen that no supplier is prepared to take on the work, perhaps because the pieces are too large—but in that case the designer, if possible after consulting the producer, can always change his original plans without causing too much upset.

But that, too, takes time. Makeshift solutions can be very attractive, but usually not when they result from shortage of time. In particular, work farmed out at the last minute is likely to prove a disappointment. I still remember how, because the designer's sketches were delivered late, a set for the Vienna State Opera (with a stage measuring some 650 square metres and an average height of eight metres) had to be completed with punctilious attention to detail within fourteen days. There being no shortage of money at the time, there was no alternative but to farm the work out on a massive scale. Some twenty-two firms within a radius of fifty miles became involved in the work. They could only be allotted half the remaining fortnight since the final touches had to be applied in the theatre workshops. One firm made the window frames, another made the doors, a third various mouldings, and so on.

After a well-organized tour of all the suppliers, the work was ready for assembly but, despite very careful preliminary discussion, it soon became clear that all was not well. On the stage centimetres can make all the difference, and measurements had gone wrong in at least half the outside work. The fourteenth working day came, and the set was on the stage. But neither the stage designer nor the workshops had cause to feel satisfied. Had the work been sent out in time, none of these problems would have arisen.

For the stage designer, in particular, time and money are of incalculable importance, for the realization of his creative work depends on a collective effort. And his work is only done when the curtain rises on his set.

Before that happens he is an indefatigable participant in the 'battle of materials'. By that term I refer to an incomprehensible artistic obsession: the resolve to cram the stage with a mass of genuine or genuine-looking materials. True, there are 'grand' operas, but they are not reason enough for cutting down a small forest. A great deal of wood may however be indispensable for the production of working frames, walls, stairs, ramps and so on, despite the use of standardized sections. Moreover, even small details on the backstage must be as apparently real as they are in the proscenium arch. Reason: opera-glasses!

Wherever it is not absolutely essential, a devotion to authenticity is not only exaggerated but looks suspiciously like a lack of imagination and a fear of originality.

Flats used to be made of painted or otherwise treated canvas on wooden frames, but plywood has gradually taken the place of the canvas. This development can be welcomed for many reasons: the flats are stable and do not become dented when they are moved from place to place. Before plywood can be painted, however, it must be covered with a thin fabric, because it is impossible to paint directly on the grain and knots of primed plywood. Plywood is often replaced with solid timber, mostly sand-blasted to achieve a rustic appearance. For large surfaces such substitutions are a waste of money.

The stage cloth is increasingly being replaced with wooden boards or artificial stone mounted on wooden frames to produce the authentic sound of footsteps. The fact that an orchestra with eighty musicians is doing its best is too often forgotten in all this thirst for authenticity. The worst is that many of these demands are satisfied just to keep the peace; after the première the genuine stone floor has often to be replaced with paint for technical reasons.

From this insistence on visual 'authenticity' the virus of 'giganto-mania' spreads to the entire set. The result is that everything is made as large as possible. Walls tower to just under the gallery: a height of twelve metres is far from uncommon. The backstage becomes the main stage, and its rear wall is given the full treatment. This area is usually some forty to fifty metres from the first row of the stalls, and the distance is frequently spanned with a raked rostrum, to increase the depth effect—with more wood. The 'battle for materials' can of course be extended even further by covering the rostrum with paving slabs or, in the case of 'meadows', with artificial turf.

The use of fabrics can also be stepped up until vast areas are involved. In a completed set, 7,000 square metres of fabric is the normal figure. But if the set is to look 'limp', perhaps for a ballet, the figure can easily go up to as much as 12,000 square metres.

I well remember the ballet set of a visiting stage designer, for which all the ninety-one trucks of the State Opera were loaded with back-drops and frames, each back-drop measuring 21 metres by 12 metres. The painting workshop was closed to every other kind of work for months. The worst excesses, however, are committed by those 'successful' colleagues to whom normal materials are no longer expensive enough, and who indulge themselves in all sorts of extravaganzas.

One, during his first season at the Vienna State Opera, plagued a whole workshop for months with his *idée fixe* that his entire design, consisting of five large sets, should be covered down to the last detail with hemp fibres torn from sacking and strips of jute to a thickness of five centimetres and that, for greater give, the fibres and strips should be sewn on the limp parts of the drops by hand. An area of 20,000 square metres had to be treated in this way.

Yet when the curtain rose, there was a set, and all that struck the audience was that they did not know how it was made: the wall was a wall and yet it wasn't one. No doubt a highly aesthetic guessing game, but did it really warrant all the effort and expense that had gone into it?

This example is typical, but not of course the only one to show that little can be achieved with much effort. The straight path is rejected because the detours seem so much more attractive. The result is invariably a kind of aesthetic traffic jam in the theatre.

However, let us proceed to what goes on behind the scenes: in the workshop, where the history of every set and even of the smallest prop begins. Generally this 'magic site' is attached to the theatre complex; sometimes, as in the account below, it is located a few miles away, and all the more spacious, light and airy for being specially built.

It is morning and everything is ready in the conference room. The model has been assembled and the technical drawings and ground plans are passed around to those present: the technical director, the head of the design studio with his staff—the heads of the various workshops—and, of course, the stage designer and his assistants. Why so many? Because the drawings are about to become reality and everything has to be crystal clear at this point. Everyone present contributes his expertise so that, if necessary, the 'impossible' may be realized.

The scenery is broken down into its elements, each numbered according to a special system. Every built piece is given a number when it is conceived, and its movements can be followed through all the workshops until it is finally brought on stage and assembled. The numbering is very important—a set can consist of up to eighty parts, and there would be indescribable confusion in an opera with several scenes if there were no means of identifying the parts. It has to be laid down precisely what material each piece will be made of, where it has to be divided for easy transport, what surface treatment it should receive, and what its special function may be. All this must be carefully recorded, since quite a long time will elapse before work on it is begun; other built pieces will meanwhile have been produced—and it is human to forget.

Such a conference may last several hours and sometimes grow very heated, especially when the participants disagree about the methods of achieving the requisite visual effects. But this impasse does not usually last long and is in any case quite understandable.

Finally the materials are discussed. The designer wants to cover certain surfaces with rusty tin, only to learn that if you take thin tin and allow it to oxidize, it will be completely rusted through by the first night.

'Well, then, I don't mind if it's some substitute,' the designer says.

'Why not let us produce a few samples and let you look at them?'

He agrees. But what do we do with the floor? It's meant to be of grass, and the available grass cloth is not nearly big enough; the manufacturers are not prepared to do a special job, and so another high-speed emergency solution is required. During the conference various firms are rung up and asked to supply a complete new cloth

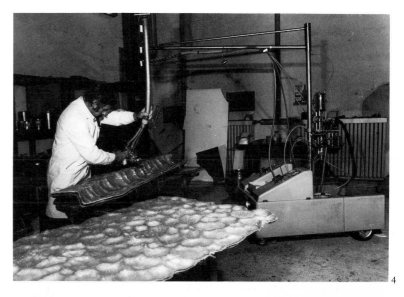

1 Practical wooden frame for a ramp, in the assembly hall. — 2 Hydraulic press with panels for the production of floor boards. — 3 Spiral staircase of wood-clad iron. Precision is of the utmost importance. — 4 Polyester resin and fine glass fibres being sprayed into the negative. — 5 The finished polymerized copy, not yet painted. An imitation cobble-stone pavement *par excellence.*

1 Latex in plaster mould. — 2 Skin being peeled from plaster mould after an interval of thirty minutes. — 3 Left: hardened latex positive; right: plaster mould. — 4 View of the paint shop from the gallery.

with unusually fine grass. In the end there is a compromise between close-cropped green raffia and a fine synthetic 'lawn'.

The last scene is discussed, and soon after the conference room empties. Before that happens a time schedule has been agreed: when the designer can look at the finished samples and when the curtains for the countess's windows can be selected.

Barely have the participants left when the internal machinery starts to hum. Every piece has to be costed and timed; a precise production schedule is worked out; orders for materials are passed on to various suppliers, and delivery dates agreed with them. At the same time the head of the painting shop is busy with the preparatory work. The artists transfer the technical drawings on to wrapping paper previously stretched on the floor, or on to old canvas, and then hand them over to the joinery or the metal shop.

During this work, which often takes a great deal of time, the plans are checked for discrepancies and, if necessary, corrected. At the same time the carpentry and joinery shops are busily getting in the wood. Long planks bought ready-made are planed, cut and glued into standard panels so that there will be no delay once the plans are handed over to the carpenters.

Very often the metal shop is involved at this stage, although most parts are made of wood, which is still the most versatile material of all.

All flats originate as a wooden frame placed over the drawing on the floor and then closed with plywood by the carpenters or covered with cloth by the upholsterers.

All ramps and rostra are supported by hinged frames. They are covered with 'practical' panels which are made to a standard pattern and can therefore be used time and again. The method of manufacture is important. In the past the boards were placed into horizontal presses and pressure was applied from the sides and the top. This process was time-consuming and the end result was not always perfectly smooth or even. Recently much more powerful vertical hydraulic presses have been tested in conjunction with special cold-setting adhesives which work much more quickly. The results are highly satisfactory.

Needless to say, the machine shop where the larger sections are cut, planed and moulded, also contains many other machines, but all have one thing in common: their waste—sawdust, wood shavings, and so on—is sucked up continuously by a central extractor fan.

In another section the cabinet-makers are at work. Furniture-making is a very special business in the theatre. The craftsman cannot rely on the drawings alone, he must also have his own sense of proportion. Often millimetres will make all the difference between ungainliness and elegance, especially with period pieces from more courtly times.

The turner's shop has to cope with delicate wooden parts—from table leg to balustrade, from imperial orbs to the sceptre of *Boris* which, once finished, will be barely distinguishable from the real thing.

The rough sections made in the joinery are fitted with loose-pin, tight-pin or strap hinges, for it must be possible to take the whole set apart for greater convenience in transport, and for any further treatment by the various workshops.

Let us now glance at the 'iron heart' of the workshop complex: the metal department. It is divided into the fitter's shop, the armourer's shop and the light-and-effects shop. In the first originate all such built pieces as railings, straight or spiral iron staircases, and reinforced frames and girders. Here we still find the old-fashioned forge which can produce, say, a wrought-iron scroll or an escutcheon for a Gothic door. This also includes such precision work as the making of bearings, special bolts, wheel flanges and all sorts of objects whose presence on the set is not even suspected. Working from scale drawings, these shops also produce trees out of wire, from the thickest branch down to the thinnest twig. As the joinery relies on glue and staples, so the metal shop relies on electro-welding, rivets and screws. Needless to say, many special effects are made here as well: Moses' rod, which suddenly turns into a snake; the dragon in the *Magic Flute* or *Siegfried*. This section is inordinately versatile.

The armourer's shop prepares for battle and war. Many kinds of swords and daggers are made here: daggers that can be telescoped to be 'thrust' into the breast of Captain Narraboth *(Salome)* or swords to fell the Commendatore after a very brief duel *(Don Giovanni)*, if possible with a built-in bladder of dye, for blood must pour generously. The blades must be genuine but blunt. The Montagues and the Capulets *(Romeo and Juliet)* do not joke during their duels. The steel must be truly tempered or else the foil will not land in Tybalt's body but in the orchestra pit.

Fire-arms must be properly made—the pistols for the Onegin-Lenski duel and the weapon with which Max brings down the eagle in *Der Freischütz*. The barrel must be blocked with paper wads and the lock must be in good order; or else, when the firing squad in *Tosca* receives orders to fire, Cavaradossi will fall without a shot, or the shot may be fired after he has fallen. Not quite the same care need be taken with armour, for which all sorts of materials ranging from wood to foam rubber can be used—metal is dispensed with except for special purposes. But it is in the metal shop that the glittering silver rose for *Rosenkavalier* or the silver tray for Jokanaan's head *(Salome)* originate. And it is in the special effects shop that all the many street lamps, the pompous rococo chandeliers and the art nouveau light brackets are made. This shop is also the birthplace of Olympia, Spalanzani's performing doll.

The modelling department employs both sculptors and 'moulders'. The latter are skilled in technique without necessarily possessing the authoritative artistic talents of the sculptor.

Because of the demand for ever more elaborate sets, this section has gained major importance, and with the increased demand the technique has changed. Copies of an ornament or a piece of architecture are no longer made from papier mâché but, in the case of large surfaces, from polyesters.

I recall an *Aida* production calling for a gigantic wall clad with some 700 square metres of stone facing. We made a mould, injected polyester resin and glass fibre and produced the facing in a quarter of the time it would have taken with conventional materials. The same problem cropped up with the production of a 200 square metre cobble-stone pavement for the narrow lanes of Nuremberg (*The Mastersingers*). We collected large stones from gravel beds and river banks, embedded them in clay and thus produced a positive; next we made a polyester negative and copied it in the requisite quantities. In all these procedures it is important to ensure that the resin is fire-resistant and that the working area is well ventilated.

For the casting of smaller objects—ornaments, stucco-work, etc.—we use a proprietary mixture of natural latex and various additives. This mixture is injected into a plaster mould and left there for thirty minutes. During this time a skin several millimetres thick has formed inside the mould; the skin is peeled off after thirty minutes and spread out for complete drying. The patterns come out very clearly, but there is a slight shrinkage. Expensive carvings on chests and furniture can conveniently be copied in this way.

There is another procedure that allows for even more exact copies. Here the mould is made of silicon resin and the latex is replaced with two fluids that foam up if a small quantity of a catalyst is added. After foaming for a few seconds, the original mixture has expanded to ten times its original volume, in solid, semi-solid or elastic form. In this way every conceivable detail can be copied. A good mould will yield up to two hundred copies, and when they are eventually painted they appear more genuine than the original.

The branches, mentioned previously, are now given their foliage. We no longer make felt leaves in Vienna, though we sometimes still buy them. Usually we make the leaves from thin fire-proof PVC sheeting. They are cut in one batch by the hundred, 'laid' in a negative mould and heat-blown. When moistened, the end product sets in the required shape. Such leaves have the advantage of not hanging listlessly from the tree—they are transparent and, on stage, shimmer in the light. Some 20,000 leaves were manufactured in this way for the linden-tree in front of 'Sachs's house'.

For support, all such vegetation demands a host of other materials including jute, synthetic fibres, sisal and hemp. The most common material is polystyrene, an expanded plastic resin marketed under a variety of trade names. It is used in the building trade for insulation, but nowadays casting would be well-nigh inconceivable without it.

Expanded polystyrene comes in slabs or blocks easily carved with a knife or rasp or cut with a hot wire; it can be turned in a special lathe, and etched with acid to produce interesting structures. Polystyrene cannot be used with all adhesives: quite a few have an 'etching' effect on it. The surface of polystyrene is easily damaged, but this can be circumvented with a protective layer of either thin fabric or paste. More recently an epoxy resin has been applied: it forms a highly resistant but elastic skin over the polystyrene without 'etching' it. If polystyrene is cut with a hot wire, highly toxic fumes must be speedily extracted. It is also important, because of its frequent use on stage, that the polystyrene be fire-proofed.

Polystyrene should always be fresh. During the winter months the store-room may be too cold and in a short time the polystyrene may be ruined; much the same happens in summer when the outside temperature is too high. When we 'foamed up' some balustrades shortly before the summer holidays and tried to use them two months later, we discovered that they were as soft as porridge. Only practice and long experience can teach one the correct procedure.

Let us return to the art department where designs and life-size parts were drawn on paper. The paint shop with its satellites—sewing room, upholstery department, dyeing department—and not least with its painters and craftsmen constitutes the heart of this section.

It is an impressive experience for the layman to step into this room unprepared; on the artist its very size ought to have the magnetic pull of a huge sheet of blank paper. Here cycloramas measuring up to 56 metres by 22 metres are painted in one piece, often posing considerable problems: a sky, with all its finer shadings but without the slightest blemish, must be evenly applied to such a gigantic surface.

The floor of this gigantic hall is made of boards, and must be very smooth since every irregularity will show on the stretched canvas or other material when the brush is moved across it. In principle, all backcloths, cycloramas and flats are painted on the floor. The painted surfaces can be inspected for shape and colour from the gallery which affords an overall view of the work.

Before a cloth is stretched for painting, it is essential to place a ground sheet underneath it. A large number of substances can be used: a PVC sheet for canvases; thin fabric for aniline painting on tulle etc. Paper is not advisable, since the wet paint makes it crinkle, producing a moiré effect on the main surface—which is useful to know if that effect should be required.

Transparent backcloths or cycloramas are made out of linen and painted with aniline dyes, a difficult procedure because every brush stroke has to be perfect. It is also possible to use latex or spirit colours, and if the cloth is synthetic it may be necessary to use special paints to avoid peeling when the cloth is rolled up. The same problem can occur with cloths painted with distemper. All cloths have to be properly primed, for not even the best-made colours will last on a brittle or friable surface.

Another delicate job is the painting of floor cloths. These stage 'carpets' are walked upon, have platforms and trucks dragged across them, and are subject to a great deal of wear and tear. A carefully measured dose of bonding agent is extremely important here because the floor is not only swept before every performance but moistened to 'freshen up' the colours.

When relatively bright paint is applied to black tulle, the ground-sheet is generally of black cotton, for if it were light the colours would not stand out so sharply.

The real problems with all these materials begin when special colours or pastes have to be used. Tulle, for instance, is usually fire-proofed by the manufacturers, and this precaution ought to be greatly welcomed. However, if gold or bronze colours are applied to impregnated tulle, the colours will oxidize into a sort of green soup. There is only one solution: to remove the backcloth and use a new, non-impregnated one pre-treated with a special gold impregnation. The best and safest method is to work with non-impregnated material and to impregnate it before painting. Much more delicate is the use of textile fillers with tulle or gauze. Here the ground-sheet must be of PVC; otherwise the filler will seep on to the floor boards.

We once rolled up a backcloth for transportation only to discover that is could no longer be unrolled. To avoid this problem, the backcloth must be turned over carefully, its back dusted with powder (not white talcum powder, of course) or sprayed very gently with pigment. The backcloth is allowed to dry and then rolled up inside out.

The workshops also simulate three-dimensional natural surfaces, from rotten wood to crumbling walls, from moss-covered stone plinths to gilded marble capitals. Earlier we mentioned the case of sand-blasted floor boards—the harder we worked at making the floor look genuine the more faked and inconsequential it looked. In the end we used a special paste, applied with a rubber roller, and produced the most convincing artificial grain. We used the same method to give tree trunks the kind of a 'barky' look we had failed to recreate with other materials. Brickwork and other building materials can be simulated with compounds of special fillers. Grated cork, sawdust and wood shavings make very serviceable fillers. A smooth covering with a paste of glue and kaolin is effective on walls and similar surfaces, and greater wonders can be achieved by adding aniline dyes, which can be applied wet on wet to produce the most attractive effects.

Very often paintings are demanded that no paint brush or spray gun can possibly produce. Generally these are structural paintings. It may be necessary in such cases to slap masses of paint on to packing paper or nylon. Dies or rollers with a teased foam rubber surface can also produce the most satisfactory results.

Finally we must not forget the painting of properties and furniture—such small objects must be treated with special care because they often draw attention: they are carried about, they move, they may be highly exposed.

It is impossible in so short a space to dwell on every possible technical variation and interesting experience with individual productions. One thing, however, is quite certain: the aim of this undoubtedly artistic department is and always will be to present its products in such a way that the boundary between illusion and reality is lost from sight.

Chapter 3   From Workshop to Stage

BY PROFESSOR GÜNTHER SCHNEIDER-SIEMSSEN

In this chapter we shall be examining that part of our story which takes place once the finished set has been transported to the stage by truck.

The first job is setting up the gridiron in accordance with the sketches and ground plans so that the flown scenery—backcloths, drops and flats—can be worked efficiently. Next the stage-hands put up such heavy fixtures as rostra, ramps and stairs. Last of all comes the assembly of the various movable objects, including pieces of furniture, set props, dressing props and so on.

Sometimes during this phase scenery from the last performance still has to be removed. I well remember talking to Otto Schenk while his *Mastersingers* sets were being taken out. 'Look,' I said, 'the opera was taken off two days ago and they're still carting this stuff away.' The stage-manager rounded on me with, 'But this is the *thirteenth* lorry we have been loading,' and Schenk added soothingly, 'What a lucky number!'

If a set involves projected scenery, it is essential to hold special rehearsals four to six weeks earlier: the stage designer must calibrate all the projection surfaces and record distortions due to angular projection. He must also discuss all lighting and related questions with the lighting designer, questions like the deployment and precise location of the various projectors. He can then prepare his slides, which must be ready before the first lighting rehearsal.

The *lighting plot* comprises the placing and alignment of the spotlights and projectors, the co-ordination of the special effects, and the possible use of film projections. Chandeliers, wall lights and other lamps are fitted at this point.

Once this work is done, the first *lighting rehearsal* can be held. The producer, the stage designer, lighting designer, chief electrician, and stage-manager now go through the entire lighting plot, marked on a piano score or in the prompt book. Filters marked with appropriate numbers are placed in the various projectors. If projections are used at all, the designer must first produce a projection plan for the electrician, and before he can do that he must hold detailed discussions with both the producer and the electrician. Such discussions may take several days.

In productions that call for quick changes of scenery, a *scene-shifting rehearsal* must also be held, first in working light and then with full illumination. Scene-shifts can be effected in many different ways: on a revolve, with wagons or manually. The experienced stage designer will often develop his system of scene changes even while designing the sets, the more so as changes—for instance in Shakespeare—have to be made with clockwork precision. Even when the designer's ideas of scenic changes prove totally impractical, they provide the stage manager with some basis for developing his own solution. In this sphere close collaboration between stage designer, stage-manager and electrician is of particularly great importance.

During lighting rehearsals costumed stand-ins are used to determine the performers' positions. This procedure is indispensable, for man is the measure of all things, and the singer, actor or dancer is the measure of everything that happens on stage. During these rehearsals flaws in any part of the scenery can be detected; the faulty parts can be sent back for repairs to the workshops or, if possible, fixed right on stage between rehearsals.

Once the lighting rehearsals and the intervening orchestral rehearsals are over, the great final spurt can begin.

The *piano rehearsal* is the first musical run-through of scenery and lighting with all the singers in costumes and masks. I call it the 'nerve test', for it is here that all the artistic elements are suddenly brought together, and it is here that the well ordered set may start to go to pieces. The lighting is wrong; a scene-shift is disastrous; a particular costume is not ready; a mask or wig does not fit; an actor has fallen ill; the stand-ins are in the bar and not on stage; a stage-hand has a fall and the ambulance must be called; the technical director rushes to the stage just as the producer is leaving it ostentatiously from the other side to inform the management that the première will have to be postponed; the lighting designer tries to make peace by ordering a break for a smoke, and the stage-manager can't understand why the rehearsal is being held up...

During the *full orchestral rehearsal,* usually spread over two days, everything hinges on the conductor and the music; that is why I call it a 'rest rehearsal' for everyone else. The singers have eyes only for the conductor, the producer checks on his progress or uses the many re-runs demanded by the conductor to make improvements in the lighting.

The *full dress rehearsal* is the last rehearsal before the first night and ought to work as smoothly as the actual performance. And yet there are always a great many last-minute hitches. Experience (or superstition) has shown time and again that a good dress rehearsal is followed by a poor first night, and that a bad dress rehearsal means a magnificent first night. The stage designer's job is now finished and he yields his set to the performers.

Chapter 4   Lighting and Projection

BY PROFESSOR GÜNTHER SCHNEIDER-SIEMSSEN

Pioneering work with stage lighting and projection over the past few decades has helped to open new vistas in the contemporary theatre. The origins of this development can be traced to Europe. Piscator was the first to use films in theatre work; more recently, prominent producers have discovered their own style in this fascinating area, among them Wieland and Wolfgang Wagner, Herbert von Karajan, August Everding, Günther Rennert and many others. A group of stage designers, too, including Heinrich Wendel and Johannes Dreher in Germany, Anneliese Corrodi in Switzerland, and Tobobeck in Britain are renowned for their use of projection on the contemporary stage.

On the other hand, quite a few prominent producers and stage designers who deliberately eschew projection and special light effects have nevertheless set new standards in the theatre. Others are positively hostile to projection techniques, which they feel have not yet been properly developed. Nevertheless, projection techniques have become as indispensable to the modern theatre as X-rays have become in medicine. It seems very likely that 'ultra-violet rays' and 'laser beams' will soon be firmly included in the vocabulary of technical theatre terms.

The move from the easel to the projection table, from working lights to the light console has already been completed in many aspects of the stage designer's work. The ability to paint with light and projection has compelled him to abandon his cramped studio for the stage and the auditorium—his new workshops, his latest experimental laboratories. And team work is increasingly replacing the contribution of the individual creator.

Projection techniques must never degenerate into mere slide-shows; projection is an artistic means of expression that must be treated with respect. It has various functions: it can be a style, a

Günther Schneider-Siemssen
Paul Hindemith: *Die Harmonie der Welt,* 1957   Staatstheater, Bremen   Producer: Albert Lippert, Model

Günther Schneider-Siemssen
Richard Wagner: *Tristan und Isolde*
Act I: On the deck of a vessel
Metropolitan Opera, New York,
1971
Producer: August Everding
Sketch

Günther Schneider-Siemssen
Richard Wagner: *Tristan und Isolde*
Act I: Love philtre and transformation
Metropolitan Opera, New York,
1971
Producer: August Everding
Sketch

substitute for scenery; it can conjure up dreams, visions, changes of place and atmosphere; it can evoke symbolic associations and illustrate the intermingling of the real world with the world of fantasy. It can also represent the stage as cosmic space, and even suggest the weightlessness of the players and the set.

I shall be discussing various projection procedures, their applications, and a number of special techniques and concepts I have developed.

By *image projection* I refer to the projection of architectural features, general views, natural objects, cloud formations and similar objects on to such surfaces as screens, sheets, gauze and many special fabrics.

Projectors strategically placed—in the auditorium, on the ceiling, or in the right and left corners of the house—are focussed on a gauze cloth, a drop scene or a curtain. On the stage itself projectors are focussed from such favourite locations as the perches on to the backdrop or the cyclorama; from the lighting bridge on to the stage floor; from the gallery on to selected areas of the stage; and from the rear of the stage for back projections. A projector must of course be pre-adjusted for the particular purpose it is meant to serve.

Structural projections are projected on to built up flown pieces, such as walls, pillars, trees, etc. They can be executed in many styles, and when used in conjunction with fabrics, wood, metal or plastics can achieve a striking alienation effect. The collapse of buildings and of natural formations can also be simulated by structural projection and with apocalyptic effect.

Moving projections are most commonly produced by the mechanical rotation between the lamp and the lens of two Plexiglas slides; or a film feeding device that turns about the projector. In both, the following effects can be obtained by using extra ribbed glass: moving clouds, rising mist; falling rocks *(Der Freischütz*—the Wolf's Glen); drizzle; cloud-bursts, running water; waves; currents *(Rheingold)*; reflections from water surfaces; waterfalls, floods; steppe fire; blazing flames; dense smoke.

In *photo-projection* various negative and positive film strips are mounted on the projection plates. The plates are then painted in different colours to produce an artistically blended whole.

In *ground projection* light is projected on to the stage by mirrors on the lighting bridge and/or on the perches. This method lends itself to a variety of applications from the most realistic to the most abstract. Used in conjunction with painted or photographic slides, it can help to simulate rock formations, branches, leaves, flowers, meadows or sand. In *Mastersingers,* Act II, the evening quickly makes way for night, and the cobble-stones can be made to look deceptively real with this technique.

Many of these new possibilities greatly facilitate the work of the stage-manager. The reflected light and shade of leaves gliding across the costumes of Pelléas and Mélisande create the illusion of a garden or a forest. But 'garden' and 'forest' do not have to be made with realistic materials—projection can convey the atmosphere just as well. Moreover, it almost completely eliminates the disturbing light circle around the protagonists caused by spot-lights.

Stencilled ground projections, which leave the stage floor completely in the dark, can suggest that rostra or ramps are floating in mid-air. In the Salzburg *Ring* very satisfactory results were obtained in that way. Elliptical segments were shifted into different positions between the scenes while various ground projections were slowly faded out and others were faded in to reveal the new positions of the segments.

Moving projections on the stage can also suggest walking through water, fire or other elements. In Ravel's *Boléro* the stage resembled a large white palette, with the dancers dressed in costumes of various colours—as if squeezed out of paint tubes—lying round its edge. Projected colour compositions flowed into one another and ensured a scintillating choreographic development.

Special effects help the designer to produce a wealth of trick effects. I can give no more than a few examples created either by specialist firms working in close co-operation with stage designers and theatre technicians, or else made in the theatre workshops. The technicians of the Salzburg Festival Hall, in particular, have made large-scale experiments in this field and have achieved striking successes, many of which have been adopted by the Metropolitan Opera and other houses.

For the *fluid effect,* liquids of different consistency are placed between three rotating glass discs. Their combination produces moving patterns.

The *fire-ball* is an invention of the Vienna State Opera, consisting of a plastic sphere with an intense light source in its centre. The transparent surface is painted to resemble flames and can be revolved about the luminous centre to create the illusion of tongues of flame and of an intense fire glow. Fire-balls are placed close to the front or rear of the projection screen etc. and rotated at the requisite speed either mechanically or by hand.

The *fire drum* or *creeping barrage* is a cylinder built on the same principles as the fire-ball. Painted in various ways, its rotations suggest floods or other apocalyptic events. The fire drum can also be used in conjunction with a slide projector aimed at a four- to eight-metre concave mirror. On the slides, which are painted black, intertwining lines of different thicknesses are scratched with a sharp implement. The concave mirror will then project on to selected areas of the set the most extraordinary combinations of movements to bizarre effect. In the production of *The Flying Dutchman* at the Vienna Stage Opera this concave mirror was rotated during the entrance of the ghostly crew, which further intensified their effect. The same technique was used for the world première of *Das Spiel vom Ende der Zeiten* in the Salzburg Great Festival Hall.

Fire wheels or *Catherine wheels* consist of two glass plates (18 centimetres by 18 centimetres) turning in the same or in opposite directions at different speeds. The individual treatment of such plates produces varied effects.

Breakwaters are pieces of ribbed glass with waving contours, painted and affixed to a cylinder. By rotating the cylinder in front of a projector it is possible to create the impression of floods and breakers. These effects have been used with particular success in *The Flying Dutchman*.

For *spiral and circular effects,* glass plates painted in various ways are rotated in the same or in opposite directions.

When the intensity of even the most powerful projectors no longer suffices, the stage designer will have to bring in special flood-lights. Perforated tin plates can be rotated in front of the lights to increase the intensity of the projection. Used in conjunction with fire-glow, water-reflection and various other visual or abstract representations, these plates can create diverse impressions. Such special devices were developed for our *Ring* project in the lighting workshops of Salzburg Festival Hall, and later adopted by the Metropolitan Opera. When the brightness of even these effects proves inadequate, perforated heat-resistant metal discs of different shapes can be used to concentrate the light intensity. Often some thirty to forty profile spot-lights are brought into play at once, and other types of spots are used to paint the stage with light. It is possible, for instance, to draw and then fuse differently coloured circles of light with three profile spots to produce a 'Northern sun' for *Tristan und Isolde*.

The *moving pillar of light* was used to advantage in the presentation of *Moses und Aron* at the Grand Opéra, Paris. That work includes a heavenly apparition; to produce it an enlarged corkscrew was positioned in front of the fire-effect mechanism of the projector. Rotations of the corkscrew and swivelling of the projector produced a pillar of fire that moved across the desert like a whirlwind. This special effect was developed by a firm of lighting engineers working on ideas I had put before them.

The *quicksilver effect* still needs considerable development, since at this stage it can only be achieved manually. Water and mercury are poured into a glass bowl placed on top of the projector. Colour is added, finely striped cellophane is pushed in with glass rods and everything kept in motion. The light is sent vertically upwards and reflected from a mirror. When I once used this effect for a ballet, it produced astounding movements and varied colours. It conjured up human organs, the beating of the heart, the movements of the stomach, the circulation of the blood, shapes of constantly changing colour of the kind that might be seen on an LSD trip. None of these movements, however, could be repeated at will.

The *shadow projector* relies on xenon light and casts very sharp shadows. During the Salzburg *Fidelio* this instrument was used to project a prison wall measuring 25 metres by 15 metres on to a forward-slanting sheet. The Plexiglas slides used measured 100 centimetres by 80 centimetres and called for a novel painting technique. (Normal projection plates, as a rule, measure 13 centimetres by 13 centimetres for use with one to three kW projectors; 18 centimetres by 18 centimetres for use with two to five kW projectors; and 24 centimetres by 24 centimetres for ten kW projectors.) This shadow projector proved effective, *inter alia,* for suggesting the ship in *The Flying Dutchman* at the State Opera in Munich, and later in Vienna.

Orcellograph and special television effects. For the entrance of the Wild Hunt in *Freischütz,* I tried to achieve an apocalypse of falling rocks and burning lava. I went to a television studio, placed a crystal ashtray on a turntable, had it photographed by three electronic cameras and then 'alienated' in the colour mixer. I then faded the final result, captured on colour film, into my set of the Wolf's Glen.

Had we filmed actual rocks and lava we could hardly have hoped to achieve the same striking effect—experience has shown that supernatural phenomena are best realized on stage by artificial methods. Cosmic fog and pulsating galaxies are far more easily simulated than reproduced. Experiments in this field are never-ending and exhilarating.

Realistic films. Only in the rarest cases have filmstrip fade-ins, sixteen or thirty-five millimetres wide, led to convincing scenographic solutions. The chief exceptions are attempts to produce documentary or alienation effects. I greatly prefer special lighting, and other techniques specially devised for the stage.

With the *eidophor* projection system it is possible to give an actor's movements outsize magnification. In August Everding's production of Orff's *Prometheus* this method proved extremely convincing.

Laser beams will undoubtedly create sensational effects one day, perhaps even of three-dimensional projection. So far laser beams have been chiefly used at the Munich State Opera for experimental plays and ballets. These beams are, at present, too unpredictable for my liking and so I deliberately do without them though I hope very much that in the near future they may be counted among proven, style-setting theatrical techniques.

Let me now run briefly through two operas and show how I have applied some of the above-mentioned techniques:

The Flying Dutchman. The interplay of reality and illusion is made manifest even in the difference between Daland's genuine ship and the Dutchman's ghost ship. The appearance of the latter can be represented in a variety of ways, for instance by painting a ship on a projection slide and bringing it closer and closer with the help of a zoom lens.

I had two model ships, sixty centimetres long, built at the Munich State Opera, and used two shadow projectors to show them in sharp profile, Daland's in full sail. Behind the screen I had that ship mounted on invisible rails and cranked towards the projector. The audience saw it coming out of the far horizon to the steep cliffs of the Norwegian coast, until it grew to the full height of the stage. Instead of building a big ship and facing all the technical complications that it would have entailed, we achieved the maximum visual effect with a minimum use of materials and equipment.

A second hurdle had to be cleared in Act III, when the ghostly chorus appears on the deck. To avoid the use of a feature film I tried to develop a special stage method. Into the shaded ship's hull I built a platform on which the sailors could be raised behind the projection screen, to loom up above the ship's rail as moving silhouettes. They busied themselves with real ropes and rigging that blended smoothly into the projected rigging of the model ship. With the fade-in of the furled sails on to the ship in full sail, with the merging of the shadowy projections of the two ships and the projection of strong wind effects, the ghostly character of the scene was sharply impressed upon the audience.

Tristan und Isolde. This opera deals with the translation of two human beings from an earthly plane to an unearthly one, both set on one and the same ship.

The producer August Everding and I decided to construct part of a realistic ship with an upper and a lower deck. Five taut sails made of projection-screen material dominated the stage; in them reflected light was simulated with projectors and spot-lights.

While Isolde hands Tristan the loving-cup, the entire ship disappears—within three seconds. This was done with projections synchronized so precisely that their combined effect simulated the total disintegration of the sails. A misty gauze cloth pulled up to a height of three metres veiled the loving couple. The elevator that removed them from the plane of reality rose unseen out of the ship, and

Tristan and Isolde were suddenly bathed in the unnaturally bright light of an unreal world. The arrival of King Marke and his retinue restored the two lovers to the real world—on the ship that became visible once more, along with the sailors upon it. This idea was developed further at the Metropolitan Opera, New York.

Let me conclude with a brief comment on the economic and administrative aspects of light and projection. Those smaller theatres whose budget is always stretched must make a point of purchasing special spot-lights and projectors. They are long-term investments that pay for themselves in a relatively short time. Projections can replace painted backcloths and built pieces, thereby economizing on the purchase of costly fabrics and building materials. Such savings ought not, of course, be achieved at the expense of the quality of the presentation.

The assumption that a great deal of time can be saved by a major shift to lighting and projection techniques is mistaken. The stage technicians will have less to do: but the electricians will have their hands full.

Chapter 5   'Plastic' Projection in Stage Design

BY HEINRICH WENDEL

In 1963 Heinrich Wendel developed his system of 'plastic' projection in collaboration with the photographer Gerd Körner.

Projection

The projector is a kind of magic lantern; it enlarges small pictures or slides and throws them on to a white screen. The heirs of the magic lantern are the diascope, the episcope, the film projector, and during the past few years, the mighty 10,000-watt projectors which have opened up vast new horizons for theatrical projection.

Formerly, the picture to be projected was painted by hand on to a glass plate: a delicate kind of miniature painting. The modern slide for stage projections ranges in size from 13 centimetres by 13 centimetres to 24 centimetres by 24 centimetres.

Photographic slides are still the exception on the stage, even though colour photography has been developed to unprecedented standards, and modern films can withstand the tremendous heat of

the large stage projectors without deleterious effects on either the colours or the brightness. The light transmission of modern films is only fifteen per cent less than that of painted glass slides. With colour photography it is possible to project large paintings and all sorts of modelled objects.

Projection and modern scenery

For all its technical perfection, projection remains the child of the magic lantern. It produces optical illusions. The more perfect these illusions the more many modern stage designers tend to question their uses. The very distinct materials employed in the construction of modern sets do not portray anything but themselves—or if they do, it is in a symbolic sense only. 'Plastic' or 3-D colour projection by contrast always portrays, even when it introduces abstract glass or metal sculptures, or synthetic materials photographed through polarizers.

If projection is to become an essential part of the set, 'illusion' must be welcomed, not avoided. It must be allowed to transform the scene as if by magic, to heighten sensation and turn images into 'imagination'. Only a few works written for the musical theatre, let alone the dramatic stage, lend themselves to such treatment.

Space and projection in space

Seen from the auditorium, painted and built scenic backgrounds have a space-confining effect. Unlike projection, they do not suggest greater depths than are actually present. Skilful use of perspective in painting or scenery building can admittedly lend the stage greater depth, but the actual scenic elements that produce this effect remain in close proximity. Projection alone can remove the 'agent'—for instance the cyclorama or, better still, a thick veil round the rear of the stage—and replace it with 'infinity'. It is possible to dissolve or dematerialize the picture 'carrier' until nothing but the projected image remains. In that sense, projection can be said to continue the real space of the set in imaginary space.

'Plastic' projection and its physiological basis

If it is possible to take a clear studio photograph of a three-dimensional model, it becomes possible to combine three effects by projection: the visual effect of a good colour photograph, the impalpability of the surface projected upon, and the space-extending and magnifying effect of projection itself.

This combination can create three-dimensional light structures of a visual force that cannot be attained with painted cloths or built pieces. Beyond that, such structures do not confine the actor but surround him with what appears to be vast horizons.

The three-dimensional effect of flat projections is the direct conse-

quence of their space-expanding properties. Objects seem to be removed to a great distance. When human eyes scan remote objects, the focal length of the eye lenses is less subject to changes than in the case of close objects, and there is also less parallax. With very remote objects these two facets of stereoscopic vision can be ignored—the eye relies almost exclusively on the three-dimensional 'feel' of the object, and on its light and shade effects. Both can be produced with photographs of specially constructed models.

The model as element of 'plastic' projection

It is impossible to project on to the stage from the spectator's angle of vision: the projector would have to be placed in an awkward spot and the proscenium frame would restrict the size of the projection. Two projectors are placed in the wings; the left half of the image is projected from the right side and the right half from the left. The two halves must meet in the middle. This poses the characteristic problems of the construction of models for 'plastic' projections.

The model must be built exactly to scale and photographed from exactly the same angle and place as that from which the projections into the stage will be made. If the model is three-dimensional, it must be built with abnormal perspectives that have first to be computed. For when viewed from the points from which it is to be photographed, the model must look as its projection has to appear to the spectator. More precisely, the left half of the model intended for a relatively high point on the right side of the proscenium must look just as the projected picture of this left half will appear to a spectator in the centre of the house. The same applies to the right half of the model, but in reverse. Hence, if an architectural feature is to appear in normal perspective, the model, though photographed from a relatively elevated part of the house, must, when projected, look like a top, not a bottom, view. Lateral effects must be treated similarly, i.e. the model must be extended to the right or left respectively.

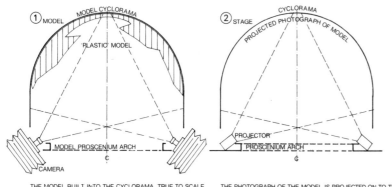

THE MODEL BUILT INTO THE CYCLORAMA, TRUE TO SCALE, IS PHOTOGRAPHED IN COLOUR FROM THE APPROPRIATE POSITIONS.

THE PHOTOGRAPH OF THE MODEL IS PROJECTED ON TO THE CYCLORAMA

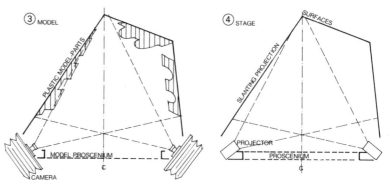

ALL POSSIBLE GROUND PLANS CAN BE USED FOR 'PLASTIC' PROJECTION. (THE NECESSARY SHIFTS IN PERSPECTIVE HAVE BEEN INDICATED ON THE GROUND PLAN OF THE MODEL.)

Wolfgang Amadeus Mozart: *Titus*
Final scene: In the Colosseum, Rome. Variable 'plastic' projections behind an illuminated, fixed rostrum.

Heinrich Wendel working on models for 'plastic' projection (1970). Below, the model for Ill. 2.

Claudio Monteverdi: *L'Incoronazione di Poppea*
Thermal baths outside Rome. Seneca and his pupils. The projected architecture and shadows help to 'extend' the set in space. Downstage, three movable ellipses constitute a variable simultaneous stage, whose background can be altered by changeable 'plastic' projections. Model carved out of plaster and mounted on a Plexiglas cyclorama with engraved lines. The shadows fall on a second, cardboard cyclorama.

45

1 Richard Wagner: *Parsifal*. Scene 1: A lake in the woods.
2 Richard Wagner: *Parsifal*. Scene 6: A temple. Instead of 'plastic' projections, flat, painted model cycloramas were projected in colour by the same method of perspective scaling. The projected trees were masked in black behind the gauze cyclorama, so that the chorus seemed to be moving between the trees and the lake.

3 Richard Wagner: *Rheingold*. Final scene. This four-part work is played on a segment of a sphere—the terrestrial sphere. Entrances from below and all around. The background is varied with changing 'plastic' projections on a gauze cyclorama that becomes transparent at times. Here the players are moving on a round black dais behind the projection.

4 Richard Wagner: *Siegfried*. Final scene. The stony parable of the Valkyries' rock appears as a series of 'plastic' projections that vary in colour, contrast, transparency and intensity, depending on the lighting.

3

4

Krzysztof Penderecki: *St. Luke's Passion.*
A large rostrum with sliding sections for a chorus of one hundred voices is surrounded by visible batteries of spot-lights in black space, or by a cyclorama with 'plastic' projections. Here 'plastic' background and ground projections place a 'steel and wire relief' over chorus, stage and players for the scene of Christ's binding with chains.

Richard Wagner: *Götterdämmerung.* The hall of the Gibichungs.
The projected building changes with the illumination. In the end it blazes up as the world is consumed in flames.

The potential uses of 'plastic' projection

With this method, all sorts of materials in any shape can be projected without loss of structure or attractiveness. The effect can be enhanced further with special light effects, for instance the fade-over of two slides of the model taken in different lights. To that end, a second set of projectors must be placed as close as possible to the two projectors on either side of the stage.

Special effects can also be produced with 'plastic' projections on gauze when the surround of the projected windows, arches, gates, etc., is masked in black. Actors can appear in projected windows, on imaginary balconies, or loom up in glassy structures. An entire chorus can make its entrance through a non-existent arch; a gigantic copper tree can arise as if by magic around a *corps de ballet*. Those who delight in naturalistic illusions can use 'plastic' projection to cause rocks and temples to collapse and bury the actors under boulders.

If used with skill and imagination, 'plastic' projections can produce everyday effects as well as the most sublime impressions.

Chapter 6   *Coping with Very Large and Very Small Stages*

BY PROFESSOR GÜNTHER SCHNEIDER-SIEMSSEN

Before I discuss the largest of all modern stages—that of the new Festspielhaus in Salzburg—I should like to consider some of the problems waiting in the wings of very small theatres.

During my student days there was the Zimmertheater in Munich; I was asked to transform two large rooms in a patrician mansion into an auditorium and a stage. A sliding glass door was our front curtain; wall brackets and chandeliers were 'sockets' for all the stage lighting. A curtained-off area served as a place of concealment, a cupboard door as the door to an unseen room. Furniture and props were always within easy reach.

When I first worked for the Lustspielhaus in Schwabing, a suburb of Munich, I was faced with a monstrously large stove that stood directly in front of the stage. My continuous attempts to make allowances for this monster culminated in a love-hate relationship. I succeeded in using it for all sorts of practical purposes, not only during the winter months but in the summer as well. It served as an advertising pillar, a shelf for papers, the corner of a house, a wrought-iron grating or a shrubbery—all of which uses forced me to extend my knowledge of fire-protection methods.

The Volksoper in Pasing, another suburb of Munich, for which I designed several comic-opera sets, had a tiny stage with a height of no more than four metres. For that reason I confined myself to details, trying to keep a balance between architectural and human proportions.

My first encounter with a 'real' theatre, as I imagined it in those days, occurred in 1951, and brought me face to face with the smallest of small stages: the Salzburg Puppet Theatre, to which I have remained deeply attached. The Mozart operas which that theatre presents during its international tours have made the Salzburg puppets world-famous.

The stages of the Salzburg Puppet Theatre and the new Festspielhaus are of the same proportions; widths of three metres and thirty metres and heights of ninety centimetres and nine metres respectively. Salzburg thus boasts the smallest as well as the largest stage in the world. This inevitably raises the question of which 'opera-house' in Mozart's city presents his works to better advantage.

I would give my vote to the Puppet Theatre, for here role, music and space are fused into a singularly harmonious whole. Until 1954 the stage had a depth of one metre, the length of an actor's arm. With the agreement of the puppeteers and stage technicians I made a number of changes. We raised the bridge on which the operators stand to increase the available playing area. As a result, the strings became longer and the movements of the marionettes benefited.

Another consequence was revolutionary: the raised bridge enabled us to deploy large marionettes downstage and small ones upstage, introducing a perspective in keeping with the built pieces. This cannot, of course, be done on the conventional stage since human proportions cannot be altered so dramatically. For tours, a light metal stage in the same proportions was constructed; it could be quickly assembled and dismantled for transportation by air.

A further innovation we added was a revolve with collapsible segments that reached up to the curtain. Finally, the lighting plant was enlarged to allow for projection.

Building scenery for a puppet theatre is of course not the same as building conventional sets. There are no windows, door frames or ceilings, all of which would impede the movement of the strings and hence of the marionettes.

While the puppet theatre uses many of the same materials as the normal theatre, much greater attention has to be paid to all sorts of details. Quite a few scenic and lighting problems are much more easily solved in the puppet theatre, which is spared a host of familiar difficulties and unsatisfactory half-way solutions. The appearance of the Queen of the Night suspended in space, the entrance of the animals, the trial by fire and water, can be staged imaginatively and yet credibly.

The entrance of the Commendatore in *Don Giovanni*—often an embarrassment on the large stage—can look charming in the puppet theatre. Don Giovanni's descent into hell seems more convincing than on any other stage. In Mozart's *La Finta Giardiniera* gardens and scenery can be shown on a seventeen-metre belt. As it moves past him the spectator can admire a varied panorama of clouds, changes in the weather, or clear, Watteau-style landscapes.

The smallest stage turns theatre into magic, into dreams. The puppet theatre has remained my laboratory for examining many aspects of artistic interpretation and dramatic communication.

The small stage of the Bremen Kammerspiele, by contrast, forces the stage designer to use every inch of available space. This problem fills the imagination with new and often surprising ideas. That is why the larger of the small theatres, for instance the Munich Kammerspiele, the Thalia Theater in Hamburg or the Landestheater in Salzburg—to mention just a few—are among my favourites.

Coping with very small stages may prove an extremely complex business: the stage designer and producer must use all their skill and ingenuity to express the dramatic tension in the relationship between man and space. The greatness of a night at the theatre is not decided by the greatness of the stage. The producer August Everding put it very well when he said, 'Before you can create the scenic space for a particular work, you must be able to describe every possible space the human imagination can conceive.'

Let us now turn to medium-sized and large stages. Undoubtedly theatre buildings with their various advantages and drawbacks, their spatial properties and technical installations, have a crucial bearing on the design of a particular set or on a specific stage conception. I can give a few examples based on my experience: for large choral operas either the proscenium is not wide enough or—as in most cases—the built pieces lack the necessary height, which is due to the low roof or the low gridiron. The history of architecture, from ancient temples through Gothic cathedrals to the latest skyscrapers in New York and Chicago, all reflect a longing for height, a sense of the grandeur of cosmic space. Theatres—with a few laudable exceptions (the Paris Grand Opéra, the Munich Nationaltheater and the New York Metropolitan Opera)—have remained deaf to this call. If one tries to find out why, one is usually told, 'The roof had to be kept low to fit in with the city plans,' or 'The grant was much too small.' In many cities with hideous skylines these answers are plainly spurious and easily rebutted. Let me illustrate this point by comparing two very different theatres of which I have personal experience: the Vienna State Opera and the Lyric Theater, Chicago.

The Lyric Theater is practical, effective, and unique in its disregard for external appearances: its home is a skyscraper with apartments and offices at the front. Behind this façade the building is exploited to its full height, giving a stage that towers to some fifty metres. All flown scenery can be pulled up so high that it cannot be seen from the stalls. This is a great technical boon that also facilitates lighting and projection, because borders and built pieces are not nearly the obstructions they are on the conventional stage.

The Vienna State Opera is another almost ideal building. The remarkable achievement of a small country, resurrecting its famous old opera in all its glory, deserves praise—although the architects and municipal authorities failed to take due account of some modern needs. The proscenium ought to be much wider than thirteen metres; spectators in the boxes near the stage have severely confined lines of vision, especially during large choral operas. The height of the proscenium is given as 7.5 metres but it can be enlarged to nearly ten metres. Nevertheless, the gridiron is not nearly high enough, a direct result of the overall architectural conception.

The enormous depth of the stage (forty-eight metres) admittedly allows for the staggering of scenery to maximum visual effect, but that is rarely important since it is impossible to gauge depth beyond a given point. This back-stage area is used chiefly for the assembly and dismantling of sets, and the temporary storage of scenery. It is also used for technical work and back projection, for which the enormous depth makes it eminently suited. It does not matter a great deal that the Vienna State Opera, like the Munich State Opera, has just one side stage; the stage designer can effect quick changes of scenery with the help of the ten-metre-deep understage and the six-piece elevator floor measuring 18 metres by 3 metres, which can be moved hydraulically to any desired horizontal position. An additional understage to the rear is a most convenient store of scenery.

Practice has taught me that normally proportioned stages are the easiest to handle. I refer to such theatres as the Vienna State Opera, the Deutsche Oper, Berlin, the State Opera, Munich, the Metropolitan Opera, New York, the State Opera, Hamburg, the Grand Opéra, Paris, the Teatro Colón, Buenos Aires, La Scala, Milan—and many that have just one side stage or none at all.

Medium-sized and very large stages necessitate the deployment of the understage to maximum effect. Many years ago the staging of the *Ring of the Nibelungs* at Covent Garden demanded the prior removal of several tons of superfluous metal reinforcement so that electrical screwjacks could be built in. Covent Garden, which has no side stages and no back stage, uses the last few metres of the stage to store scenery, the built parts being stacked up right to the ceiling. Quite apart from the fire risks this entails, the dimensions of the remaining area introduce grave problems for the producer and stage designer.

In general, the difficulties in coping with very small and very large stages do not spring exclusively from architectural miscalculations. Labour regulations, casting problems and artistic and technical demands expose all who work in the theatre to constant pressures, and these are often more of a hindrance than even the worst buildings.

There are two distinct ways of designing sets:

The set can be created for a particular stage. The designer takes its technical equipment into account when planning his presentation. Such sets cannot, of course, be taken on tour.

The set can be designed without relying on specific stage machinery, and be modified to suit a variety of theatres.

Let me give a few examples:

The Salzburg *Ring*-ellipse in the new Festspielhaus is based on rollers and sliding segments. The ellipse moves in its own orbits, and changes the scenic space into which the different parts of the four operas can be fitted without assistance from the stage machinery. For Horvath's *Geschichten aus dem Wienerwald* (Tales from the Vienna Woods) at the Burgtheater and the Munich Kammerspiele, a special system of scene-shifts and projection had to be invented for this ellipse. It was set up with its existing technical aids, with comparatively little expense.

For Shakespeare's *As You Like It, The Taming of the Shrew* and *Much Ado About Nothing,* Otto Schenk and I devised certain sets which could be modified to serve in all four plays. All of our sets allowed for quick scene changes. With every one of these sets it was possible not only to develop up to fifty different ground plans and playing areas, but also to give guest performances on large and small stages alike.

The development of new scenographic systems with inbuilt technical devices was the subject of experimental studies at my seminar at the International Summer Academy in Salzburg. We tried, for instance, to develop an extended stage for the three Shakespeare comedies just mentioned that would allow for different styles without visual repetition.

Financial and cultural factors may well force the musical theatre to consolidate its stage area. Research into more flexible stage design should take this trend into account.

Stages of different size can offer acoustic problems. Let me mention just one episode in this connection: for the re-opening of the Theater an der Wien *The Magic Flute* was staged under Herbert von Karajan's musical direction and in Rudolf Hartmann's production. I tried to tailor my design to the special needs of this house, but the set was later—and to me quite unexpectedly—transferred to the Vienna State Opera, where it had been built. This transfer caused no technical problems because the stage of the State Opera is larger, but the acoustics of the two houses are quite different.

Originally, when Professor Hartmann and I agreed that the Queen of the Night would emerge from the depths of the earth and move downstage to sing her taxing *coloratura* aria from behind gauze, I was afraid that von Karajan might object on acoustic grounds. When I put it to him he said, 'Don't bother about the music; I'll get round it somehow—the main thing is to have it look good and convincing.' Lucky indeed is the stage designer whose conductor is as concerned with the visual presentation as with the sound!

Three years later, when the sets were transferred to the State Opera, the work was to be conducted by Josef Krips, whose Mozart interpretations I hold in very great esteem. He wanted all the sets shifted downstage as he could not hear the voices. Had I done as he asked, the première would have had to be postponed, for considerable changes would have had to be made. I tried to solve the problem in a most unconventional way—I changed nothing at all.

The task of coping with very large stages like that of the new Festspielhaus in Salzburg, invariably brings about a clash of interests for the stage designer. Usually, he must try to come to grips with the work first, but in this situation he has to deal simultaneously with the stage and the message of the play. Instead of a continuous work process he is drawn into a work conflict: the opera *vs.* the stage, the stage *vs.* the opera.

The relative shallowness of the new Festspielhaus stage poses a problem only when back projection is called for—the width of the stage and the short distance between the back projector and the cyclorama can cause the projected picture to look 'like a stamp on an envelope'. The cyclorama has to be moved forward by several metres, which reduces the upstage acting area. At this point let me quote from my 'Man and his space in the Festspielhaus' (*Opernwelt,* 1974), an article that dealt chiefly with the problems of very large stages:

> Again and again one is asked about the shape and size of the ideal opera stage. The ideal would no doubt be to present every work—from the chamber opera to the great choral opera—on a stage suited to its size and form.

> This ideal has been realized in Salzburg, which has stages for every shape and size of presentation. The new Festspielhaus, with its cinemascope stage and amphitheatrical auditorium, forms a striking contrast to the traditional opera-house with its picture-frame stage and towering tiers of seats. For that reason the great stage of the Festspielhaus calls for a specific type of dramaturgy, and for works whose spiritual import and greatness are at one with the magnitude of the stage.

> Conversely, whenever works written for the normal opera-house are put on in the Festspielhaus, producer and stage designer must use the added potential of the huge forestage with great sensitivity. In particular, they must not reduce the size of the stage so as to destroy its proportional relations with the auditorium.

> The artistic and technical demands we now make of an opera-house are generously met in the new Festspielhaus, whose shape helps to create acoustic conditions that can only be described as superb. If we compare its visual qualities with those of other opera-houses the Festspielhaus comes off best as well. In particular, the side seats and stalls in many opera-houses afford unsatisfactory viewing conditions while in the Festspielhaus the entire stage can be seen from every seat. The spectator has the best auditory and visual conditions wherever he sits.

The work as the starting-point

When designing a set for the new Festspielhaus, the first question must be: 'How can I do justice to the work?' Dramaturgy determines the scenic solution...

The liberating and living theatre does not depend on stages boasting all the latest technical refinements. An over-equipped theatre does not necessarily guarantee the quality of a production; indeed, it threatens to do violence to the author's intellectual conception by diverting it into purely technical channels. There must be full freedom to take or leave the magnificent technical aids the modern stage has to offer, and this freedom can only be attained by those who accept that stage technology must be the servant of dramaturgy.

One should only employ a revolve if its use is demanded by the work, if it has a real function in the stage presentation. For that reason I welcome the absence from the Festspielhaus of a fixed built-in revolve. Like every opera-house, however, the Festspielhaus is not without flaws. The technical director Herman André has had to expose a number of rigid technical structures; flexible battens, cycloramas and light metal trucks are but a few innovations from which both the artistic and technical sides of the Festspielhaus have greatly benefited.

Compared with its width of thirty-three metres, the stage is relatively shallow. But this is not too great a disadvantage because perspective arrangements and constructions can often help to simulate stage depth.

The height of the stage (eight to nine metres) is not what it might have been—the content of many works demands great height. The maximum height of the stage is determined by the height of the gridiron, and the whole by the size of the façade which, in the event, is a protected monument. A more harmonious solution should have been sought by the municipal planners. As it is, the stage practitioner has to revert to a tested traditional means: borders to mask the flown scenic pieces. This is particularly important for the expensive seats in the front rows, all of which have a full view of the top of the stage...

The curtain at the Festspielhaus cannot be manually operated because of its weight. This is due to the extreme width of the stage, and it often poses special problems, for the motor closing the curtain must be perfectly synchronized with the score.

We saw how difficult it often is to move a set designed for one opera-house to another. A set created for the Festspielhaus is unlikely to fit into a normal opera-house. The Kremlin Theatre in Moscow is the only house of a comparable order of magnitude, and hence the only one to which such a transfer would be possible.

Because every theatrical director, designer and stage-manager tends to worry about the expense of a set, it must be pointed out that the large costs incurred in this house are due not only to the demands of particularly exigent works, but also to the very size of the stage. This is a matter of simple calculation. From one backcloth built for the Salzburg Festival Hall it is possible to make two to three backcloths for an opera-house of normal dimensions. The same ratio holds for most other built pieces...

Man in light and space

Human relations and their expression on the stage pose some of the most difficult problems the producer and designer have to solve. The simplest entrances, exits and groupings have to be developed in specific ways.

Light and projection are here, as everywhere, decisive elements of the set. The theatre in general and the Festspielhaus in particular can no longer be conceived without the adjunct of modern lighting techniques...

Since the theatre is in a continuous state of evolution, ever new demands are being made of this large stage that can accommodate every possible form of dramatic expression—from the simultaneous setting (tryptichon) to the opera, the cosmic theatre and the concert.

[*Op. cit.*, pp. 31-4.]

Chapter 7   *The Stage as Cosmic Space*

BY GÜNTHER SCHNEIDER-SIEMSSEN

Before we treat the stage as cosmic space, I would refer the reader to *Die Bühne als kosmischer Raum. Zum Bühnenbildschaffen*, (The Stage as Cosmic Space. On Stage Designs) by Günther Schneider-Siemssen, published in Vienna by the Bergland Verlag in 1976. Its authors—Kurt Becsi, Walther Birkmayer, August Everding, Joachim Kaiser and Georg Pirckmayer—investigate this aspect of my work from several distinct viewpoints. Since the book is still in print all I shall do here is to sum up its most important points.

On the origins of my approach I should like to quote Heinz Haber, Professor of Astrophysics, who says in his *Der offene Himmel* (The Open Sky), 'The universe is a gigantic spectacle that unfolds before our eyes. The stage of this universal spectacle is space or,

Günther Schneider-Siemssen
Arnold Schönberg: *Erwartung*. Royal Opera House, Covent Garden, London, 1957. Producer: Peter Ustinov, Sketch

Günther Schneider-Siemssen
Richard Strauss: *Die Frau ohne Schatten*. Act III: Final scene, State Opera, Vienna, 1964. Producer: Herbert von Karajan, Sketch

Günther Schneider-Siemssen
Paul Hindemith: *Mathis der Maler*. Opera House, Nuremberg, Producer: Peter Lehmann, Sketch

Günther Schneider-Siemssen
Carl Orff: *De temporum fine comoedia*
World première, Salzburg Festival,
1973. Producer: August Everding

more precisely, cosmic space.' The existence of so magnificent an astronomic spectacle in space and time can only be suspected by those who understand the greatness and glory of the universe, its tragedy and transformation. According to certain contemporary cosmological theories, it is an apocalyptic display: one that depicts a tragic decline, but points to a higher, other-worldly form of existence.

In this connection it should be remembered that a scene on the normal stage also points beyond the immediate events to a cosmic, existential nexus. This explains my attempts to represent the stage as cosmic space, my liking for plays and operas that contain cosmic features or perspectives. In general, the idea of a 'cosmic' theatre not only reflects the cosmic consciousness of modern man, one who has walked on the moon—but also that unfolding of cosmic consciousness which is characteristic of all great cultures. It is the job of the visionary designer to integrate the new world of cosmic experience into his designs, to express linguistic or musical emotions lyrically or dramatically against cosmic space. The creation of such space demands an innate musical sense—the sensitive treatment of all inner and external events as symbolic expressions, the infusion of spirit into the most abstract ideas. One of my projects was the creation of a set in which gravity had apparently vanished. This was achieved in several scenes of Wagner's *Ring* and *Tristan und Isolde,* in Strauss's *Frau ohne Schatten* and in Carl Orff's last work, *Das Spiel vom Ende der Zeiten.*

Others before me had already gone a good part of the way. Jacques Polieri with his *théâtre total,* Oskar Schlemmer with his *Bauhausbühne,* Egon Vietta with his *spherical theatre,* inspired by Indian religious ideals, and Pierre Garnier with his *théâtre spatial* all made progress in this direction. Mention should also be made of the many interesting designs for new theatre buildings, for instance Ernst Pischke's plan, inspired by the architecture of a planetarium; and of the importance of lighting on the modern stage, as advocated by Adolphe Appia and Edward Gordon Craig among others. The

turning-point, however, will only come when contemporary writers for the conventional and musical stages enter upon new paths and set new standards as part of a general collaboration between the liberal arts and space research.

Pointers to this development can be found in Goethe's *Faust,* in Richard Wagner's music theatre, in Strindberg, Apollinaire, Claudel, Tagore, Lorca, Priestley, Wilder *(Planetary Mind),* Brecht, and in the existentialist theatre and the theatre of the absurd (Sartre, Camus, Ionesco, Beckett).

Of the attempts to present this ideal on the stage I consider the following worth mentioning here: *Boris Godunov* (in Herbert von Karajan's production, Salzburg, and in Otto Schenk's production, Vienna); *Fidelio* (Otto Schenk); *Parsifal* (Dieter Haugk, Munich); Schönberg's *Expectation* (Peter Ustinov); Britten's *Midsummer Night's Dream* (Werner Düggelin); *Frau ohne Schatten* (Herbert von Karajan, Vienna, 1964); Stravinsky's *The Rite of Spring* (Vienna); *Pelléas et Mélisande* (Herbert von Karajan, Vienna).

The stage designer's art will not, in the future, be considered a subsidiary branch of theatrical activity, but creative work *sui generis*—something that can help to shape the work creatively. The theatre of the future will no doubt portray cosmic emotion and awareness based on spiritual and religious strivings. It is bound to have a decisive influence on the development of all the arts.

I should like to conclude this brief digression on the stage as cosmic space with a quotation from Albert Einstein's *Cosmic Religion* (Covici, Friede, New York, 1931):

> ... The individual feels the vanity of human desires and aims, and the nobility and marvellous order which are revealed in nature and in the world of thought. He feels the individual destiny as an imprisonment and seeks to experience the totality of existence as a unity full of significance.

To develop and foster these ideas, to convey them to the spectator and to help him experience them for himself—that is how I see my task for the future.

Chapter 8   My Work as Producer and Stage and Costume Designer

BY JEAN-PIERRE PONNELLE

I became a producer after long experience as a stage designer had convinced me that I was unable to present my work as I wanted. There were too many differences and misunderstandings with producers, and I discovered that I could no longer answer for my work. I decided to refuse all commissions that did not give me sole responsibility for the entire production.

In this combined role it is all the more important to study the score—not just the piano arrangement—very thoroughly. There are some composers, Mozart amongst them, whose orchestral technique is of the utmost importance to the producer. The very choice of key can illuminate certain emotions or psychological situations. Mozart's use of a particular modulation may be said to dictate the choice of production, lighting, stage and costume design. I also filter the libretto through the screen of my analysis of the score with the 'sediment' constituting the basis of my interpretation.

Experience has taught me that when the roles of producer and stage designer are fused, it is the latter who really suffers. My chief interest is the concept, the realization of the work. If one is merely a stage designer there may be a temptation to concentrate too fully on the purely graphical aspect of the set; it can become a pleonastic illustration of the producer's concept. This is something I deplore.

The time the normal stage designer spends on the elaboration of the producer's concept—on sketches and technical drawings—runs to hundreds of hours a year. I feel certain that fifty per cent of this time is wasted on pointless work: the making of sketches for the sole purpose of satisfying the producer and of explaining the effects to be achieved. I am only too happy to forego this sort of work; I greatly prefer to hand my drawings straight to the workshops. This system saves me a lot of time; sometimes I need less time now to build all the sets and to produce the work than I would have needed just to make the sets for another producer.

Combining the roles of producer and stage designer also has disadvantages. When a producer's concept lives in symbiosis with a stage design, the benefits to both are self-evident: one knows even at the first rehearsal how the set will look in its final form. At subsequent rehearsals there will—at most—be changes of costume due, say, to physical assessments of certain actors; or to a change in my original concept, leading to a very subtle alteration in the character of a role. However, I am deprived of the benefits accruing from discussions between producer and stage designer, which can be extremely fruitful. This enriching exchange of ideas cannot be achieved by any amount of self-analysis. Sometimes I badly miss a partner, a critical partner. In the opera-house, I often do find him in the person of the conductor, whose artistic judgement I greatly prize.

I dispense with scene-shifting rehearsals completely. They serve only to obstruct the whole operation and they cost a fortune. I think that able producers should do without them.

I have never yet allowed the curtain to rise at a first night without the conviction that I had done all my homework and presented the opera as best I could. Nevertheless it does happen that in retrospect the scales fall from my eyes—sometimes even at the first night—and I suddenly have the feeling that I must do better next time.

The set is but one of many elements in the dialectical process constituting the theatre. When I was a designer and nothing more, I naturally—and wrongly—considered my work to be an independent art form.

I no longer believe in aesthetic conceptions; it is a matter of utter indifference whether a set is beautiful or ugly—all that really matters is whether it is 'right' or 'wrong.' The proper function of a set is to render a particular production more comprehensible. The designer's concept is part of the vocabulary of the overall dramaturgic concept, to which it must subordinate itself in the same way as the lighting design, the costumes, the pantomime and all the rest.

Chapter 9   Professional Ethics

BY JEAN-PIERRE PONNELLE

Opera, like every other form of dramatic art, is affected by fashion; if one's own approach happens to be in tune with the prevailing trend it is obvious that success will come more easily. But such success, by its very nature, can never reflect the true merit of a work of art. Admittedly, one has to be very careful with such concepts as 'art'. The theatre presents one particular form of art in one particular place and addresses it to one particular audience. After a few years, or a few months, that form may seem antiquated, for all too often it has ceased to reflect social, historical and sometimes economic realities.

However, when one considers that most producers and stage designers are intent upon presenting the results of their studies and reflections as well as they possibly can, and not only to gain easy popular success and rave reviews, then we automatically introduce the concept of 'qualification'.

In my view that stage designer is 'qualified'—or 'professional'—who combines craftsmanship and skill with the intelligence to probe into the deeper essence of a work of art, and who has the imagination to present his knowledge as attractively as possible.

Needless to say, presentations are often beset with financial problems. But lack of money—and there are many examples—is not always a handicap. Very often definite limits, or 'corsets', are highly desirable, particularly when they stem from economic, not politico-cultural, considerations. I am against the squandering of money in the theatre, the more so as high costs are often due to lack of teamwork.

Serious differences of opinion can often be attributed to the 'blindness' of producers. Very often they cannot conceive in space what they accept in the stage designer's two-dimensional draft or scale model. Then expenditure escalates, as the set travels between workshop and stage for constant corrections.

Professional competence means, moreover, that if a producer or stage designer comes to the conclusion during the preparatory phase, that the work does not suit his talents, that he is not the right or the best man to stage it, then he ought to refuse the commission. In all such cases I consider it a matter of course—contract or no contract—that artistic integrity should take precedence over the letter of the law.

Chapter 10   *Stage Design Today*

BY GÜNTHER UECKER

The citadels of music—are they needed, are they places that move the world?

They are rather places of piety, courts at which the bequests of the great composers are interpreted, transformed into feasts of delight, ritualized into conventions.

Here artificial form celebrates itself; no original interpretation can find more original expression.

Such cultural institutions as opera-houses and museums, hand-me-downs from the past, could, when filtered through their own dust, find essential expression in the originality of artists representing themselves.

I believe that the 'opera-house', as a Noah's ark, ought to be abandoned, and that the music theatre must be matched to the intellectual demands of the day.

Performing tasks ought to be delegated to artists, writers and composers.

Here I should like to dilate on the task of the artist as stage designer.

To leave greater room for the music, the set must be a visual space in which the music can find flowing, floating, spatial and temporal expression.

Movements, structured by static means, present themselves as a visual score. The set is no longer illustration but instrument.

Music is made visible; it is perceived in the interstices of the visual structures.

The set is functional, it offers the singers choreographic positions that lend clarity to the sung literary form.

This approach has proved itself in my designs for a ballet, Bach's *Suite No. 1;* for a composition by Schnebel; for an opera, Döhl's *Klangszene;* and in *Fidelio* and *Parsifal*.

In every case, the closest possible collaboration with the producer, the conductor, the choreographer, the chorus master and, in *Fidelio,* the author, was a prerequisite of a harmonious presentation.

By transcending the originality of the individual, by verging towards complex phenomena treated as a whole, the musical theatre has been able to retain its original fascination and vitality.

Opera Production

Hans Hartleb

These comments, based on my long and varied experience as an opera producer in fourteen countries in Europe, America and Asia will be subjective, but no one can write of matters close to his heart with complete detachment. I should like to stress that it is not my intention to extol the producer's profession, or to present it as the be-all and end-all of opera.

Nevertheless, I believe that opera in its present form is essentially moulded by the producer, and in particular by his efforts to suit it to the conditions of our age. I am aware that no matter what his positive achievements, he is also responsible for a host of distortions and failures.

Opera as Paradox

Opera, fathered—or concocted—by cultured Florentine nobles, quickly became the favourite form of court entertainment. It was absorbed intact into nineteenth-century bourgeois culture, and continues to attract broad strata of the population in both the democratic and the socialist republics. Currently experiencing a great revival of interest, opera derives its extraordinary vitality from the tension between music and speech, a tension that clamours for resolution. Moreover, though opera may lack the expressive force of the dramatic play, it excels over it in direct sensual appeal.

The Apollonian and the Dionysian impulses, Ratio and Eros, inhabit both forms of the stage but it is a characteristic of the dramatic stage that Ratio should predominate, while Eros reigns supreme in the musical theatre. This explains the direct sensual appeal of opera, which is its basis and moving force, and the cause of prolonged bursts of applause no less than of the most derisive catcalls.

Riddled with paradoxes that are hard to analyse, this strange and enchanting art developed its astonishing vitality, its adaptability to the most divergent social structures out of the friction generated by its inherent contradictions. Because it moves along two tracks, it calls for two kinds of driver: a conductor and a producer. The former is in charge of the musical apparatus, the latter of the stage and everything appertaining to it. The final stage product is, or ought to be, the result of an essential and continuous dialogue between these two. Only after resolving—or at least reducing—conflicts by dialogue culminating in co-operation, can even vaguely satisfactory solutions emerge. Perfection, alas, must remain a dream, an ideal, particularly in this complex and capricious art form with its vast, unattainable possibilities.

But all this is what, in the final analysis, constitutes the great appeal of opera and ensures its special position in the theatre. Difficulties spur us to greater effort, entice us to seek new and better solutions. They prevent rigidity, set up tensions and create interest in the best sense of that term.

At the beginning of this century the programmes at German court and municipal theatres would state the name of the producer but not yet of the conductor. That was to change soon afterwards, when the conductor became the star, while the producer remained the indispensable controller of entrances and exits. At the same time the footlights—out of range of the producer's modest directives—emerged as the favourite parade ground of the singers.

When new dramatic effects were introduced by Verdi and Wagner, the call for artistic stage direction was heard with growing insistence. Gluck had attempted innovations much earlier, and the childlike genius of Mozart had anticipated these accomplishments with the help of da Ponte and Schikaneder. Libretti had increasingly drawn their inspiration from literature. Puccini was inspired by Prévost and Murger, Richard Srauss by von Hofmannsthal and Oscar Wilde. Textual demands increased, the roles became more scintillating and refractive, scenic life more complex, technical requisites more complicated. And so the producer stepped on to a rudimentary form of what we know as the set today.

The Opera Producer

Let us leave the tempting but easily beclouded realms of aesthetic speculation, to enter the more solid ground of practical work. Let us ask what the craft of the opera producer consists of, and whether it differs from that of the producer of drama.

The answer is that it does. Opera brings a new dimension to the stage: it introduces music. Music is its spring-board, determining its style and colour. When Giorgio Strehler was interviewed by Sinah Kessler, he had his say on the subject:

> Should the opera producer heed the word rather than the music? This is an idle and misleading question. Of course he must heed the music in opposition to the word not the word in opposition to the music. Their synthesis ought to be taken for granted, as it is in a very few operas. But since it is not in most, one must try to integrate word and music, music and word. Once one has to ask whether greater heed ought to be paid to the one or to the other, something has clearly upset the artistic equilibrium.

In other words, the very presence of the music introduces and demands something that is absent from the spoken drama because it is not needed there. Music imposes a special attitude even on those who disdain it.

The presence of music largely determines the style, colour and dynamism of an operatic presentation. It helps the producer by adding its own emotional and expressive force to that of the scenery, and provides the actor-singer with a standard and guide. Music also complicates the producer's labours because its very rhythm and form affect the dramatic development, entrances and exits—sometimes unequivocally so.

Music introduces an emotional as well as a time factor. Deliberate efforts to 'work against the music' invariably confirm its presence, and can, indeed, be legitimate artistic devices since they, too, must be genuinely related to the score.

Let us take a practical example: the stage presentation of a complicated ensemble, a septet with chorus, for instance. The ensemble must of necessity be so placed as to allow the several voices to produce the desired overall effect. It can also impose movement, when new vocal combinations are needed. Moreover, many ensembles include subsidiary singers who are introduced for purely musical reasons and sometimes merely to allow for special rhythms.

Verdi uses second tenors who owe their stage existence to such requirements alone. In Rossini's *Mosè in Egitto* (Moses), too, the figure of Aufides in the first finale has a predominantly musical justification; the action could easily dispense with him. The producer as stage director thus has an additional task of casting the main and subsidiary roles to best advantage. The outstanding case is the finale of *Figaro*, Act II. When certain producers boast that they are about to tackle a new work, while claiming that they cannot tell one note from another, they are either joking or remarkably naive.

Of course, even an outsider can achieve great things, precisely because he comes to the work with an open mind. It happens in every profession. In opera, Gustaf Gründgens's *Figaro* (1931) and Jürgen Fehling's *Flying Dutchman* (1929) were two impressive and highly individual productions whose performance in Berlin's famous experimental theatre, the Kroll Oper, made theatrical history. In both cases eminent stage directors, new to the traditions of the lyric theatre and lacking musical expertise, produced outstanding interpretations. Their achievements were due to the fact that, respecting the music and trying to come to grips with it, they set out deliberately to achieve 'total art'. The assistance of two renowned stage designers—Gründgens worked with Teo Otto, Fehling with Ewald Dülberg—stood them in very good stead as well.

We all know of outsiders, lacking the wisdom of experience and therefore not hardened by it, who have hit upon astonishing solutions. That is to the good, but only so long as inexperienced critics, those least qualified to judge, do not turn it all into a religion or a dogma.

The Craft of Opera Production

The producer's first task is to formulate a general approach to the work he intends to interpret. On that basis he must decide on the style, the period in which the work is to be set, the scenery and the costumes. He will have to familiarize himself with the chronological, artistic, cultural and political background of the work, to analyse its bearing on the author's life and times no less than on his own.

If he is unfamiliar with the work, the producer will have to study first the piano score, then the full score and, of course, the libretto.

Records and tapes may prove invaluable aids. This work is extremely time-consuming; my own preliminary study of Alban Berg's *Lulu*, whose German première I gave in the Essen Opera-House, followed by a Dutch première during the Holland Festival in Amsterdam and in The Hague, took more than six months.

Contacts with the conductor cannot come too early, for only with him is it possible to determine the dynamics, tempo and enunciation of, for instance, the recitative of a Mozart opera, which is crucial to the stage development and the general understanding of the plot. Unfortunately, such early understanding is rare in practice, because technical progress has turned just these two men into constant travellers, strolling players in a modern world.

Altogether indispensable, however, are early contacts between producer and stage designer, for their understanding is a *sine qua non* of success. The producer will usually come to their first meeting with a more or less coherent set of ideas which he must discuss and clarify. Differences of opinion are best ironed out at this stage, though it may take a long time before general agreement can be reached. The relationship of producer to stage designer is nothing short of the marriage of two artists. It has its honeymoon, its ups and down, its occasional raptures. Both partners must yield and occasionally stand up for themselves. But despite their battles, they often reach so deep an understanding that it finally becomes impossible to tell which idea was whose. In doubtful cases the producer must always have his way because he cannot inspire those with whom he works to do their best on a set and in a scenic atmosphere he believes is not appropriate to the opera he has to interpret. If the stage designer feels that he cannot accept the producer's concept, he ought to withdraw from the common project—half-heartedness cannot be the basis of artistic creation.

It must be emphasized that the stage designer is the producer's crucial partner. Often enough he is able to persuade the producer to change his approach, altering the course of the whole production. I know how much I owe to such famous masters of their trade as Herta Böhm, Wolfram Munz, Wolfram Skalicki, Josef Fenneker, Gerd Richter, Hein Heckroth, Rudolf Heinrich, Jörg Zimmermann, and especially Ekkehard Grübler, Paul Haferung, Helmut Jürgens and Ita Maximowna.

The co-operation of stage designer and producer on the preparatory work often extends over a considerable period of time. The planning of our Munich and Buenos Aires *Falstaff*—in two versions adapted to two very different stages— kept both Ekkehard Grübler and me busy for approximately ten months; the Swiss première in Berne of Cikker's *A Play of Love and Death* required more than a year.

Once the size of the stage and the set have been agreed on, appropriate costumes must be designed. Many stage designers also design their own costumes, which may produce either greater homogeneity or uniformity, a visual impoverishment. If the stage designer confines himself to the stage and the sets, a special costume designer has to be brought in.

The extent to which costumes can help to mark out an unconventional style is something I discovered quite recently during rehearsals of *The Bartered Bride* in Düsseldorf. I had aimed at the elimination of all the ridiculous nonsense and operetta-style folklore that attaches to this beautiful though easily superannuated work. I am largely indebted to Martin Schlumpf for his striking peasant costumes and to Hermann Soherr for his down-to-earth sets, both of which helped enormously in the implementation of my plans.

Soloists and chorus must have memorized their musical parts by the time the stage rehearsals begin. In a German state or municipal theatre the opera producer is usually allowed six weeks of rehearsals, somewhat longer for particularly demanding works. Let me show how I used this time to prepare my Düsseldorf production of *The Bartered Bride,* a work of average difficulty:

Rehearsal room: 23 rehearsals with piano on a marked-out set. Rehearsals averaged three hours, but some took longer.

Main stage: 16 rehearsals with piano and complete set. Rehearsals lasted three hours.

5 stage rehearsals with full orchestra and full set. Rehearsals lasted three hours.

2 lighting rehearsals, total eleven hours.

1 dress rehearsal with piano. The entire cast in costumes and masks. Full set, full lighting. No time limit.

1 dress rehearsal with orchestra. All soloists in costumes and masks. Chorus, ballet and extras in costumes without masks. Full set, full lighting. No time limit.

1 full dress rehearsal, as performance. No time limit.

The chorus was rehearsed exclusively on stage, for a total of twenty-three rehearsals. In addition to the forty-eight stage rehearsals already mentioned, there were numerous ballet rehearsals and special rehearsals of the circus scene, for which outside performers had to be brought in. In all operas involving a ballet troupe, the producer must reach an understanding with the choreographer even before the rehearsals begin, especially for a work like *The Bartered Bride,* in which the dance must blend smoothly into the rest of the action, and so-called 'ballet interludes' must be avoided at all costs. The producer must take an active interest in the ballet rehearsals. Things are quite different with the ballet scenes in, say, *I Vespri Siciliani* (The Sicilian Vespers) or *Aida,* which are intended as spectacular interludes, though they, too, must be in tune with the basic style of the production.

Outside German-speaking countries rehearsals can take a great variety of forms. Let me mention two examples from the USA and Argentina as illustrations of the working methods of international opera-houses that do not play throughout the year and practise the *stagione,* or season, system. In that system a cast of opera stars from all over the world is engaged to appear in a particular opera for a fixed number of performances in a relatively short time, all during a single season. They give the work in the original language, except for operas of Slavonic origin in which the linguistic difficulties generally prove too great.

Years ago I produced *Figaro* and *Don Carlos* at the Lyric Opera, Chicago. Georg Solti was the conductor of both and the outstanding cast included such famous names as Giulietta Simionato, Tito Gobbi, Walter Berry, Jussi Björling, Anna Moffo, Eleanor Steber and Boris Christoff. Two young Broadway stage designers whose names I have forgotten, I am sorry to say, provided the sets and the costumes. For each of the two operas we were given sixteen days from the first stage rehearsal to the première. At the Teatro Colón in Buenos Aires I produced *Falstaff, Don Giovanni* and *Idomeneo,* one after another. *Falstaff* was conducted by Previtali, the two Mozart operas by Schmidt-Isserstedt. Ekkehard Grübler designed the *Falstaff* set; Ita Maximowna that of the two Mozart operas. The cast included Geraint Evans, Elisabeth Grümmer, Luigi Alva, Ilva Ligabue, Eberhard Wächter and Oralia Dominguez. The total time available to me from the day of my arrival to the evening of the third première was some six and a half weeks.

This may sound rather daring by Central European standards, but it was not so in fact. In Chicago and in Buenos Aires we had highly qualified and very experienced performers, as near perfect musically as one could have wished. Soloists were prepared to rehearse for almost unlimited periods—we often worked from morning until late at night with relatively few breaks. Fixed rehearsal times were of course set aside for chorus, ballet, extras and orchestra.

Since such star casts are very well paid, costs have to be kept down by time-saving measures; and because the singers had other engagements throughout the world, everyone was prepared to work with the utmost concentration. Rehearsals could, moreover, continue late into the night, since none of the stars had to give evening performances. The rehearsals were extremely thorough, and the presentation of the three operas clearly reflected this fact.

European repertory theatres achieve excellent results even with a constantly changing cast. Needless to say, this calls for longer rehearsals; moreover, singers who are expected to perform in the evenings cannot be expected to rehearse for as long as we did in Chicago and Buenos Aires. If a particular production is staged for years in succession, it demands regular and fairly frequent 'refresher' rehearsals. The fact that these are often omitted—from indifference, poor organization or lack of authority—is only too painfully obvious from the performances of quite a few famous opera-houses. Many smaller ones are run far more vigorously and can serve as excellent examples.

The many assistants and assistant producers—his closest collaborators—whose services the producer must enlist frequently before he can stage an opera can only be mentioned in brief, though all make a considerable contribution. There is the technical manager and his staff, the wardrobe mistress, the make-up section, the prompter, the property master, the lighting engineer, and, of course, the stage-manager, who is responsible for the entrances of soloists, chorus, ballet and extras, for raising and lowering the curtain, for the length of the intervals and many other matters. Mention must also be made of the *répétiteur,* who plays the piano during stage rehearsals and often doubles as lighting assistant by signalling the various light cues to the lighting crews in time with the beat.

Lighting

Stage lighting is of critical importance in all modern opera productions. The light may be harsh and all-dominating, casting sharp shadows as an additional means of expression. It may be used to accentuate dramatic moments directly or by dwelling on contrasts. The producer has the choice of the various means of projection, and of the considerable possibilities of back projection. He can veil the stage from the audience with subdued mood lighting. He can choose between smooth and gradual or quick lighting changes, or use the so-called follow spot-light which picks out individuals. In all these cases light helps him to produce striking effects, to clarify and interpret actions proceeding on the stage. Lighting is an art *sui generis,* to be learned after long practice.

The lighting of an opera always demands a great deal of time. I, for one, have always numbered the lighting designer and his team among my most important colleagues. I well remember that my Munich production of *Re Cervo* had 132 different lighting locations; for our Dortmund production of Levy's *Trauer muss Elektra tragen* (Mourning becomes Electra) we made do with eighty-seven; for our Frankfurt production of Gluck's *Orpheus* there were ninety-six.

It should by now be clear that opera production, though an art, is also a highly technical affair—increasingly so since the Second World War. I must also mention the effect of television, which provides the stage producer with a new field of experience. My television productions of *Wozzeck, La Bohème* and *Simplicius Simplicissimus* (K.A. Hartmann) have had direct repercussions on my stage work. Attention to detail is of the utmost importance in television, simply because the camera can focus upon it at will. Television work teaches us to be scrupulously accurate and reminds us time and again of the dangers of the kind of laxity that so easily creeps into stage productions.

Producer and Soloists

Work with soloists is a psychological as well as an artistic task. It is impossible to convey artistic intentions and insights without the help of psychology, for the producer has the job of persuading a group of men and women of widely divergent talents, intellects, artistic sensibilities, and drives—a group differing in age, experience, education and musical knowledge—to adopt a single style, to subdue their own personalities for the sake of a common goal.

This need for understanding and fact becomes clear when we consider that most opera and stage stars are egocentric introverts, a quality that enables them to play so many different characters before large audiences.

The producer's position alone no longer assures him the authority he needs to keep his team together. This is fortunate, for this helps to eradicate the incompetent. Dictatorial producers, formerly the very cream of their profession, are becoming an extinct race—the general atmosphere is no longer congenial to them. The producer no longer demands obedience without question, but must try to inspire the loyalty of the group. The aim has remained the same but the means have changed. This does not preclude the respect due to any leader of a group of men; but this respect has to be earned, it can no longer be taken for granted.

Even so, the producer, as the central creator of the stage presentation, has a duty to translate his ideas into scenic realizations. He must be able to channel discussions, to cut short fruitless argument, and to encourage useful dialogues. In particular, he must stop trivial chatter, which is often a substitute for real work. Every theatrical production needs a guiding hand that can settle differences of opinion and assume responsibility for the whole—that is something the group cannot do for itself.

Among the singers there are some with enormous talent, whose intellectual powers are, however, no match for their vocal abilities. This type, which used to prevail, is in a minority today—opera singers have set unprecedented standards over the past few decades, in direct response to the growing demands of the contemporary opera stage. Films, and occasionally television as well, have greatly increased public expectations. Opera has had partially to surrender its former role of gourmet entertainment, but it has grown in stature. This is, no doubt, in response to the modern call for artistic integrity, and to modern dissatisfaction with spectacular but otherwise threadbare performances.

The opera singer's stage personality is different from the actor's, but it has long since ceased to be inferior. His technique, his dependence on the music, his reliance on his vocal cords—all this gives him advantages not enjoyed by his theatrical colleague, but also presents disadvantages and special difficulties. Some of his dramatic powers are dissipated because of the attention he has to pay to the music. Yet the precise performance of his musical task helps him to achieve his most expressive effects. By providing him with standards and setting him limits, music binds him to a world of forms that prevents him from using a purely private idiom. At the same time, the music of an opera, by virtue of its alienation effect, endows the stage on which he appears with an artificial atmosphere.

The combination of great voices with high dramatic skills is no longer confined to a few leading opera-houses—the term 'provincial' can no longer be applied in a derogatory way to all medium-sized and even small theatres. On the contrary, these theatres have become important training grounds for young artists—one of the great advantages of the repertory over the *stagione* system—and several important operas in the last few years have been given in the 'provinces'. I am thinking, for instance, of the Darmstadt *Wozzeck,* of Henze's *Re Cervo* and Zimmermann's *Soldaten* (The Soldiers) in Kassel; of Křenek's *Karl V* in Graz, and of Rossini's *Moses* in Berne and Lausanne. Moreover, Wozzeck owes its breakthrough, not to the Berlin première, but to its performance in the small municipal theatre in Oldenburg.

The inordinately rich, variegated and multinational tapestry which is modern opera has not been woven exclusively or even predominantly in Vienna, Munich or London, in Paris, Leipzig or Milan, in New York or in other world centres; its colour and pattern cannot be imagined without the naive strength that springs from the absence of snobbery and intellectual hyperaestheticism found in those regions that used to be dismissed as mere 'provinces'.

It is one of the producer's most important tasks to create a coherent ensemble out of the profusion of individuals placed under his charge. He must work with people, not against them and since this is something he can only do by persuasion, he must be something of a therapist. As such, he can rely on words or gestures, on the intellect or the emotions, depending on the situation. But whether he explains a particular walk, movement or emotion in words or demonstrates it in action, he must be able to inspire and interest his cast. He must help them to shed inhibitions or to appear more subdued. This calls for a great deal of insight, self-examination and respect for those with whom he has to work, an excess of good will, patience and self-control—a rather demanding list. Wild shouting, temper tantrums, and harping on one's authority just will not do the job today. Effort, restraint and tolerance—these are essentials. Quite obviously, all this calls for thorough spade-work, and close familiarity with the libretto and the music.

The stage no less than the purely musical production of an opera is an intellectual and technical process. It calls for the judicious combination of a great variety of nationalities, talents, temperaments and qualities into one valid presentation of a work of art, based on the ideas of its authors and informed by the critical expectations of one's own period.

Hans Niedecken-Gebhard who, as sponsor and leading light of the Göttingen Händel Festivals rediscovered the stage works of that great composer in the 1920s, put it as follows: 'Opera production demands a total sense of style and must be the cultural expression of the age.'

The work must be seen in the light of its period, and in terms of the intellectual outlook and awareness of our own. Today no opera of the past—meaning prior to the Second World War—can be presented without some alteration, unless it is treated as a formal aesthetic object.

Producer and Chorus

The producer must proceed with the chorus just as he does with the soloists, except that he must apply group, rather than individual, psychology. All permanent choruses have a remarkable store of experience; under expert guidance they can rise to remarkable heights. Enjoying economic security with little threat of dismissal, they can also contain the second-rate performers, and those who prefer threadbare routine and hiding in the crowd to any serious exertion.

But when the producer knows how to appeal to them as responsible individuals, he finds that the chorus will usually rise to the occasion. And the chorus often plays the chief 'role' by the side of the soloist, as in *Cardillac, Carmen, Oedipus Rex, Turandot, Moses and Aron, Lohengrin, Mathis der Maler* (Matthias the Painter) and *Aida*—the list could be greatly extended.

When outside choruses are brought in, the producer will profit from the natural desire of musicians to perform as best they can. The extra chorus must be incorporated into the permanent chorus so that the amateurs are able to lean on the professionals.

The engagement of stage extras poses much more difficult problems, for mistakes are readily spotted by an audience. Here the leading opera-houses, most of whom have a regular contingent of extras under a permanent leader, have a great advantage over the smaller ones. Many operas make great demands on the extras and often call for dramatic feats that are beyond the layman's power. In such cases it is possible to enlist the help of drama students from various academies and universities or from the special workshops now attached to all great opera-houses.

Language

The question of whether or not an opera should be performed in its original language is a complex one. I myself would never buy a record or a tape of an opera in any language but the original. Generally, a work of art finds its purest expression in its original form. For that reason many operas are now performed in the original language throughout the German-speaking world and gradually in the Francophone world as well.

In Britain and the United States this has been the custom for a very long time, so that the whole problem would have passed them by had not the opposite trend made itself felt in recent years: *The Magic Flute* sung and spoken in English at the New York Metropolitan Opera House, English performances of *The Mastersingers of Nuremberg* and *Der Rosenkavalier* (The Knight of the Rose) at London's Covent Garden, for example. London's Sadler's Wells and American music schools and universities—whose performances are often near-professional and of remarkable distinction—also give most of their operas in English as does the City Center Opera in New York. The same is true of the Royal Opera-House in Stockholm, where I produced the Swedish première of Alban Berg's important work *Lulu* in Swedish.

Needless to say, the language problem is of the utmost importance to the opera producer who must, after all, try to present his art to the broadest possible audiences.

But as in all spheres of human endeavour theory is a long way from practice. This is particularly true in the German-speaking world, because opera plays a much more crucial role in the theatrical life of these countries than it does in, say, Britain or the USA.

To this day Germany, Switzerland and Austria—and to a much lesser extent France and Belgium—have a subsidized municipal theatre with a permanent cast and daily performances for at least ten months a year. It is based on a tradition that goes back well over a hundred and fifty years and has deep popular roots. To this day the German opera-house has remained a cultural focus for broad strata of the population. The ordinary opera-goer in these countries expects performances that he can enjoy dramatically as well as musically. Opera lovers in these parts are intimately familiar with Puccini's 'Che gelida manina' in German.

I should therefore like to examine what factors have been responsible for the recent insistence, particularly in the German-speaking world, on the performance of foreign operas in the original language. In this connection, the following points deserve special consideration:

Everyone who values this magnificent expression of western culture must be concerned about the preservation and development of opera. In view of increasing costs, the solution must be to attract the widest possible audiences, not reliance on the 'fans' who are the main justification for presenting an opera in the original language.

It should, however, be said with emphasis that ever since Gluck and particularly since Verdi and Wagner, and quite definitely since the turn of the century, the dramatic element in operas has increasingly come to the fore, so that opera has ceased to be music plus scenery, becoming instead an integrated form of art that appeals not only to the ear or the eye, but also to the intellect, to the aesthetic sensibility. And it is precisely this fact that constitutes the enormous impact of opera. Concertante performances as opera substitutes can never replace the total effect, the union of music and scenery of a dramatic performance. An opera-house that can easily fill its auditorium for twenty performances of, say, L'Africaine (The African Girl), in a single season, would barely need a single repeat performance of a concertante presentation. Opera music is bound to the stage, the operatic word to the music—that is the ultimate meaning of opera. However, without wide and constant public support opera qua music-and-drama has no future. Will a broad public be prepared to keep supporting performances in a foreign language it cannot understand?

Does not the refusal to employ a generally comprehensible language constitute a wholly incomprehensible cavalier attitude to the dramatic content of an opera? Are Otello, Don Giovanni, Pelléas and Mélisande, Manon Lescaut, Death in Venice, Eugene Onegin, Thaïs, Kát'a Kabanová, Dido and Aeneas, Anna Bolena, Les Troyens (The Trojans) or Gluck's operas, based on French texts, mere excuses for music-making, are their texts so unimportant that the public can be spared the trouble of following them? Are we really entitled to cut a work of art in half, to prevent it from making its impact as a whole?

In an age that prides itself on its social awareness, can we really ignore the fact that a foreign opera in its original language is only accessible to a small, linguistically gifted élite?

It was plainly his refusal to agree to that proposition which persuaded Giorgio Strehler to give his Fidelio at the 1969 Maggio Musicale Fiorentino in Italian. He has offered the following explanation:

> We were faced with the difficult, but to us important, problem of including Fidelio in the repertoire of Italian opera from which it has always been absent. That is why we had it sung in Italian by Italian singers. This method had its pros and cons but helped to make the opera more like 'one of our own'. I believe that this kind of 'sacrilege' is justified if, as a result, Fidelio ceases to be the unusual work, the extraordinary opera it has been, to become a familiar friend of Italian opera lovers.

Is not such familarity precisely what the German-speaking world must seek to achieve with Pelléas and Mélisande, Falstaff, Les Dialogues des Carmélites (The Carmelites), Billy Budd, Boris Godunov and so many other masterpieces? The parallel call for English versions of German operas in Britain and the USA is equally justified. In this connection, the reader would do well to recall that Verdi insisted on having his operas sung in German at German performances, urging his friend Giulio Ricordi to publish translations as soon as possible.

While even smaller opera-houses may put on Italian operas in the original, what German company is capable of singing The Bartered Bride in Czech, Eugene Onegin in Russian or Faust in French? Pelléas and Mélisande sung in French can be heard throughout Germany—in Munich no less than in Aachen; but what of Yugoslav and Bulgarian operas sung in the original or of Halka sung in Polish? The occasional attempt to have Boris Godunov sung in Russian must remain confined to a few of the very largest western opera-houses.

One more thing; do we not have truly brilliant translations of all the great operas? Is it not a fact that Levy's masterly Mozart translations have considerably widened the horizon of German opera lovers, or that such leading musical publishers as Ricordi in Milan, Bärenreiter in Kassel and Universal-Edition in Vienna are constantly working on new opera translations that are as satisfactory in literary respects as they are musically justified?

Hans Hartleb

Richard Strauss: *Die schweigsame Frau*. Design: Helmut Jürgens; Costumes: Sophia Schröck, State Opera, Munich; opening of Munich Opera Festival, 1962

Hans Hartleb
Igor Stravinsky: *Oedipus Rex*
Design and costumes:
Ekkehard Grübler,
State Opera, Munich;
Munich Opera Festival, 1970

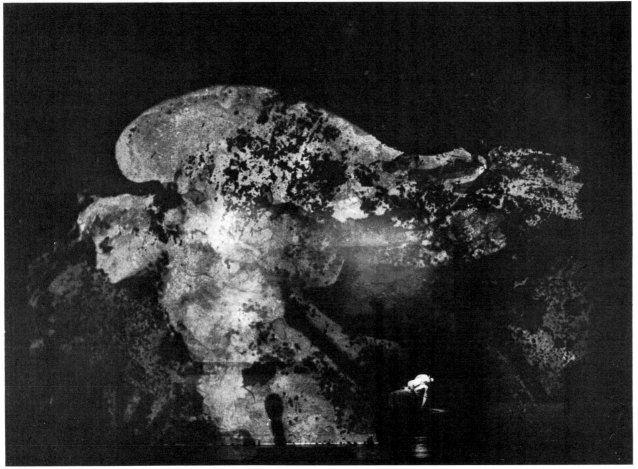

Hans Hartleb
Benjamin Britten: *Death in Venice*
Design and costumes:
Ita Maximowna
State Opera, Munich,
March 1975

There are well-known works—for instance *Tosca* or *Aida*—whose plots are so straightforward that they can be understood even in the original language. But what of the most brilliant examples of *opera buffa: Falstaff* and *Gianni Schicchi;* what about *Così fan tutte,* whose charming allusions and bitter truths must be understood to be appreciated?

The Bavarian State Opera used to give *Figaro* alternately in German and Italian, and it became clear that contacts between the performers and the audience were incomparably more intense during the German performances, and the overall impact incomparably stronger. I have given German performances of *Falstaff* at the Munich Festival, of *Così fan tutte* in Karlsruhe, and of *Schicchi* in Graz, and every time it was brought home to me how much more directly and strongly *buffa* in particular appeals to the public if its spoken as well as its musical message is made clear.

Is not the use of the original language at any price the result of an armchair abstraction? I believe that the whole problem needs re-examination with special attention to the question of whether the stylistic and aesthetic gains are not counterbalanced by a serious loss in genuine theatrical impact.

Another thing: can the 'Italian' that is normally heard on our stage really be called an 'original language'? I do not usually get that impression. And while it is possible to find audiences in Berlin and London, in Munich and Vienna, in Paris and New York, in Salzburg and Glyndebourne, who prefer performances in the original language, things look quite different elsewhere. In any case the living reality of the theatre ought not to be sacrificed on the altar of a snobbish aestheticism.

Music and Scenery

I have always thought it would be ideal to have the conductor present from the first stage rehearsal. Unfortunately this has long since ceased to be the custom, leaving many problems concerning the co-ordination of scenery and music unsolved. It is important that the conductor and producer agree about the length of a pause during which a certain action is to be performed on stage: a glance, a withdrawal, a movement of the hand, an approach. There is a famous pause in the last act of *La Bohème,* when Schaunard realizes that Mimi is dead. It is a pause that cannot be determined with a metronome. Here the conductor must understand the producer and *vice versa:* they must reach a complete agreement based on the singer's powers of expression.

In this and many other cases a common determination to achieve an artistically satisfying result is essential. Yet the conductor and producer often pull, or seem to pull, in different directions, creating emotional conflicts due to touchiness, self-assertion, vanity and temperament, that must be reconciled. A score is much more precise than a scenario which can be interpreted in many different ways.

The conductor places so many obstacles in the producer's way and *vice versa!* It is important, for example, to have perfect agreement about the conductor's tempi from the very first stage rehearsal. There is always a difference between the tempi used at the musical rehearsal in a room or hall and those used on the much larger stage. I consider it essential that the conductor and the producer should meet as often as possible.

Unfortunately lack of time and the increasingly hysterical tempo of successive productions make this kind of collaboration exceptional. I have known the conductor of a new production appear for his first meeting with me during the first technical rehearsal with full orchestra. Fortunately this is not the rule, but a growing number of conductors hold two posts—one with an opera-house and another with a symphony orchestra in some distant city. It is always the opera which suffers, for its complexity and versatility make the continual supervision of a powerful musical leader and intellect imperative. Sometimes producers divide their time between two institutions, with equally baneful results.

Opera Today

André Malraux has described western art as a continuous process of self-questioning, not as a path leading to the permanent establishment of paradise on earth. And yet noble though it indubitably is, the attitude to which Malraux refers can become dangerous if it leads to total cultural pessimism and to passive acceptance of what is allegedly inevitable; if it misleads us into uncritical acceptance of destructive philosophies. Every genuine quest implies a will to find an answer, and culture, the sum total of men's yearnings, experiences, desires, disappointments and hopes, can show us how to find it. And the theatre in its many forms is an integral part of culture.

One of these forms is opera, and opera plays a central and increasingly important role in European theatrical life. While the stage at large has lost its old certainties, suffering both from lack of public interest and from a reciprocal contempt for the public, the direct intellectual and sensual impact of opera is being increasingly appreciated, particularly by the younger generation. The declining importance of the theatre is no doubt essentially due to its didactic approach, its neglect of what Brecht has called its special function: entertainment.

This danger hardly threatens opera, which is, in essence, without dogma. Even works with so predominantly political a background as *Fidelio, Tosca* or *The Carmelites* owe their impact to their operatic character; the evil that all three pillory becomes all the more tangible thereby, and the spectator is rendered more thoughtful than by the dry and unvarnished truths of many a dramatic production. The appeal of Zimmermann's *Soldiers* is drawn from the same sources, and the fate of Marie points the spectator in the direction of humanity.

Those who have made an analytical study of opera know that certain formulae, legitimate and most effective only a few years ago, have become empty conventions, and that established customs have been exploded overnight. It is only natural that the precipitate transformation of our world view, the realization that major changes are round the corner, should also be reflected in the arts—in attempts to arrive at new, unconventional and, in the main, radical creations. The natural initiator and mediator of all such attempts is the producer.

Change, permanent change, is the hallmark of all life. If, however, it is treated as an independent value and fostered by force, it can become an impediment to vital development. The new becomes an end in itself, and those who suffer anguish lest they be mistaken for 'squares' elevate these pseudo-novelties into idols—falsifying the vital values without which man is mere flotsam.

In our time the general ideal is the quest for a series of superlatives: the fastest car, the most seductive woman, the cleverest crook, the most sensational performance. In music a plethora of new groups and schools exist, each determined to run the whole show. One side insists on the strictest adherence to established forms, claiming that nothing but the traditional rules of harmony can help us out of our rut; the other side rejects all but dodecaphonic music. Both paint everything in black and white, tolerating no shades of grey. The quality of the music is sublimely unimportant to them; only its form matters. Bernard Shaw might have had an inkling of this development when he wrote that the true musician finds nothing more distasteful than the attempt to pass off musical forms for music.

In the opera reviews of the sensational press, in particular, artistic criteria are blatantly ignored. A performance is often judged by the sensation it causes, prolonged catcalls being a guarantee of quality, while long runs and loud applause are certain signs of Philistinism.

A hankering after a radically new approach may well be a justified attempt to transcend dead conventions, to blow away old dust. But to treat the so-called 'bah-effect'—the contempt for the audience—as an end in itself, or to serve it up as a stroke of genius is not only tragi-comic but a sign of what can only be called 'futurist dilettantism'.

Opera does seem to be in a sufficiently healthy condition now to withstand all sorts of experiments. Resilience based on formal perfection is the basic characteristic of its greatest contribution. That very strength provides the reason for its rejection by the representatives of cultural anarchists, who look upon the conservative element in culture as a barrier to total change—to destruction.

Many traditions have had to be altered, and often to good effect. The repertoire, in particular, has changed markedly over the past few decades. There are many losses but also many gains, most of which have been drawn from works of the past.

Pagliacci (The Strolling Players) and *Tiefland* (The Lowlands) have lost much of their box-office appeal, and formerly successful operas like *Mona Lisa* or the works of Schreker are hardly known by name today. In compensation revivals of such classics as Gluck's *Iphigénies*

take modern audiences by storm. *Così fan tutte* has become a great hit, as have Verdi's *Don Carlos* and *Macbeth*—two operas that were not often heard outside Italy until after the Second World War. Moreover, Verdi's early operas—*Masnadieri* (The Brigands), *Attila, Luisa Miller* and *Giovanna d'Arco* (Joan of Arc)—are included in many modern repertoires. Rossini's *Moses,* Meyerbeer's *Les Huguenots* and *The African Girl* have also been revived. Opera-goers are increasingly turning back to 'Grand Opera' with its strong theatrical appeal.

Modern and contemporary works appear to have fallen into neglect, and do not figure largely in the repertoires of most companies. Now and then, it is true, these may include Stravinsky's *Oedipus Rex,* Schönberg's *Erwartung* (Expectation), *Moses and Aron,* and—far too rarely—his one-act comic opera *Von Heut auf Morgen* (From Day to Day), Křenek's *Karl V.* More frequently performed are Alban Berg's *Wozzeck* and *Lulu,* works by Egk and Orff, Klebe and Honegger, Walton and Levy, Henze's *Boulevard Solitude* and *Junger Lord* (The Young Lord), Zimmermann's *Soldiers,* together with several Italian, English and French operas.

Few of these works enjoy the number of repeat performances on which eighteenth-, nineteenth- and early twentieth-century composers could count with certainty. The concert-going public is much more conservative than the art-loving world—perhaps the ear is more critical of novelty than is the eye. It would be useful in this connection to study whether or not some of the most recent musical creations are deliberately designed to offend on the principle of 'épater le bourgeois'.

Repertory theatre still takes precedence over the *stagione* system in Central Europe because the permanent opera-house plays a fixed part in the cultural scene. Its advantages are obvious. It is the ideal training ground for young singers, conductors, stage designers and producers. It can offer a comparatively wide repertoire, and, since it is not wholly dependent on box-office revenue, it can experiment with the very latest works. The repertory does not depend on the often dubious glory of great names, and it can count on a regular audience. Its disadvantages include a general tendency to follow the beaten track, and a proliferating administrative machinery that threatens to overwhelm the creative element whose inspiration requires an unfettered atmosphere.

The *stagione* system occasionally does produce outstanding performances, but by its very nature it is guided more by an ambition to assemble the greatest number of international stars than by a purely artistic spirit. It is no secret that even the most brilliant cast is no guarantee of a great performance. What the *stagione* system lacks is the chance to interpret contemporary works. It is hard to imagine a *stagione* consisting of Stravinsky's *Oedipus Rex,* Henze's *Re Cervo* or Nono's *Intolleranza* (Intolerance).

For some years a mixture of repertory and *stagione* systems has been gradually emerging. Permanent casts grow smaller and are joined by guest performers in increasing numbers. But even this mixed form cannot prevail without the firm foundations of repertory opera. The direction of this trend depends much more on the development of society at large than on the sagacity of theatre management.

In any case opera seems now to be a robust and stable form of art, perhaps because its corner-stone—the trained human voice—is the result of craftsmanship and control. No argument, no temper tantrum, no flight of fancy, will avail in the end—high C must simply be sung. Even the most introverted and self-assertive producer has to accept certain laws and fixed values, keeping his vanity in check. Opera remains a triumph of form, a fact that does preclude the discovery of horizons, the search for that ultimate that sets its own standards. Our world would be poorer without *Don Giovanni, Falstaff* or *Tristan,* to mention just three out of an impressive number of masterpieces.

Our success in preserving and developing the lyric theatre will depend largely on whether or not the theatre administration—personified in the general manager—will be able to resist those fashionable tendencies that are obviously intended to destroy our culture. Some managers are embracing those tendencies. Those most afraid of seeming out of date and 'square' tend to forget that the most fashionable is often the most transitory. I believe, moreover, that the ideal opera manager of the future will be a cultured, artistically discriminating man who devotes his energies to running his house without engaging in artistic activities. Under modern conditions the management and administration of an opera-house are responsibilities that leave neither time nor strength for other duties.

In the various contributions to this book the reader will discover a welter of conflicting views and notions. He may gain the impression that opera is in a state of flux, that its future is quite undecided. He might, however, conclude that the diverse and apparently incompatible stylistic exercises that are presented on the modern opera stage are proof of the vitality of this form of art. People do not, after all, argue about old hats, or invest in dead ducks. A wealth of opinion, effort, happy inspiration, humiliation, beauty, ugliness, failure and success, fills the frame of the contemporary opera picture. If this book has helped the reader to form his own critical opinion of opera today, its authors can be well satisfied.

Should Beauty still be Portrayed?

Everyone must be familiar with the phenomenon of bad faith, must know the turmoil and fear that plague modern man as much as doubt in the rightness of traditional moral and artistic values, in the veracity of created form. The roots of this uncertainty lie in a past stained with crime. We feel highly sceptical about mankind's path in general, and about form and beauty in particular.

How can anyone believe in the value and the magic of beauty when beauty was the declared ideal of a humanity whose faults and errors have become so starkly obvious in our day? One of the chief aims of that art form we call 'opera' is precisely the creation of beauty—beauty as a source of liberation, of fulfilment, of purification and delight—and so opera becomes inevitably a victim of our doubts.

But is the lofty ideal of beauty necessarily impure because it grew up on impure ground? I am not referring to formal beauty alone, but also to beauty as an agent of existential concentration, as a source of strength. In this sense, Alban Berg's *Wozzeck* and *Lulu,* two works of dark tragedy with despair as their basic element, can also be called creations of the purest beauty, of that hard and crystalline beauty that shuns sentimentality in all its forms. And are things any different with the works of Rembrandt, Dürer, Titian and van Gogh; of Shakespeare, Racine, Goethe, Manzoni or Tolstoy?

That the conventional theatre—or at least a whole series of conventional theatres—has come to reject beauty in favour of the cult of ugliness—which includes the telling of the unvarnished truth—may be understandable as a process of purification, an elimination of spurious sentiments. The fact that this inherently laudable attitude tends to degenerate into aesthetic nihilism, into a determination to expose every form of beauty as a philistine self-deception, is a direct consequence of that German thoroughness that kills the flowers with the weeds.

Such thoroughness is rearing its head even on the opera stage. Opera, as an integral part of the world of artistic and aesthetic creation, is the least suitable vehicle for the transport of ideological and political slogans. This in no way diminishes its cultural importance, as its humourless, and totally prosaic opponents would have us believe it does. Opera, more than ever before, touches that precise point in the sphere of human emotions which is impervious to utilitarian ideas. That it is making so much headway today, particularly with the younger generation, may well be a direct result of this fact.

The general disillusionment that set in quite rightly after the political and military catastrophes in the years 1930 to 1945, has done its laudable work of purification. It is now time to lift up eyes that have probed deep into the filth with which this world is riddled and to look towards brighter horizons—at the beauty that may prove the best cure for all our misery. Just as 'keep smiling' can produce a crude distortion of human relationships, so 'keep frowning' is nothing but a lugubrious display of a *Weltschmerz*. Both attitudes have grown out of a fashionable conformism, whose dictates all too many have swallowed without challenge, lest they be considered behind the times. Fortunately, attitudes seem to be changing, and the first songs of praise to beauty have begun. Let me quote two passages from a most readable essay, Joachim Kayser's anything but sentimental 'Unbehagen gegenüber dem Schönen':

> …Beauty prevails—that beauty which, as it were, confirms or rejects the essence or testimony of a work of art. Created beauty, even when enjoyed superficially, is always more than mere nourishment. It ousts indifference, which explains why Negro spirituals, for instance, prove more powerful and effective reminders and warnings than any number of essays or tractates on slavery…

...Are all those, to whom the beautiful and consoling fitness of great works of art of the past is anathema, simply refusing to be accomplices in, and propagandists of, classical and traditional achievements? Every distortion denies the power of past achievements. Since it seems impossible to construct valid modern antitheses, talented outsiders exploit their chances and set out deliberately to crush the great theses of human art history. They mean no harm, they are mere critics. That is how 'discomfort in the face of beauty' acts and reacts today.

And on the importance of form, Konrad Lorenz had this to say in a valedictory essay written for the eightieth birthday of Carl Zuckmayer:

...The true artist is bound to laws that are not one jot less strict than those that bind the scientific researcher. Identical claims are made on the probity of both...

The reader will know why I included these three quotations in this book. They can all be applied to opera, a phenomenon bound to form and beauty. Discontent and dissatisfaction with beauty do not diminish the value of beauty itself, for beauty is timeless and unaffected by changes in fashion.

Selected Operas

*Interviews and Reports Compiled
and Adapted by Wolfgang Haefeli*

Don Giovanni

A horseman galloping wildly through the night, with unbridled passion, forever in search of amorous adventure, afraid of nobody and nothing: a figure that inspires fear—and secret envy. He seems to be omnipresent, so quickly does he change the scene of his crimes and surmount vast distances. The peasants are afraid of him, hiding their wives and daughters away and hoping fervently for a chance to destroy this satanic ruler of their lives. He laughs at their threats, commits fresh outrages, slaying when he has to, and moving remorselessly towards self-destruction.

Mozart took only a few months to write the score to a text submitted by da Ponte, the librettist who had earlier proved his worth with *Figaro*. The magnificent overture, it is said, was composed only one day before the première in Prague in 1787. It was a great success; Don Giovanni, or Don Juan of Spanish legendary fame, took the world's opera-houses by storm. The awe-inspiring finale, in which the 'wicked debaucher' is dragged down by demons, was a concession to the spectators' sense of justice, not a true account of the end of the quasi-historical Don Juan de Manara, who repented, entered a monastery and, after his death, was revered as a saint by the Spanish people.

On stage it was long the practice to omit the epilogue, or second finale, and have the opera end with the dramatic disappearance of Don Giovanni. But da Ponte called his piece a 'dramma giocoso', a humorous play, and in older piano extracts it bore the sub-title of 'opera buffa'. The propitiatory ending in which the characters moralize upon Don Giovanni's fate, far from being redundant, is absolutely essential if the overall character of the opera is to be maintained.

The quick scenic changes and absence of appropriate musical transitions pose an urgent problem. The perplexing speed with which the dashing Don Giovanni makes his entrances and exits must be rendered credible; even the shortest break after an exit is likely to spoil the continuity of the action and hence bore the audience. The idea of using an 'all-purpose' stage, on which the demand for continuity can be satisfied with minimal changes, seems attractive, but has always been found wanting in practice because, although it holds the spectators' attention, it fails to rival the excitement of a headlong rush through a welter of ever-changing scenes. And it is precisely this sense of involvement, of shared fears, of joint sighs of relief during moments of respite, of delight in the strains of the optimistic finale that, no less than the music, make *Don Giovanni* the fascinating experience it invariably is.

In 1896 the Munich Residenztheater, that splendid rococo building designed by François Cuvilliés, was the first to employ the revolving stage invented by Carl Lautenschläger for a performance of *Don Giovanni*. Ernst von Possart was the producer, Richard Strauss the conductor. These two great interpreters put on the opera in the German version of Hermann Levi, the famous conductor who, with Possart, ushered in the Munich Mozart renaissance (*Figaro*, *Così fan tutte*).

A word about the textual problem: as a producer I have always tried to make sure that the spectators appreciate the humorous passages in *Figaro* or *Così fan tutte* and that they acknowledge them as generously as they do the recitatives in *Don Giovanni*. Sticking to the original language at any price, however incomprehensible and no matter what loss of direct impact it may entail, strikes me as far too great a sacrifice to the majesty of the playwright's pen. It is significant that Mozart's early works, *The Abduction from the Seraglio* and his stage legacy, *The Magic Flute,* were composed to German texts. In the German translations by Levi and Georg Schünemann, moreover, we have excellent versions that are both heedful of the original and musically satisfying.

The choice of Mozart's opera was made quite deliberately in the knowledge that modern stage aids offered us great new possibilities, and the breath-taking, uninterrupted succession of scenes did, indeed, prove a triumph.

This impetus from the famous Munich Mozart renaissance ought to be utilized in all current and future performances of *Don Giovanni*. Monotonous stylizations, however tasteful, cannot hope to do justice to the lightning tempo of this opera and its compelling music. The highly advanced technical resources of the modern theatre allow of many and varied applications; the revolving stage has not remained the only solution. For all that, the complete fulfilment of the dramatic demands we have tried to set forth must continue to be the mainspring of every stage production.

Rudolf Hartmann

Scenes

1.1	Garden in front of the Commendatore's palace. At night.
1.4	Street. At night.
1.16	Garden with two gates, opening inwards. Two bowers.
1.20	Brilliantly lighted ballroom.
2.1	Street. At night.
2.7	Dark ground-floor hall with three doorways in Donna Anna's house.
2.11	Fenced-in churchyard with a statue of the Commendatore. Moonlit night.
2.12	Chamber in Donna Anna's house.
2.13	Room with laid table in Don Giovanni's palace.

1968, SALZBURG FESTIVAL   GROSSES FESTSPIELHAUS

Producer: Herbert von Karajan — Stage designer: Günther Schneider-Siemssen — Costumes: Georges Wakhevitch — Conductor: Herbert von Karajan

Herbert von Karajan's production was based on a discriminating characterization of Don Giovanni, who has been considered the embodiment of male aspirations, and a figure reminiscent of Goethe's Faust.

An essential element of this interpretation was von Karajan's insistence on 'seamless' transitions. In view of the large number of scenes, this could only be achieved with the help of the drop curtain and the rebuilding of the set between the scenes.

Günther Schneider-Siemssen, who has called the stage of the Great Festival Hall 'one size too large for *Don Giovanni',* has recorded his 'tremendous respect' for the composer.

> I believe Mozart needs no scenic clutter; the crystal-clear purity of his music must be allowed to dominate. There is no place for naturalism or for realistic sets; to achieve an alienation effect in keeping with Mozart's spirit, all that is needed is a set of huge moulded tablets.
>
> The central element of my set was a rhomboid rostrum, allowing some scenic concentration on this large stage. The set was reduced to the enormous sculpted tablets, which reflected the simplicity and linearity of Mozart's music.
>
> These elements were the architectural corner-stones of our production. With them I was also able to create the galleries of the banqueting hall or the impression of a lane in a park. Despite the lack of realism I took pains to make my sets as credible as possible.

Don Giovanni is 'a very difficult and problematical work' and not only for the producer; it 'invariably imposes a burden' on the stage designer. In retrospect, Günther Schneider-Siemssen feels that today he would 'find it easy to master this stage conception and even to improve on its execution'.

Report by Wolfgang Haefeli
after an interview with Günther Schneider-Siemssen.

1971, COLOGNE   OPERNHAUS

Producer: Jean-Pierre Ponnelle — Stage designer: Jean-Pierre Ponnelle — Costumes: Jean-Pierre Ponnelle — Conductor: István Kertész

This presentation of *Don Giovanni* no less than that of the *Magic Flute* was based on a synthetic approach to the entire 'Mozart cycle'.

In this interpretation Jean-Pierre Ponnelle did not attach paramount importance to the figure of Don Giovanni.

> He is much too colourful a character to be forced into a straitjacket. Were the entire production to revolve around him part of the audience would feel deeply frustrated—everyone projects his own fantasies into this *bon vivant,* and women do so quite differently from men. Moreover, Don Giovanni is not an expressive character and the few purely philosophical, almost metaphysical dicta that da Ponte has placed in his mouth strike me as being rather feeble.

Ponnelle's primary concern was to discover how Don Giovanni affects those around him, what he means to Donna Anna and Donna Elvira, and what effect he has on Zerlina and Masetto, the couple considered by Ponnelle the most important of all. In his view Leporello and Don Giovanni keep flitting between the nobility and the peasantry. Don Giovanni's importance stems less from his personal problems than from his social relations with the secondary characters, who alone can enlighten the audience about Giovanni's ideology.

> Within my overall stage conception I tried to create a set that could tell a parable from that period and convey whatever information the audience needed to follow the story. Windows, doors, trellises, curtains, blinds and walls could all be moved quickly and soundlessly while the action was continued with

concertante pieces in front of the drop curtain. The Spanish elements on my late baroque set were represented in roughly the same proportions as they are found in Mozart's score—very sparsely indeed.

Don Giovanni is a work that makes the highest demands on the producer's skills and faces him with an inexhaustible challenge.

Report by Wolfgang Haefeli
after an interview with Jean-Pierre Ponnelle.

Producer: Franco Zeffirelli — Stage designer: Franco Zeffirelli — Costumes: Franco Zeffirelli — Conductor: Josef Krips

Our preliminary discussions were held in May 1972. Zeffirelli was preparing his presentation of *Don Giovanni* at the Vienna State Opera, elaborating the production as well as the scenic conception. He did so with the artistic verve we know so well from his films.

His visual ideal was an exquisitely pretty and charming set in Watteau colours, suffused with all the technical magic the opera-house could provide.

On a steep and foreshortened slope that ended at or dissolved into the sky, scenic elements sliding on rails or flown in from the grid-iron appeared as if by magic to fuse into an ever-changing tableau. The resulting scenes with their kinetic impact enhanced by exquisite lighting intended to give the effect of engravings; their characteristic horizontal striations were to convey the impression of 'air vibrations'.

It is easy to reproduce these strokes on a piece of paper, but to do so in three dimensions is quite a different matter. This problem preoccupied Zeffirelli a great deal, and at first it was difficult to see how the theory could be put into practice.

A few days had passed since our first meeting; Zeffirelli had made

numerous sketches, but had not yet hit upon a satisfactory solution. One day at about noon we were sitting in his studio in Rome, discussing the problem and illustrating our points with sketches. Some colleagues from Vienna were there too, with, of course, Zeffirelli himself and his assistants. When it seemed to me that there was no practical solution to our predicament, Zeffirelli suddenly walked out of the room. Soon afterwards he reappeared, beaming with delight; he held a packet of spaghetti in his hand, found in the larder.

For a moment I was unsure whether or not this was an invitation to a traditional lunch. Then all became clear. 'I've got it,' he exclaimed. He spread some glue on a sheet of glass and stuck pieces of spaghetti horizontally across it to produce what looked like a three-dimensional flat.

'This can be done with tubes two to five centimetres in diameter. If we use lateral drops and a few backcloths one behind the other which we can move up and down, we'll have air vibrations!' We saw at once that he was right.

The construction of the backcloths, needless to say, proved much more difficult than sticking spaghetti to glass. We had to cut up some 17,000 metres of PVC conduit into twenty-metre tubes and thread them on thin wires at intervals of one to two centimetres, the final result resembling a gigantic blind. Next, these 'air vibrators' were painted and Zeffirelli was right: the effect of these unorthodox contrivances on the stage was sensational.

This was just one facet of a stage conception overflowing with sparkling ideas. I should need several pages to describe our collaboration in detail; I confine myself to this one example, because it was so typical: the spaghetti idea could not have come to Zeffirelli out of the blue, he simply chose it as a visual demonstration of a solution that had been maturing in his mind. Banal things like this best demonstrate an artist's relationship to his material, and his talent for

Costume designs, Franco Zeffirelli

clarifying complex ideas by simple means. God knows how many others I have encountered who take the opposite path and represent simple ideas by the most complicated means.

Despite all the technical difficulties my work with Zeffirelli proved a lasting theatrical experience and confirmed my view that the great masters are simple men at heart, and that only petty minds are complicated.

Workshop report by Pantelis Dessyllas.

1972, AUGSBURG   STADTTHEATER

Producer: Peter Ebert — Stage designer: Hans Ulrich Schmückle — Costumes: Sylta Busse — Conductor: Hans Zanotelli

Don Giovanni presents the producer with one of the most fascinating operatic tasks of all—and one of the most mortifying. There is probably no way of finding an answer that satisfies beyond the evening of the première. This opera is one of those few which every producer should be forced to tackle as a recurrent duty.

After several attempts to recapture the mentality of Don Giovanni in a traditional way, I realized that the use of such external paraphernalia as realistic doors, pillars, rooms and gardens, only serves to stifle the extremely complicated landscape of changing emotions. The characters themselves are no less unique and breathtaking than their interrelationships. The distillation of the dramatic essence and structure is so brilliant—despite the added interludes—that not a bar must be omitted. The very perfection of the score allows an unrivalled freedom of interpretation: for as subtle as is the characterization of the various figures, so broad is the range within which their closely interwoven destinies can be presented.

It now seems incomprehensible that Don Giovanni should have

been depicted as an indefatigable philanderer in his prime, when in fact the opera deals with the twenty-four hours of a man whose life is in a state of pathological decay. This exhausted organism can no longer add to his amorous conquests: he fails with Donna Anna, and cannot even seduce Zerlina, deeply impressed by him though she is. Everything seems to revolve around Don Giovanni, but when we look more closely we find that life inexorably passes him by.

Hans Ulrich Schmückle and I were agreed that we would try to recapture the right spatial architectural and environmental atmosphere for every one of the widely differing scenes. Our next most important task was to portray the 'crumbling' facets of Don Giovanni's personality. To do so convincingly, we felt that the interplay of the characters could only be expressed by an abstracted scenic presentation.

This presentation promised an additional bonus: it allowed a seamless sequence of scenes. I am firmly convinced that every interruption of that sequence—if it lasts longer than the applause that normally greets the end of a scene—produces a drop in the temperature and a lessening of the spectators' attention. The most striking element of this approach is the 'cut' between the downfall of Don Giovanni and the looming up of the sextet. The sudden emptying of the stage—achieved without any musical break—the magical disappearance of anything reminiscent of Giovanni, strikes me as being by far the best solution to this problematical element in the presentation of the opera.

Don Giovanni offers a surfeit of problems. To consider the finale again: how are we to cope with the problem of the Commendatore's statue? He did not place his monument in the churchyard during his lifetime, and the statue did not make the arduous journey to Giovanni's dining-room. In other words, we must assume that the alleged identification of the statue in the churchyard and its appearance in Giovanni's palace were the hallucinations of a disintegrating mind; and that the force of Giovanni's personality was so great that his delusions were shared by Leporello and Elvira. I do not believe that the product of his delusion can be portrayed by a figure walking or rolling on to the stage, no matter how filled it may be with theatrical fog. In my view we did much better when we gave the statue a spectral aspect, represented by a schematic drawing on Don Giovanni's dining-room wall. Naturally, in our version the statue cannot take its leave of Don Giovanni with a handshake, as the libretto specifies.

Instead, after the Commendatore's request, 'Dammi la mano in segno', Giovanni steps up to the spectre. He is pulled towards it as if by a strong magnet and remains chained to it by an invisible power. With his cry of 'No, no!' he manages to tear himself away, but only for a brief moment. The ensuing antics of the demons—once again the product of Giovanni's feverish imagination and a clear sign of his complete mental breakdown—prevent him from regaining his freedom; he is, as it were, kept on a short leash until the magnet (the Commendatore) chains him back to the wall. Immediately *before* Don Giovanni's last scream—if possible just an instant before—a

Costume designs, Sylta Busse

blackout extinguishes his life and the sudden transformation mentioned above is completed during the brief orchestral epilogue. Before the beginning of the next musical passage bright light floods the apparently infinite black set in which the epilogue was enacted. Giovanni, and everything connected with him, have vanished without a trace.

Countless questions have to be answered by any producer of *Don Giovanni,* many of them involving small details that have an important bearing on the delineation of a particular character. Does Giovanni wear a mask when he calls on Donna Anna? I doubt the idea of adopting a cheap disguise for this great adventure would have occurred to him. Why does Giovanni kill the Commendatore? Giovanni is no common criminal. He does his utmost to avoid an armed confrontation, and nimbly parries the thrusts of the incensed but pugnacious old man. Only when he loses his hat during the fight and is recognized by Anna's father does he feel compelled to kill the Commendatore. Anna should leave the scene of the duel at exactly the right dramatic moment, before her father starts his duel with the unknown intruder. It is important to portray Don Ottavio as a strong character, even during his first recitative, in which Mozart-da Ponte make him appear almost taciturn.

Donna Elvira is another interesting figure. She is the only woman in the opera who understands Giovanni; she idolizes and loves him to the point of humiliation. I used this trait in the solution of a particularly delicate problem: Giovanni's escape at the end of Act I, when his enemies have cornered him. If Giovanni extricates himself by knocking the sword out of Don Ottavio's hand, then Ottavio merely looks ridiculous and the scene does not have a strong dramatic effect. I felt it was more appropriate—and more logical—to let Donna Elvira stay Ottavio's hand just as he is about to slay his adversary. In the ensuing confusion Giovanni and Leporello make good their escape—a surprising but convincing conclusion of the scene.

Such problems occupy a major part of all discussions of any *Giovanni* production. They must be resolved organically by a completely realistic presentation of the plot. The most fascinating aspect of every attempt to stage *Don Giovanni* is the casting and characterization of the various roles. It would be idle to attempt a comprehensive account of all the possible interpretations in so brief a note. I believe that the player determines the mood and phrasing of the vocal passages no less than his gestures and choreographic expression. The recitatives, in any case, offer him the greatest possible scope for characterization.

Peter Ebert

Before I discuss my general approach to scenic space I would like to explain what prompted me to adopt my particular solution, and why I prefer it above all others.

It is generally acknowledged that the many quick changes of scenery demanded by this opera cause grave problems. This was not, however, the crucial factor in my decision to evolve a mobile solution.

The real impetus came from Bernhard Gugler, who wrote a remarkable article on this opera for the Stuttgart *Morgenblatt für gebildete Leser* (Morning News for Educated Readers) in 1865:

It is said that the action ends with Don Giovanni's destruction, that we do not care what happens to the other characters, that it makes no difference to us what Elvira and Leporello intend to do, and whether Octavio will lead his Anna to the altar straightaway, or only after one year of mourning. And this observation is just. However, what happens in this horrific scene cannot be the last word; the sensitive spectator feels certain that there was meant to be another. He does not care to emerge from the theatre into the streets reeling with shock, but demands a gradual relaxation of the tension before he returns to his everyday world. In purely musical terms the opera as it is currently performed has no proper ending. The music stops but it does not fade away.

These lines helped to harden my conviction that my own stage conception must hinge on a satisfactory solution of the finale.

Because it is impossible to present the sextet in the destroyed space of Don Giovanni's downfall, I opted for a radical alternative. I set this scene in infinite, empty black space, thus marking it off sharply from the rest of the action.

I had to devise a general presentation that would incorporate my final scene to maximum effect while doing full justice to the producer's ideas.

I decided to construct a street set into which scenery could be shifted swiftly on wagons. The set was constructed of skeletal architectural elements and a profusion of trellises, evoking the Spanish baroque and an atmosphere of decay. The scenic area could—as dramatic needs dictated—be enlarged or constricted at will, so that no one scene was like any other.

I refer to scenic elements that can be moved or mounted on rails as 'screens'. Thanks to the exclusive use of sidelights, and to their great height and their peculiar relief, such elements gave the set as a whole an overpowering alienating character, half real and half mystical.

The resulting scene-shifts, during which no technical aids or stage hands appeared on the set, were carried out smoothly in full view of the audience. The finale of the opera now proved as effective as I could have wished it to be: after a few seconds of total blackout only the ensemble was left in a large, bare and intangible space. After the destruction of Don Giovanni it must have seemed as if the entire décor had been swept off the stage. In this way the sextet was completely divorced from the operatic action, and Gugler's demand for a 'gradual relaxation of the tension before we return to our everyday world' received its scenic and optical fulfilment.

I also found it necessary to convey the passing of time, the better to drive home the point that the action of the opera is completed within twenty-four hours. To suggest this idea, I designed a screen

(in the normal sense of the word) and produced the required atmospheric impressions with the help of back projection, which was treated as an indispensable complement to the rest of the set.

Hans Ulrich Schmückle

1973, BERLIN   DEUTSCHE OPER

Producer: Rudolf Noelte — Stage designer: Jürgen Rose — Costumes: Jürgen Rose — Conductor: Lorin Maazel

The action begins at nightfall and ends next morning: the Commendatore dies after the sun has set, Don Giovanni before it rises again. 'The night is fairly well advanced' when Giovanni intrudes into Anna's chamber, killing her father a short while later.

In the subsequent street scenes it is 'quite late'. The remaining scenes of Act I and their headings contain no indications of changes

in the time of the action. Elvira enters 'late'; the villagers' procession takes place 'late'; the peasants' improvised banquet is held 'late' and is meant to last 'into the night'; Leporello's catalogue will contain ten names more by 'tomorrow morning'.

The heading of Act II gives no new time indications either. The action continues without interruption; it is 'late', or 'toward evening'. Then, during the masked scene, it 'gradually becomes night'.

The moon shines on the cemetery; it is a 'lovely night, brighter than day', the time 'not yet two o'clock'. The supper jointly held with the Commendatore takes place a little later. Giovanni and Leporello leave the cemetery—at about two in the morning—to prepare 'a fine meal'.

The supper is held just before dawn, and then the Commendatore's prophecy is fulfilled: *before* dawn the laughter has died on Don Giovanni's lips.

The traditional view that the action spans several days, or that 'it takes almost exactly twenty-four hours', is uncorroborated. This interpretation is based on a mistaken analysis; it is advanced by numerous musical critics who refuse to eclipse the 'Spanish sun' in favour of a nocturne...

They object that 'Leporello addresses the Commendatore's statue even before the Commendatore has been buried'. This idea is based on three errors: a tomb or statue can be erected even before death; the statue in the cemetery is not demonstrably the 'statue of the Commendatore'—in the manuscript it is merely called 'la statua'. It becomes the 'statue of the Commendatore' during the supper, when the guilt of Leporello is exacerbated and inflamed with wine.

The inscription on the plinth of the statue is of Leporello's own invention, a ruse to coax his master away from the cemetery. Leporello previously assured him that he had not learned to read by moonlight. 'For goodness' sake, come quickly, no longer let us stay!'

And yet the product of Leporello's terrified imagination was so preposterous that Giovanni would surely have dismissed it, had not his own head been befuddled by feasting and wining. The stage direction 'Leporello reads' is significantly absent from the original libretto. 'I wait in prayer and patience until my murderer by his own act is punish'd.' Who could have written this preposterous inscription?

There could only have been one author: Leporello. His motives were fear, a bad conscience, and an impossible order: 'Read, I tell you.' His dubious response deluded Don Giovanni into believing that he was standing by the Commendatore's grave, as it did those critics who refuse to grant that the entire action takes place in one night. The longer the duration of the action is assumed to be, the more incredible and illogical the story becomes. Giovanni is completely dehumanized into a 'Prince of Voluptuaries' and endowed with 'monstrous, demonic forces' that 'tire as little of using him as the wind tires of raging'.

Anna becomes a 'victim' because 'Don Giovanni has had his will of her in the dark of night.' The proof: 'Don Giovanni's indifference to her which shows that he has possessed her, just as he has possessed Donna Elvira and so many others, and also her wish to be avenged by Don Ottavio...'

The belief that Anna is a 'victim' is widespread, even though the theory that Anna's own account is false is not borne out by any passage of the libretto—or by the music.

All these misinterpretations are the result of erroneous views about the duration of the action. The fact is that, in the few hours between the Commendatore's death and his own, Don Giovanni had no opportunity to woo Anna all over again—this is the real explanation of his 'indifference to her'.

The original text does not support the view that she wanted to be avenged by Don Ottavio; she merely calls on Don Ottavio to avenge her father—an understandable request to one's fiancé made immediately after such a murder.

The text says nothing about her refusal to 'belong to Don Ottavio'. She asked him to grant her a year of mourning, another reasonable request at this particular time.

All these critics clearly prefer construction to textual interpretation of the original sources. Anna, though she assures Ottavio of her devotion and fidelity most convincingly, becomes a liar and Don Giovanni an inhuman monster.

His own explanation of the encounter is simple and much more convincing than that of many of these critics, not least because it is so down to earth and human:

'Today...all's going badly.'

Today—during this single night in the life of Don Giovanni: his last!

Translated from: Rudolf Noelte, 1974, pp. 7–11.

In our view the action of *Don Giovanni* takes place during a single night, beginning in the late evening and ending early the next morning. This approach determined our choice of setting, costumes and lighting. The continuous light gradations—from dusk, through moonlit night and thunder-storm to dawn; the contrasting brightness of candles, lanterns and torches—became the crucial optical components of our presentation.

The long succession of scenes called for a set that lent itself to quick transformations. Between scenes a black curtain came down; no scenes were played in front of the curtain while the set was being rebuilt behind.

Our basic structure was a steeply raked rostrum on a scale of 1:10. It ran symmetrically from the apron to the back of the stage, with entrances upstage right and left, downstage right and left (behind the stage portal) and, in a few 'street' scenes, to the rear of the stage. This area was reached by a broad stairway and used, for instance, during the entrance of Donna Elvira in Scene II.

The rostrum was covered with velvet cloth the colour of moss; it stood in the middle of an autumnally sombre park. The trees were drops made in the old way: painted on canvas, cut out, stiffened and staggered for perspective effect. In some scenes they were set off in silhouette, against an illuminated background; in other scenes they were deliberately lit from the side. They ran deep into the back of the stage and fused into a precise optical whole with a back projection that changed from scene to scene—indicating different parts of the landscape or 'town'.

I had the projections painted to scale, before they were photographed on colour slides.

Every scene was now given at least one realistic architectural complement: a wrought iron gate overgrown with foliage in the courtyard of the Commendatore; a well and two wall sections with lanterns to light up the 'street'; two symmetrical, baroque stone benches set amidst lush flowers in the 'palace garden'; stone balustrades with rich bowls of flowers, an oak table and numerous baroque chairs, fronted by the terrace of Giovanni's palace; the ivy-covered 'family tomb' of the Commendatore with the statue of death and other gravestones.

All these props were overgrown with vegetation to blend with the autumnal trees and reflect the southern atmosphere. The entire scenic conception was inspired by eighteenth-century paintings. The furniture and set pieces were exact copies of originals, and the costumes were in late eighteenth-century style.

Jürgen Rose

Berlin, 1973   Noelte/Rose

Cologne, 1971   Ponnelle/Ponnelle

Augsburg, 1972   Ebert/Schmückle

Don Giovanni

'Garden in front of the Com-
mendatore's palace. At night.'

Salzburg, 1968   Karajan/Schneider-Siemssen

Vienna, 1972   Zeffirelli/Zeffirelli

Don Giovanni

'Street. At night.'

Costume design, Jürgen Rose, Berlin, 1973

Vienna, 1972   Zeffirelli/Zeffirelli

84

Augsburg, 1972
Ebert/Schmückle

Salzburg, 1968
Karajan/Schneider-Siemssen

Berlin, 1973   Noelte/Rose

Cologne, 1971   Ponnelle/Ponnelle

Augsburg, 1972   Ebert/Schmückle

Salzburg, 1968   Karajan/Schneider-Siemssen

86

Don Giovanni

'Garden with two gates, opening in-
wards. Two bowers.'

Vienna, 1972   Zeffirelli/Zeffirelli

Berlin, 1973   Noelte/Rose

Don Giovanni

'Fenced-in churchyard with a statue of the Commendatore. Moonlit night.'

Berlin, 1973   Noelte/Rose

Vienna, 1972   Zeffirelli/Zeffirelli

Augsburg, 1972   Ebert/Schmückle

Salzburg, 1968   Karajan/Schneider-Siemssen

Cologne, 1971   Ponnelle/Ponnelle

Don Giovanni

'Room with laid table in Don Giovanni's palace.'

Cologne, 1971   Ponnelle/Ponnelle

Vienna, 1972   Zeffirelli/Zeffirelli

Augsburg, 1972   Ebert/Schmückle

Berlin, 1973   Noelte/Rose

Salzburg, 1968   Karajan/Schneider-Siemssen

Die Zauberflöte *(The Magic Flute)*

Nearly two hundred years have passed since the première of this opera in Vienna, in 1791, shortly before Mozart's death. Ever since it has enjoyed undiminished vitality in thousands of performances and hundreds of different productions on stages the world over. Compared with the meteoric rise and equally sudden decline of so many other contemporary operas, its continuous appeal seems almost inexplicable. The brilliant score alone cannot explain its spell, for audiences also expect to be enthralled by visual effects and dramatic developments on the stage. Perhaps it is the stylistic quality of *The Magic Flute,* so difficult to specify, the fact that its theatrical components are derived from a wide spectrum, ranging from the popular *Singspiel* to grand opera, that have assured an abiding success to this extraordinarily happy alloy of humour and high seriousness. Mozart's score, always in step with the colourful scenic changes, comprises the simple stanza no less than the inspired aria and duet that, under his unique pen, transcend the 'Italian' idiom, and the sweeping and solemn choral scenes of the final phrases. All these elements combine into melodious speech, voicing Mozart's presentiment of his impending death and thus imbuing the whole work—the serious portions no less than the gay—with mystical wisdom, the token of eternity.

It was a unique chance that Mozart's genius should have been fired by Emanuel Schikaneder's libretto and, soaring high above it, should have fashioned an unequalled chain of melodious gems of his own inspiration.

Schikaneder's libretto has often been criticized and, indeed, decried as 'patchwork'. It is true that a fairy story set to music by Wenzel Müller and published at about the same time forced Schikaneder to make a number of quick alterations to his original text with the result that much of *The Magic Flute* is confused, the main and secondary themes in particular being mixed up. Even so, this librettist *cum* stage director, this experienced artist, whom Oskar Bie once called 'a manipulator, nice enough fellow, impudent and lively', wrote the most effective scene sequences with obvious gay abandon. As his own role he invented the figure of Papageno, one of the most beloved characters in opera. Using masonic ideas, with which he and Mozart were both familiar, Schikaneder turned his fast-moving plot into a rare glorification of humanitarian principles. The contrast between the dark realm of the Queen of the Night and the bright sunlit world of Sarastro—effective confrontations of 'evil' and 'good'—helped him to write scenes of the highest dramatic tension.

Personal experiences with countless productions and interpretations have confirmed me in the view that *The Magic Flute* lends itself, like few other works, to a host of stage presentations, all of them 'right' provided only that they follow their chosen path consistently. For this opera, apparently born of chance, proves to be exceedingly vulnerable to thoughtless violations and illogical distortions, though it will tolerate an astonishing variety of approaches. By that I am not merely referring to the treatment of the three youthful messengers from the realm of the Night who turn into friendly guides in Sarastro's world; there are also many other, at first sight confusing, individual characteristics that must, in one way or another, be blended into a logical whole.

Ever since Schinkel's classic architectural solution, many inventive designers have followed the most divergent paths. The strict stylizations of Alfred Roller and Hans Wildermann, whose Egyptizing forms and colours were intended to symbolize the masonic background, were followed by the sets of Traugott Müller, Ludwig Sievert, P. Aravantinos, Leo Pasetti, Emil Preetorius and the younger school of stage designers, who were able to create a more convincing fairy world with the help of the latest space-creating lighting techniques.

The interpretative possibilities have been far from exhausted, although certain conventions are now generally accepted: the scenic space must not be too large lest it detract from the dialogue and the more intimate scenes; there must be no break in individual acts.

It is to be hoped that all future productions will lend a sensitive ear to Mozart's music. Producer and stage designer, working in re-creative artistic association, can do no better than remember Richard Strauss's words: 'Mozartian melody is God's ultimate gift to mankind', not least because *The Magic Flute* is the last theatrical work of that immortal genius.

Rudolf Hartmann

Scenes

1.1   The stage represents a rocky place, dotted with trees; on either side there are hills which can be walked upon, and there is also a temple.

1.6   The hills divide, and the scene changes into a resplendent chamber. The Queen is seated on a throne which is studded with diaphanous stars.

1.9   As soon as the scene changes into a sumptuous Egyptian room, two slaves enter, bearing fine cushions and a splendid Turkish table, and spread carpets on the floor.

1.15   The scene changes into a grove. At the back, a beautiful temple with the inscription 'Temple of Wisdom', from which colonnades lead to two other temples: the 'Temple of Reason' on the right, and the 'Temple of Nature' on the left.

2.1   The scene changes into a palm-wood; all the trees are silver, the leaves gold; each of eighteen leaves supports a pyramid and a large black horn set in gold. The largest of the pyramids and the largest of the trees are in the centre.

2.2 Night. Distant thunder. The scene is changed to a forecourt of the temple, with ruined pillars and pyramids and some thorn-bushes. On either side there are practicable Egyptian doors suggesting other buildings.

2.7 The scene changes into a pleasant garden; there is a horseshoe of trees; in the centre is a bower of roses and other flowers in which Pamina is asleep. The moon shines on her face. In front there is a grassy bank.

2.13 The scene changes into a hall in which the flying frame can be deployed; it is surrounded by roses and other flowers and has a door. Right in front are two grassy banks.

2.16 Three boys arrive in the flying frame covered with roses. In the centre is a sumptuously spread table. One of the boys carries a flute, another a chime of bells.

2.20 The scene changes to a vault beneath a pyramid; Chorus and some Priests. Two Priests carry illuminated pyramids on their shoulders; each Priest holds a transparent pyramid, the size of a lantern.

2.25 The scene changes to a garden at the front of the stage.

2.28 The scene changes into two mountains. On one there is a waterfall, which one can hear rushing and roaring. The other mountain spits out fire; each mountain has a jagged grating through which one can see fire and water; where the fire burns the horizon must be bright red, and where there is water there is a black mist. There are two iron gates for passing through the fire and water.

2.29 The scene changes back into a garden.

2.30 There is a loud clash of elements: thunder, lightning and storm. All at once the whole stage is transformed into a sun.

1967, NEW YORK   METROPOLITAN OPERA HOUSE

Producer: Günther Rennert — Stage designer: Marc Chagall — Costumes: Marc Chagall — Conductor: Josef Krips

Every new production of *The Magic Flute* not only poses the question of intellectual interpretation and of a new approach to this truly 'incommensurable' work, but also of the scenographic starting-point, and, in this particular case, of the scenic material. The issues involved here are more complex than merely whether the dominant element is the colourful fairy-tale or the miracle play, the popular work or the philosophical drama, or whether the dominant visual element is colour, architecture, or movement. The mythological substance of this work is inexhaustible; the symbols allow endless new possibilities of visualization, ranging from the confinement of the imagination imposed by the stage properties to complete abstraction in which the contents are evoked by pure association...

When Sir Rudolf Bing invited me to produce *The Magic Flute* in New York in collaboration with Marc Chagall, I realized that I was about to embark on one of the greatest scenic adventures possible in my field. Would an artist with so marked a personality be prepared to make any concessions to others? Would not the laws governing the construction of scenery constrict the world of his own imagination?... Could we co-ordinate our efforts to enhance not only the pictorial impact but also the musical effect?...

During our first conversations it became perfectly clear that my chief problem would be to give the painter a meaningful exposition of dramatic problems, of what is involved in a 'scenic score'...

We would first have to agree on the scenic space in which to set, without breaks, the struggle between the Queen of the Night and Sarastro, the trials of Pamina and Tamino, and Papageno's antics. I had a simple model built, on which the course of the action could easily be shown. It was a boxed-in stage on which, following the old baroque method, flats and drops could be freely deployed as the twenty-four scenes demanded. ... I made sure not to engage Chagall in purely technical discussions, so that he could work at his drawing-board without this extra burden, an especially onerous one in *The Magic Flute*. [Rennert, 1974, pp. 71–74.]

It seemed obvious that ours would be a fairy-tale *Magic Flute*, one in which this painter was so much at home. Hence I gave a great deal of thought to the best way in which I could bring home to him the three distinct levels of this opera: the cathartic drama, the popular play and Sarastro's overriding, nomological world. It was accepted from the start that Chagall's colour scale had to be given full scope to create artistic symbols appropriate to these three worlds.

It proved relatively easy to come to grips with Papageno's world, which lent itself well to Chagall's fairy-tale approach, while Sarastro's lawful and orderly world had first to be translated into special terms that could be given visual expression in Chagall's particular language. In the process we deliberately eschewed Egyptian or Masonic stereotypes and other conventional representations, and looked instead for forms in which a painter could render law and order visible.

We arrived at such basic forms as the circle, the isosceles triangle and the rectangle which, in various combinations and transformations, and always enriched with an immense colour sense, kept recurring in the painter's scenic backcloths.

We now had a common sign language that helped us to arrive at clear pictorial conceptions, applicable to all three levels of this most difficult of all theatrical productions. In this way there emerged some sixteen pencil sketches—sheets from which the whole work could be constructed like a house of cards. . . .

During the next stage we had to develop three-dimensional theatrical areas from two-dimensional sketches. I cut out individual parts of the sketches, and some were duplicated. I had the cut-out segments freshly painted and recombined into a perspective model in accordance with the original sketch.

Space was thus born out of the elements of the first primitive sketches. This process was fascinating because the transformation of two-dimensional surfaces into three-dimensional space struck me as marking the turning-point in the painter's work. [*Op. cit.*, p. 76]

Two formal stylistic problems—the representation of the Queen of the Night and that of the Sun—which seemed insoluble to even a painter of Chagall's stature, were the subjects of lengthy discussions.

It was extremely difficult to talk to Chagall about darkness. He dreads the dark itself, but not the colours by which it can be represented, like dark blue, deep red and grey. . . . During lighting rehearsals of the scenes with the Queen of the Night the stage could never be bright enough for him although we were fully agreed this way was to be a shadowy world. [*Op. cit.*, p. 76]

In the end, Chagall abandoned the idea of investing the Queen of the Night with the customary brilliance and invented an absolutely fitting 'demonic dark glow'. A light midnight blue with an almost silvery motif of rays dominated a scene that could not have been more beautiful. I have never seen a more convincing presentation of the Queen of the Night. This one was, if anything, even more fascinating than Schinkel's classical model, which I adore.

At the end of his libretto, Schikaneder specified: 'The stage represents a sun.' This was one problem Chagall considered insoluble from the very start. And so he finally decided, like so many great stage designers before him, to paint several suns, intended to signify the requisite radiance. Even so, as late as the première itself, Chagall nearly succumbed to a remarkable malady: an inability to paint the sun. The intellectual realization that one can only represent, not paint, finally persuaded the great artist to deploy a whole battery of spot-lights, which he had quickly installed during the intervals of the first performance. This proved unconvincing, however; the idea of representing the sun by a multiplicity of painted suns was much more effective and was, in any case, a perfectly legitimate theatrical solution.

The Magic Flute involves so many changes of scene that it stretches the technical resources of the stage to the utmost. The set we constructed allowed smooth scene changing at great speed and without the use of a drop curtain. Instead, the gridiron, the complicated system of stage traps and the overlarge side stages were used to the fullest possible extent.

Thus conceived, and dominated by the infinite intricacy and artistic distinction of Chagall's world of colour, *The Magic Flute*—fairy-tale, miracle play and popular entertainment—was to be performed without any breaks. For the cast, we envisaged three distinct forms of gesticulation, each in accordance with the form, colour and content of the scenic picture. This made great demands on the singers, all of whom went out of their way to meet them and to play their roles with great sensitivity.

Compiled by Wolfgang Haefeli after
an interview with Günther Rennert.

1967, SALZBURG FESTIVAL   GROSSES FESTSPIELHAUS

Producer: Oscar Fritz Schuh — Stage designer: Teo Otto† — Costumes: Teo Otto† — Conductor: Wolfgang Sawallisch

In the course of our lives we are likely to be presented with *The Magic Flute* in a variety of guises. It is so complex a work that no general approach can be laid down once and for all; each new production tends to emphasize one aspect or another. It is the combination of mystery play and popular Viennese comedy that has always proved the greatest stumbling block: either the final conception fails to match Sarastro's world or else it does not correspond to Papageno's. Producers came up against this problem every time they were forced to operate with the sets of the old illusionistic stage, which *The Magic Flute* basically demands.

Starting from this realization, and conscious of the difficulties posed by the vast stage of the Salzburg Festspielhaus, we deliberately refrained from both a historical interpretation resurrecting the old Viennese folk theatre, and also from any attempt to reflect the classical ideal.

Instead, tempted no doubt by the iron curtain of the Festspielhaus, we arrived at a solution that involved a confrontation with mannerism, an approach that, endowed with the authority of El Greco, seems to be very much in vogue again. Building on the basic structure of Hoflehner's curtain, we paid special attention to the fusion of the two apparently contradictory worlds of the Queen of the Night and of Sarastro, treating one as the mirror image of the other.

Since neither the realm of the Queen nor the monastic world of Sarastro seems to have fixed sociological or historical foundations, we placed our set in a dream world accentuated visually by a profusion of architectural styles and plants, together with a labyrinthine world which combined the coldness of metal with the transparency of glass.

This unreal, mannerist world—which throughout the opera makes itself felt with particular force in Sarastro's internal realms—was framed by an eye represented in various forms. The French architect Boulle had developed this idea, along with many other futuristic concepts. His 'eye' fascinated Teo Otto all the more because it conveyed the idea of composition, a reflection of the entire course of events in the detached eye of an observing god.

The set included architecture from the fantasy world of the imagination; we used some projection as a deliberate stylistic aid, introducing illusionistic detail to break up over-large surfaces and especially to shape the ground area of the enormous amphitheatre of the Festspielhaus.

The dream-like atmosphere was maintained throughout the production by means of continuous open scene changes; the result was a permanently shifting world, reminiscent of the smoothly blending sequences of a dream. We paid particular attention to the continuity of the final build-up to the Temple of the Sun, in which two thirds of the scenes take place at night.

The aspirants, too, journey through dark and forbidding ruins before finally reaching fire and water, and we made no attempt to portray this by illusionistic techniques.

Despite the special problems posed by the mammoth Salzburg stage, we were agreed from the outset not to reduce its overall size in an effort to bring out the intimate character of the opera. The resulting proscenium arch would undoubtedly have made the audience feel that they were watching developments as if through a window.

Instead we constructed an arrangement of bars that included the forestage, an effect we did not produce with equal success in all the scenes.

We were particularly conscious of the fact that Papageno—no matter how ably interpreted—would be lost in this gigantic stage, if he were not given some kind of optical reinforcement. To that end, we filled the stage with vegetation so that he could make his entrances from between trees and branches that suddenly sprouted out of the ground, providing at the same time a landscape in which he could catch his birds. We even decided to allow the spectator a view of the large side stages on which rocks, distant caves and subterranean cities would be displayed, suggesting an infinite landscape. Technical reasons unfortunately prevented us from doing this, and in our opinion the production suffered as a result.

Oscar Fritz Schuh

1970, MUNICH   BAYERISCHE STAATSOPER

Producer: Günther Rennert — Stage designer: Joseph Svoboda — Costumes: Erich Kondrak, Anneliese Corrodi — Conductor: Rafael Kubelik

Joseph Svoboda induced me to employ anonymous scenic spaces consisting of nothing but light and colour, challenging me no less than had Chagall. Since I wanted neither to copy nor to vary the New York performance, I had to start from different premises. The dramatization of the initiation and purification mystery—in psychological terms the individuation of two human beings—would be central to the new production, and have to be presented by unconventional means.

This view accorded fully with that of Joseph Svoboda. His conception of scenic space is, in any case, one that eschews décor in favour of a constructive spatial solution. I felt that a subtle lighting technique, in a black stage box articulated into different stage levels, was perfectly adequate for the portrayal of the various dramatic levels of this opera, and for its fairy-tale element.

Admittedly, this interpretation throws up special problems, including acoustic ones. It is obvious that, in the pianissimo passages, it is difficult to make the presence of Tamino and Pamino felt as strongly on a stage measuring 15 metres by 20 metres as on a baroque stage which, moreover, is much fuller of colour and light than the much larger area on which only particular areas can be highlighted.

This is more or less true of all intimate scenes, such as the conversation between Sarastro and Tamino, or the playful sequences with Papageno in which, for dynamic reasons alone, one might wish for a shorter stage, one on which the effect of not a single word might be lost. On the other hand, I felt that this sober and bare area offered me a unique chance to deploy a large cast to best advantage. Scenic aids were confined to bare essentials, so it was all the more important to pay careful and detailed attention to the characters. Choreographic elements, in particular, became far more important.

The organization of the ensembles and choruses in this empty box turned out to be a scenic and dramatic task of some difficulty, in contrast to what happened in New York, where I was hard put to it to bring the characters to life in so great a surfeit of pictorial inspiration. The Munich performance with Svoboda, its world of light and space so unlike Chagall's, may serve to demonstrate how many and varied are the approaches and optical interpretations to which *The Magic Flute* lends itself.

Günther Rennert

My starting-point was Dr. Rennert's proposal to reduce the staging of *The Magic Flute* to the barest necessities in an area defined by light and the most important props alone.

The basis of my scenic conception was a mirror-like passe-partout measuring 13 metres by 10 metres. It could be shut by two systems of wings, the first of which was attached to the front of the frame with special hinges, like the wings of a gate. When they were fully closed a circular opening, three metres in diameter, was left in the centre of the passe-partout.

The second system of wings was attached to the rear of the passe-partout. It was made up of four wings that could be closed in the same way as in the other system but the wings of this one were sickle-shaped and formed a kind of hyperbolic aperture.

The passe-partout was placed three metres behind the stage portal, its two lower wings—the inner and outer—constituting the playing area. The space behind, covered in black and bounded by the lateral wings, had a width of twenty metres and a great depth that provided large projection areas. It was broken up by a relatively small, oval rostrum with a maximum depth of seven metres but stretching across the entire width of the stage. The stage was completely closed off by a projection screen of dark grey foil on to which laser beams and other light could be projected. To avoid scattering, I constructed the screen as a pyramid truncated in the direction of the projection. I used four 5-kW projectors for showing 18 by 18 centimetre slides, and also a laser projector.

Joseph Svoboda

1972, COLOGNE   OPERNHAUS

Producer: Jean-Pierre Ponnelle — Stage designer: Jean-Pierre Ponnelle — Costumes: Jean-Pierre Ponnelle — Conductor: István Kertész

When Claus Helmut Drese and István Kertész first asked me to produce a Mozart cycle I was taken aback—I had not thought before of treating Mozart cyclically. At the same time I was fascinated by the idea of confronting this composer within a much wider context than I could in a single work.

At first I found it very difficult to discover a common denominator in an 'opera seria' such as *Titus* or *Idomeneo,* an *opera buffa* such as *Così fan tutte,* or a *dramma giocoso* such as *Don Giovanni,* and for a while I wondered whether there was, in fact, any point in pursuing that search. On closer examination, however, I became convinced that a historical approach could provide the answer—an approach based on the composer's own outlook and not on an intellectually dishonest projection of hindsight knowledge.

Accordingly, I tried to see all Mozart's works in the spirit of his own age: as the most perfect expression of the eighteenth century, the century of the Enlightenment and of humanism. With this key I arrived at a common dramatic denominator, a continuous 'red thread'. Even so, I could hardly have produced the cycle had I not been my own stage and costume designer. In the cycle I tried to give the different works a more or less similar ground plan. The result was a theatrical and vocal arena on which fixed architectural elements, together with lattice-work and painted screens, set the period, and on which scene shifts did not interrupt the flow of the play. Lighting which gave a monochrome effect in black and white and the use of camaieu décor were intended to produce a distinctly functional style that may perhaps have seemed unjustified when taken on its own, but that was validated by the greater dramatic action.

All the scenes involved two distinct planes, with a pronounced emphasis on the central axis and the entrances: an echo, a paraphrase perhaps, of the baroque theatre. This terraced, or stepped, construction enabled me to place the members of the ensembles at different levels so that, in accordance with the score, they were brought into a permanent, almost dialectical, relationship with the music. My intention was not so much to provide a visual illustration of the score as to convey its meaning and structure on the stage. I believe this is as essential in staging Mozart as conveying the right dramatic effect.

The ground plan I mentioned not only had a dramatic function, but was meant to improve the acoustics of the opera-house. I created a kind of funnel box that directed the rich sounds of the orchestra into the auditorium without drowning out the voices. I believe that with this arrangement I was fairly successful in creating optimum acoustic conditions for the performance of Mozart's music.

The deliberate choice of a black-and-white colour scale was an equally essential facet of my general conception: Mozart does not strike me as a 'colourful' composer. Lighting and a variety of costumes, some full of colour, helped to set off the performers all the more sharply and poignantly from a fairly anonymous background—in full accordance with Mozart's intentions.

Quite a few of the operas are set in Spain, a country that appears bleached by the baking sun. This colourless environment is undoubtedly bound up with Mozart's world—a world in which man, characterized with great insight, invariably constitutes the central point.

As part of the general approach, my interpretation of *The Magic Flute*—certainly Mozart's richest and most mature work—was guided by the belief that the opera must be presented without cuts or any of the traditional 'witty' stage effects. I consider every kind of omission, especially with Mozart, a kind of sacrilege; the usual cuts in the dialogue of *The Magic Flute* contribute nothing whatsoever to the understanding of the plot.

I deliberately took the road back to 'high Schikaneder', as an important step towards the elucidation of the relationship between the Queen of the Night and Sarastro, of the story of the succession, and also of the Masonic ideal whose expression is, after all, not superficially confined to a few appeals to 'Isis and Osiris'.

Jean-Pierre Ponnelle

young man intended às Sarastro's successor had simply to prove himself before an unchallenged authority.

In 1974 we had been invited to the Vienna State Opera by R. Gamsjäger, whose Berlin production we remembered as an example of enthusiastically executed stage conception. True to Felsenstein's dictum that one must face the work one intends to perform without bias, we re-read this libretto only to discover novel issues and structures—a quite different interpretation of the distribution of good and evil.

We found that two contradictory realms existed side by side and that neither one could do justice to the fullness of life without the presence of the other: the rational, planning world of the initiates built on intellectual discipline; and the vegetatively proliferating realm. Like the Quuen, who, driven by genuine maternal grief, alcause. Since both are one-sided and incomplete, they try to find each other, to fuse in the younger generation. Concepts from the Indian Tantric doctrine provided us with powerful symbolic parallels.

Thus, while the initiates miss no opportunity to express their misogyny, the ladies of the Queen seek to lure a man into their realm. Like the Queen, who, driven by genuine maternal grief, allows herself to press a hybrid claim to power, the initiates are still groping for true humanity. Slaves, driven by a Moor, help them to reap the fruits of their studies; the administration of justice is rough and ready. Mozart's music unmistakably expresses the jubilant and utopian hope that such polar opposites may become fused harmoniously in the future, and reflects it in the chorus of people who, as a third force, raise their voices significantly in this opera.

We preserved the elements Walter Felsenstein had clarified and those that ought, in any case, to be quite obvious to anyone who has

1974, VIENNA   STAATSOPER
1975, LEIPZIG   OPERNHAUS AM KARL-MARX-PLATZ

Producer: Joachim Herz — Stage designer: Rudolf Heinrich† — Costumes: Rudolf Heinrich† — Conductor (in Vienna): Christoph von Dohnanyi; (in Leipzig): Gert Bahner

Rudolf Heinrich was stage designer, and I was Walter Felsenstein's assistant during his production of *The Magic Flute* at the Komische Oper, Berlin, in 1954. That performance has made theatrical history: the boxes at the side of the stage were embellished in Indian baroque of the most massive construction, with South German baroque providing a playful counterpoint on the stage. The world of the initiates was good, that of the Queen of the Night was bad. Whatever did not fit this interpretation we analysed away. The optimism of the new start in the early post-war years did not yet admit the many questions glossed over by such life-affirmative views. The

Costume design, Rudolf Heinrich, Vienna, 1974

read the libretto: for instance that there is only one Moor and that there are no female initiates. Instead of scrapping the trio—unfortunately phrased in the original—we adopted a new solution and went on to plan scene after scene during our customary walks, this time in the Vienna woods. New transitions were added and a smooth succession of scenes devised. A constantly changing forest maze allowed us to let Tamino and Pamina miss each other in amusing ways. The actual presence of animals and especially of the snake was taken for granted by all of us. Moreover, we made sure that the mysterious temple of the initiates literally eluded Tamino's questions. For the ordeals by fire and water we borrowed freely from the puppet theatre, but we did not allow anything to detract from the deadly seriousness of the tests. The scene with the three genii became a colourful mass spectacle: country people dyeing cloth for the initiates.

In Part II the 'full stage/forestage' principle was implemented to bridge dialogue scenes, which involved a number of transpositions in the otherwise unaltered dialogue.

The initiates realize that the three ladies wish to influence the two aspirants but approve of this intervention as a crucial test: it shows that the aspirants can no longer be beguiled by the enemy. The test of silence is imposed on the initiates unbeknown to the spectators, who learn of it only at the tragic end of this scene, when a tent-like partition rises up to confront the initiates with the Isis chorus. The three genii peel Pamina out of a giant gourd, and the Queen's last assault is directed at the solar circle (illusory or real?), which suddenly floods the stage with light and destroys the attackers.

'The stage is transformed into a sun.' 'The kingdom of error to truth yields the day.' Taking these injunctions literally, we have the crowd step on to the now-golden disc of the earth, with the young couple in their midst. Sarastro has become dispensable; he quietly abandons the jubilant circle and disappears from view.

A fabulous set, a great deal of stage magic and the rollicking fun of the Viennese Punch-and-Judy show were the declared objectives of our joint effort. We decided against an Egyptian solution for this reason, and also to draw more freely on the other source of the opera: Wieland's fairy-tale, eastern world of *Dschinnistan*. As for the Masonic ideas, we dispensed with their optical symbols, but expressed them through the fundamental and vigilant pursuit of compassion, enlightenment and the fraternal ideal.

Joachim Herz

We were anxious to tackle this work not with an accumulation of dusty traditions, but with incisive realism. Long, fruitful discussions and shared critical pleasure in creative work allowed us to be perfectly frank with each other, with the result that our interpretation, too, was straightforward.

On the basis of a fundamental agreement on the contents, we now tried to arrive at scenic elements that I could create and transform

and that Joachim Herz was able to fit smoothly into his own conception.

At the centre of the set I placed the earth, an uneven disc accessible to the players on all sides. It barely changed throughout the play and thus served as a symbol of universality, which allowed two worlds as distinct as the Queen's and Sarastro's to coexist.

The lunar world of the Queen was represented by lush vegetation in a hothouse atmosphere. Here there were no sharp angles; everything ran riot, springy and untrimmed, full of birds and colour, with green predominating. This world of turmoil and complete harmony was fashioned from such plant material as raffia, and from gold and brilliant green silks deliberately turned inside out to suggest the primitive. We deliberately eschewed elegance; improvisations served to intensify the wildness of nature, its jungle character. The scene was divided into three dimensions: the first was the earth on which the actors disported themselves; next came the natural space independent of man; and finally, the great cosmic time dimension with its glittering golden clouds promising the morning sun.

The division itself provided a link between Sarastro's solar realm and the lunar world. The world of the initiates which, in our production, resembled that of Zen Buddhist monks, created a stark contrast.

Here all colour was banished; stark wooden gates and pillars—reminiscent of Samurai architecture—helped to avoid the least impression of a resplendent palace. We tried to stress the fact that the ideals of the initiates were universal and not subject to geographical limitations. The dominating ascetic atmosphere was slightly relaxed by the orange scintillation of the priests' silk cloaks. The ideas of nature and love, the symbolic expressions of the night and the sun, and of the slaves and initiates—which embodied reality despite the fairy-tale language—were thus portrayed by specific theatrical techniques. Within this general scenic conception, which placed no restrictions whatsoever on the producer, I attached the utmost importance to the finale.

Sun and earth become as one in Schikaneder's idea that 'the stage is transformed into a sun'. And so, the black background was suddenly replaced by a yellow-white curtain, flooded with 'sunlight'. The earth—in fact the floor of the stage, covered with a brilliant sheet of gold foil—reflected this light straight into the auditorium, thus drawing the spectators into the solar circle, and giving tangible expression to the universal appeal of *The Magic Flute*.

Compiled by Wolfgang Haefeli after an interview with Rudolf Heinrich (31.7.1975).

The Magic Flute

'The stage represents a rocky place, dotted with trees; on either side there are hills which can be walked upon, and there is also a temple.'

Munich, 1970   Rennert/Svoboda

Vienna, 1974   Herz/Heinrich

Salzburg, 1967   Schuh/Otto

Costume designs, Rudolf Heinrich, Vienna, 1974

Cologne, 1972   Ponnelle/Ponnelle

101

New York, 1967 Rennert/Chagall

The Magic Flute

'The hills divide, and the scene changes
into a resplendent chamber. The Queen
is seated on a throne which is studded
with diaphanous stars.'

Costume design, Rudolf Heinrich, Vienna, 1974

Munich, 1970 Rennert/Svoboda

Cologne, 1972   Ponnelle/Ponnelle

Salzburg, 1967   Schuh/Otto

Cologne, 1972   Ponnelle/Ponnelle

Salzburg, 1967   Schuh/Otto

Munich, 1970   Rennert/Svoboda

Vienna, 1974   Herz/Heinrich

The Magic Flute

'The scene changes into a grove. At the back, a beautiful temple with the inscription "Temple of Wisdom", from which colonnades lead to two other temples: the "Temple of Reason" on the right, and the "Temple of Nature" on the left.'

New York, 1967   Rennert/Chagall

Cologne, 1972
Ponnelle/Ponnelle

Munich, 1970   Rennert/Svoboda

106

The Magic Flute

'The scene changes to a vault beneath a pyramid; Chorus and some Priests. Two Priests carry illuminated pyramids on their shoulders; each Priest holds a transparent pyramid, the size of a lantern.'

Salzburg, 1967   Schuh/Otto

Munich, 1970   Rennert/Svoboda

Salzburg, 1967   Schuh/Otto

Leipzig, 1975   Herz/Heinrich

The Magic Flute

'The scene changes to a garden at the front of the stage.'

Cologne, 1972   Ponnelle/Ponnelle

New York, 1967   Rennert/Chagall

The Magic Flute

'There is a loud clash of elements: thunder, lightning and storm. All at once the whole stage is transformed into a sun.'

Leipzig, 1975   Herz/Heinrich

New York, 1967   Rennert/Chagall

Cologne, 1972   Ponnelle/Ponnelle

Munich, 1970   Rennert/Svoboda

Salzburg, 1967   Schuh/Otto

Fidelio

Basing himself on a play by Jean Nicolas Bouilly, the Viennese author Joseph Sonnleithner wrote the libretto of *Fidelio or Conjugal Love,* a three-act opera with music by Ludwig van Beethoven. The première at the Theater an der Wien on 20 November 1805 was a disappointment—and there were three performances all told. A year later Stephan von Breuning condensed the three acts to two and the composer made appropriate alterations to the score. The name of the opera remained unchanged, but the libretto was now restyled *Leonora or the Triumph of Conjugal Love.* The new version, too, was taken off after two performances and forgotten for several years.

A third version, dating from 1814, came from the pen of Georg Friedrich Treitschke, an able dramatist and producer at the Vienna Court Opera. Beethoven wrote some music for this production, including the E-major overture. The performance in the Theater am Kärntnerthor at last earned the opera the lasting fame it has enjoyed ever since.

In its final form, the sub-title was omitted and the work was simply called *Fidelio.* We know that Beethoven himself would have preferred to call his opera *Leonora,* but that he allowed himself to be dissuaded. As a result, the stress was shifted from the heroine and marital fidelity to the hero.

And yet marital love is the mainspring and the very heart of this opera. The defeat of tyranny remained a side-issue and though it has often been highlighted, especially after periods of political or military unrest, all such interpretations smack of cheap journalism. The uniforms of Pizarro and his soldiers, which were intended to be period pieces have—unfortunately—been changed time and again to illustrate contemporary events, for no part of the world has entirely escaped the tyrant's heavy hand. In *Fidelio,* however, Don Pizarro does not symbolize political power. He is a villain in his own right, and one who ruthlessly pursues personal vendettas and abuses his powerful position in the process. The authority of the state, of which Pizarro is, in fact, afraid, appears in the person of the King's Minister in the final scene, and when it does, metes out justice and restores liberty.

Through Beethoven's music there runs like a red thread the preparation for his last great hymn, to the glory of human love in its highest, most noble, sense. Marcellina's fervent and lyrical aria is followed by a marvellous quartet in canon form; Leonora's great solo scene is a fitting counterpart to the visionary allegro of Florestan's recitative in the dungeon; the jubilant duet of the reunited couple blazes the trail for the radiant brilliance of the tremendous finale. In all these passages the text reflects but a single idea: 'Let hope sustain my trembling heart... and love to joy will guide us...'; 'My heart has told me so, before one word he said...'; 'Fair light of hope, point me the way, that love may safely find it...'; 'To him, my one and only one, my course unfalt'ring presses (in the German;

"My plighted troth sustains me"...)'; 'My angel, Leonora, my angel, my wife. She leads me to freedom and heavenly life...'; 'Oh joy, beyond expressing, when heart finds heart again...'; 'Happy he whom God has granted to be lov'd by such a wife. Praise we now the noble lady, saviour of her husband's life.'

The history of the work proves the arduous struggle Beethoven waged before he arrived at the final version of *Fidelio.* For his only stage piece he discovered and developed a musical form that transcended all current ideas about the true nature of an opera. The magnificent finale has an unmistakable affinity with the final chorus of the Ninth Symphony; the human voice is more than once pushed to the very limits of its instrumental possibilities.

The producer and stage designer must cope with unusual difficulties. The beginning is reminiscent of the popular operas of an Albert Lortzing, and the 'bourgeois' atmosphere of the private world of the chief jailer must be made to blend smoothly into the subsequent, sombre scenes—there should be no break. The dialogue poses grave problems; it is advisable to shorten many turns of phrase that sound too archaic to the modern ear. But the spoken passages leading up to the musical renderings and preparing the ground for them—for instance the phrase introducing the quartet in Act I ('Still, meinst du ich könne dir nicht in's Herz sehen?' [Hush, do you think I cannot read your heart?]) ought to be retained in their emotional, original form.

The main protagonists stand out clearly through most of the work. The somewhat conventional pair, Marcellina and Jaquino, no less than their surroundings, must accord with the increasing seriousness of the plot, as must the equivocal figure of Rocco, who so ably combines avariciousness with the execution of his unpleasant duties. Don Pizarro offers a wide field of interpretation, ranging from lust after political and military power to sadistic mania. The embodiments of the main motif, Leonora and Florestan, must remain uncomplicated throughout. The King's Minister, Don Fernando, is no hermit from *Der Freischütz,* and it is of the utmost importance that this part be played by an outstanding singer of great authority.

No matter how the stage is conceived, the final scene can dispense with every decorative embellishment; liberating floods of light will serve the soloists, now rid of petty ambition, together with the chorus, as the best setting for the grandiose finale.

Rudolf Hartmann

Scenes

1.1 The courtyard of the state prison. At the back is the main entrance with a postern gate and a high wall overgrown with trees. Beside the entrance is the gatekeeper's lodge. To the left are the prisoners' quarters; all the windows are barred and the numbered doors have metal furnishings and heavy bolts. In the foreground is the door to the jailer's house. On the right are trees surrounded by railings and a gate to a garden.

2.1   A dungeon. To the left, a cistern covered with rubble and stones. At the back a wall, with irregular openings made secure by gratings through which a flight of steps can be seen leading down to a prison door on the right. A lamp is burning.

2.7   Parade-ground outside the castle with statue of the king.

1968, SALZBURG   GROSSES FESTSPIELHAUS

Producer: Günther Rennert — Stage designer: Rudolf Heinrich† — Costumes: Rudolf Heinrich† — Conductor: Karl Böhm

Before every new production of Beethoven's *Fidelio* one has to ask oneself to what extent one's own concept is in tune with the spirit of the age. Like all important works of art, *Fidelio* allows of several distinct approaches. After the war, for instance, the emphasis was on the conflict between a brutal tyrant and a determined individual ready to make the supreme sacrifice. The atmosphere of the concentration camp and its destruction by liberal forces became the central elements of many stage presentations. [Rennert, 1974, p. 91.]

What attracted us in this work was the determination of one individual to stake his life in order to save another's, to defend freedom against dictatorial repression, and the chance that this determination might win through. Leonora's total commitment to her husband is what ultimately decides the issue and constitutes the chief fascination of this opera.

We quickly agreed that the 'cinemascope' stage of the large Festspielhaus called for the projection of this individual struggle on to a communal or national plane, which meant articulating the overrid-

ing idea of freedom all the more emphatically. In our view the whole work would be ruined if any other approach was used on this mammoth stage.

We realized from the start that we had to reduce the stage to human proportions, and to make Leonora appear as the dominant character on it. To that end we devised a large set that narrows down to the actual playing area, the area to which the prologue leads up.

To vary the width of the stage, Rudolf Heinrich designed a series of massive, almost oppressive, metal partitions, devised as mobile towers and based on the iron curtain of the house, which symbolized power, oppression and terror. For the first scene the towers were moved together to reduce the width of the stage considerably. Before a radiant background there rose up the 'idyll'—an island of quiet and peace. The completely realistic exposition of this small, intimate scene helped us to set off the gloom of the prison courtyard and dungeon all the more poignantly.

The metal partitions drew back to reveal a double-storeyed structure, also constructed of heavy metal plates. The guard, on broad gang-planks, held a commanding position over the prisoners. The whole area, shut off without a glimpse of the sky and filled with hopelessness, conveyed a sense of terror and enslavement.

The dungeon was built on the same principle used in the first scene: the reduction of the stage by means of high walls. A stepladder reaching from the gridiron down to the stage floor suggested the abysmal depth of this dungeon.

A complete contrast was the setting of the hymn to freedom: a relief of white, moulded figures spanning the entire width of the stage (thirty-five metres) and extending the chorus, which was drawn up in several clusters and dressed in bright national costumes, into infinity. This was our way of presenting the idea of freedom with maximum visual effect. [*Op.cit.*, p. 91]

We agreed that this particular space with the appropriate architectural stresses would be the right setting for my conception on this outsize stage.

Compiled by Wolfgang Haefeli after
an interview with Günther Rennert.

1969, FLORENCE   TEATRO COMUNALE ENTE AUTONOMO

Producer: Giorgio Strehler — Stage designer: Ezio Frigerio — Costumes: Ezio Frigerio — Conductor: Zubin Mehta

Our presentation did not solve the many complex problems posed by this unusual and contradictory opera—one that, though basically misunderstood, is generally recognized as a masterpiece. The problems were musical as well as dramatic.

The first task we tackled was a difficult and, to us, important one, of adding *Fidelio* to the repertoire of Italian opera companies, from which it was unfortunately missing. To that end we decided to have it performed by Italian singers. This choice had its pros and cons,

but it did help make the opera seem more like one of our own. The sacrilege could be justified if it helped to turn *Fidelio* from a relatively unknown opera into one with which our opera-going public becomes familiar.

Fidelio confronts its interpreters with a series of questions. Which of the many revisions Beethoven produced is the correct one? By which performances of the past ought one to be influenced? How does one concentrate the spoken dialogues to lend greater impact to the work as a whole? How are certain dramatic moments best emphasized to enhance the scenographic logic, and the psychological portrayal of the characters, without exploding the conventions? Which of the many plausible solutions offered in the past is most in keeping with the 'sense' of the action and with history?

I believe that all serious interpreters have had to ask themselves these questions, and I am sure that they will continue to do so in the future. *Fidelio* is open to all interpretations. And although we bravely but humbly arrived at our own version after much thought and long discussion, we cannot claim to have discovered its crux.

All we can offer are suggestions for a possible *Fidelio*. With little hesitation, we decided to use the 1814 version, which includes the 'Fidelio Overture' but not the 'interpolation' of the third Leonore overture before the last scene—a great loss, musically speaking.

In his 1814 version Beethoven reached unparalleled heights, or so we believe. We chose a logical approach to the dialogues; that is, we wished only to preserve their substance. When cutting, we kept the psychologically significant phrases, and those that throw light on a particular character's overt or covert behaviour. Our aim was thus a sober, terse and sensitive recital, not an eloquent justification of some point or action.

Here we were unmistakably arbitrary. But when all is said and done no other solution would have been possible or just. We are by no means certain that the omission of phrases that interpreters have come to love through long usage, is the best solution. But it is no doubt a possible and consistent one.

In respect of scenic logic, we did not attempt to make every action or movement seem real in terms of neo-realistic psychology; we merely tried to render the stage presentation credible and to transpose every dramatic moment, however incongruous, into mus-

ic. There is a whole literature on the recurring inconsistencies and logical fallacies in *Fidelio,* which purports to justify changes in the development of the plot and even in the characters. Thus we have been shown Rocco as an inflexible jailer, a Nazi officer, a traditional warder with keys and chains, a notorious or even sadistic wretch, or a good-natured old man bowed down by his fears. Rocco is probably the best exemplar of the variety of interpretation to which *Fidelio* lends itself. This is by no means coincidental. In any case, when trying to solve the practical or psychological scenic problems, for instance the duel scene when Leonora, as if by a miracle, suddenly holds a pistol in her hand, we took pains not to exaggerate, and to eschew the rhetoric of the old operatic tradition.

The pursuit of 'revolutionary novelty' is no less dishonest than slavish and uncritical adherence to conventions. We sought to represent psychological reality on two levels, the plausible and the conventional, and to fuse them dynamically in such a way that music, action, word and gesture became an inseparable whole. For the rest, we believed that the only essential truth of this opera is the transformation wrought by music; music has precedence over words and actions, though it must not become isolated in the process.

We did make one transposition in the 1814 version: we advanced Rocco's 'gold aria' ('Love will not suffice for marriage'), which is often omitted because it proves a dramatic embarrassment. This decision was carefully considered. It seemed to us that, as a result, the opera would evolve more evenly from the everyday and familiar world to a level of sensibility on which the rules of melodrama are superseded, where everything finally culminates in non-action so that the opera becomes pure music.

One final remark: we set the action in Spain, as the libretto specifies, but chose, not the eighteenth century, but the period in which the opera was written. It seemed to us that this interpretation would help to clarify Beethoven's human and political attitudes. Perhaps this is the most easily justified of all unjustifiable solutions; it was to us, in any case, the most pleasing, or at least the most fruitful, and not only in regard to the historical perspective.

Translated from: Giorgio Strehler, 1975, pp. 149–54.

1970, VIENNA   STAATSOPER

Producer: Otto Schenk — Stage designer: Günther Schneider-Siemssen — Costumes: Leo Bei — Conductor: Leonard Bernstein

If I agree to take on a work, it is usually one I have loved since my days 'in the gods'—that is, since I was a child—or else one that sparks me off on first acquaintance. If neither is the case I will not entertain the idea of a production—nothing can make up for a lack of direct contact.

In the case of *Fidelio* I have always been enchanted by the tremendous musical power of this glorification of human love set to music,

The courtyard of the state prison. Designs for sets, Günther Schneider-Siemssen.

found attractive enough in this text to conjure up such marvellous music. The vogue nowadays is to scoff at the libretto, to dismiss it as a touching but incredible fable and to forget that Beethoven must have believed in it. Reason enough to look more closely into the matter.

The story is a naive one, with a magnificent human background, involving the barely credible idea that a woman could live among men for months and be taken for a man the whole time. Hence it is essential to create a place and an atmosphere in which this story can be believed. Since experience has shown that the public has an almost boundless will to believe, all that seemed to matter was to tell the story in a consistent way. My intention was to make a very simple beginning and then, quite suddenly, to let humanity burst the bonds to bring us to the very heart of truth. Had I created a 'heroic' opera, I would, in my opinion, have stripped *Fidelio* of all its meaning.

This homely tale begins with the words: 'Come, sweetheart, at last we're alone,' followed by a petty squabble amidst the tangible threat posed by the authority of the State. Many people hold that *Fidelio* is a fractured work, one that starts as a comic opera and ends as an oratorio, but I have never felt that way. To my mind it only achieves its momentous effect because of the playful and idyllic preludes; because a simple, small-time hanger-on happens to be the jailer; because his daughter wants to marry a woman; and because of the 'gold aria', which is occasionally and fatally omitted although it describes precisely what that world is all about. This confrontation between the idyllic and the ominous threat of the State is what fascinated us, and caused us so many scenic problems.

We imagined a courtyard, a place with a touch of Spain, an 'eternal idyll' in front of a prison. The result was *The Beggar Student,* Act I: a merry prison. We realized at once that our 'idyll' would have to be produced differently, more simply. The prison lacked the wonderful simplicity of Beethoven's music.

We used another approach: our prison would have a form befitting the Beethoven stage. We believe that every good production should be a guest performance by a Verdi, Wagner, Mozart or Shakespeare troupe on a workaday stage. We considered what scenery our Fidelio troupe might have brought with them and what simplifications we had to introduce. The idea of a stage with a full system of wings appealed to us; here the ominous prison could loom up from behind a scenic idyll. The result, alas, looked more like a *Singspiel,* or a kind of puppet-show, perhaps befitting *The Magic Flute* or *The Abduction from the Seraglio*—but quite out of keeping with our conception.

We then took a look at the way grim stage prisons used to be built in the past, and came up with the idea of a set constructed of walls. At the same time we relied on hints contained in the work itself. Thus when the prisoners make their entry with: 'Here we are watched and overheard,' we are made to feel that there is a rampart above from which guards look down on an oppressive atmosphere.

The idea of a prison courtyard was conveyed very well through the use of walled passages and flats. A rampart with a grating dominat-

but on the other hand I have never been able to accept the relatively inferior quality of the libretto. I accordingly asked myself what a man like Beethoven—who was nothing if not critical—could have

ed the scene; the entrances were closed in to suggest the idea of towers, those eternal symbols of oppression or force. A simple but utterly depressing area was created. The prison courtyard was hidden behind a wall in Act I, which enabled us to set off the 'idylls' with an ironing-board and a line with some washing. The towers were visible without appearing directly threatening.

For the last scene we searched for a visual symbolization of freedom. We found the answer in Pizarro's order to his officers: 'Six men day and night on the drawbridge.' Shortly before the chorus began, a drawbridge flanked by towers swung into our walled-in courtyard world, and the relatives stormed in from outside to embrace the semi-conscious prisoners who barely grasped what was happening to them: 'Hail happy day, day of rejoicing.' The towers still loomed on either side of the stage, but the scene was now open to light at the rear. A realistic effect, people might say; we do not share that view since we tried only to create theatrical verisimilitude.

We made it a point to be sparing with backcloths and machines, and to solve all scenic problems in the most practical, simple and uncomplicated way possible. The action alone was meant to be complex and ardent—in keeping with Beethoven's music.

Otto Schenk

Producer: Georg Reinhardt — Stage designer: Hermann Soherr — Costumes: Liselotte Erler — Conductor: Günther Wich

I have loved Beethoven's music since my youth, especially this opera which so many producers scorn, believing that little can be done with it.

I take the opposite view: the frame in which Beethoven's declaration must be invested with meaning in our day leaves the interpreter more than enough scope.

The work fascinates me because it demands a humanistic approach to the dramatic events it portrays. Beethoven not only built a lasting monument to marital love, but celebrated the victory of light over darkness in immortal sound. This is something that has to be rendered both visible and tangible in space. I felt I had no need to devise particularly 'modern' drops, suggesting solid prison walls and the like, but looked instead for the simplest, most plausible and human way of symbolizing what the author tried to convey.

I wanted to present this many-layered avowal of faith in such a way that the burning passion and classical greatness of its music would be transformed into dramatic fire and a timeless symbolism. I

Costume design, Liselotte Erler

tried to create a crystal-clear, sharply outlined performance that dispensed with idle theatrical display while avoiding exaggerated sobriety. The contrasts would have to be tied together, though not with abstracting ideological bonds; on the other hand, the opposition of tyranny and the love of freedom would have to be brought out by unconventional means, with careful avoidance of the operatic cliché.

The sombre reality of hopeless imprisonment stamped the entire performance. Only after the 'liberation' did the dark space with heavy black bars make way for the dazzle of bright daylight: the white landscape of freedom.

The awkward style of the spoken dialogues was 'dusted off' as far as possible and shorn of sanctimonious pathos; the play was condensed to its essential elements; positions and movements were stylized into geometric relations; but life, the spiritual confluence of like minds, was never denied. The whole production was aimed at infusing dramatic life with symbolic force; economical use of props and stage aids was intended to achieve expressiveness.

A timeless interpretation of the work—deliberately avoiding allusions to Spain and Seville—seemed to me the only practical and credible way of doing justice to Beethoven's intentions on a modern stage.

Georg Reinhardt

Fidelio holds a special place in opera repertoire; it was the first opera to be written with serious intent. The question of its social meaning becomes superfluous in the mass dungeon; the choice of Spain is explained by political developments at the time it was written, but is unimportant except in respect to the costumes. The marital bonds between Leonora and Florestan and the whole problem of oppression are timeless.

This explains the wish for stylization. After rejecting rock or freestone scenery, however excellent, we decided that the only correct solution was the bare décor of an iron cage around the entire stage, in front of a black backcloth. There would also be a large sliding gridiron on the steeply raked stage, for the entry and exit of the prisoners' chorus. To close off the ominous scene at the top, movable iron galleries of five to seven metres would be mounted by soldiers during all the choruses—visual symbols of inescapable hopelessness.

In Scene I we would use a low, whitewashed partition across the stage; a bench and projected shadows of trees. For Florestan's cell, a full-length, damp, greyish-black vertical pillar, a steep iron staircase leading down from the galleries, and slabs on the floor for the grave.

The finale would take place against an open background, a large white doorway, giving on to a dazzling white backstage.

Hermann Soherr

1974, BREMEN   THEATER AM GOETHEPLATZ

Producer: Nikolaus Lehnhoff — Stage designer: Günther Uecker — Costumes: Günther Uecker — Conductor: Hermann Michael — Spoken text: Hans Magnus Enzensberger — (Title of opera: Leonore)

Beethoven's *Fidelio* was not only the composer's problem child; theatres, producers and the public also have ambivalent feelings towards this opera. The spoken dialogues with their naive turns of phrase are certainly one reason why Beethoven's only opera is not the most popular of his works; much more crucial, however, is its inorganic dramatic form, the wooden juxtaposition of *Singspiel,* musical drama and oratorio.

The *Singspiel* scenes right at the beginning are perhaps the greatest stumbling block of all: they are too long, and never properly integrated into the main plot. The *quid pro quo* of the expositon is interrupted by the entry of Pizarro, and is then forgotten. The spectator loses sight of Marcellina until her re-entry at the end of the opera, when with her astonished cry of 'Oh father, father, what has fate decreed?' the spectator is suddenly reminded of the protracted opening scenes and, not infrequently, reacts with amusement.

For the Bremen version I accordingly decided to omit the introductory scene with Marcellina and Jaquino, and also Rocco's 'gold aria', so that the Marcellina theme became of subsidiary importance. Jaquino, whom Beethoven himself treated in a rather cavalier manner, was thus relegated to an even less important role, with the result that the dramatic presentation gained in tenseness and strength.

After a close scrutiny of their dramatic function I decided to dispense with all spoken dialogues, none of which helps to develop the action. After some hesitation I decided to use a narrator who could repair whatever misunderstandings might arise from the omission of the dialogues. The idea of a compère in the no-man's-land between stage and auditorium actually does not appeal to me and I agree with Brecht that it is almost impossible to introduce a narrator without attaching a didactic significance to him.

For the new textual arrangement I was fortunate in being able to enlist the collaboration of Hans Magnus Enzensberger. We agreed on a presentation in which the narrator would stand in the auditorium to address the house during four sutures in the work: after the Leonore overture; before the entry of Pizarro; before Florestan's aria; and after 'Joy beyond expressing.'

Enzensberger's text bears formal resemblance to a litany, and as such leads well to the oratorical conclusion. In terms of its content, the text exists on two levels: a meta-level of reflections about the 'opera', and a direct or demonstrative level. The two are linked by the central concept of appearance, the opera being conceived as a disguise.

To make the dramatic structure more visually compelling and convincing, Günther Uecker and I decided in favour of a simultaneous setting, on which the nocturnal world of the dungeon is contrasted with a diurnal Utopia. The main action, beginning with Marcellina's aria and ending with the fanfare of Leonora and Florestan's 'Joy beyond expressing,' is played out in the nocturnal world. The finale is treated as a commentary, a reflexion. Before the spectators' eyes the two gigantic stone walls of the black dungeon between which Florestan seems hopelessly hemmed in collapse suddenly, leaving Leonora and Florestan standing in a white space through which people dressed in white approach them. The narrator's white suit was conceived as an anticipation of the finale, during which the gap between stage and auditorium is bridged: the narrator steps on to the stage and becomes part of the 'white collective'. The finale is not the conclusion of a real action, but is enacted on that meta-level which the narrator inhabits from the start.

On the stage, the narrator at first assumes the function of the

Leonora's aria

Leonora's vision of freedom

The reality of imprisonment: the vision of freedom is destroyed

Demonstration of power

minister. We have, instead of the breaking of the chains, an imitation of the initiation ritual of *The Magic Flute*: the symbolic clothing of Leonora and Florestan in white. At that moment all the actors have given up their roles, becoming 'narrators' who carry the white light into the audience, incorporating it into the scene. The final hymn should really be sung by everyone together.

The black world of the prisoners—the world of mankind at large—determines the active part of the opera. During Marcellina's opening aria a timeless pendulum of light and of death moves slowly over a field of corpses, while Leonora steps into this prison world from the depths of the stage as a figure of light. A trajectory of light forces its way through the field of corpses; the light runs ahead of

Leonora, representing the principle of hope. This trajectory will also point the way from the dungeon into the white Utopia, the 'Joy beyond expressing,' before the black world bursts into shreds of canvas, and proves to have been a disguise in Enzensberger's sense of the word.

Naked power is the centre of Pizarro's world. In its black space I posted thirty-two anonymous, invisible, black figures in a choreographic arrangement, each carrying a vertical, silvery lance. In their midst stands Pizarro, the prisoner of his own system.

Leonora tries with all her inner strength to break this system. At the end of her 'aria to hope' during the prisoners' chorus, I had her fall into a dream, glimpsing a vision of a liberated humanity. The vision overpowers her—Leonora 'awakens'. She hears the voices of the prisoners in the depths; she has a presentiment of the coming liberation. Filled with joy by the prisoners' jubilation, she turns around spontaneously, hoping to face liberated men. At this moment I had sixty long wooden stakes descend slowly into the prisoners' choreographic tableau. Leonora's vision of hope is brutally destroyed by the stark reality of the prison. She breaks down in despair, while a prisoner sings the warning, 'Remember there is one forbidden word that never may be heard...'

Nikolaus Lehnhoff

Lehnhoff rings up. Suggests I do the design for *Fidelio*. Grand opera awes me as much as monumental sculpture. I am surprised to find him a young man: imagined a reverential figure from the musty world of opera. Have a very broad discussion of the history and contents of *Fidelio*. Come round to Ernst Bloch's 'Principle of Hope,' which I have just read—Lehnhoff points out that it was suggested to him by *Fidelio*...

First step is to buy some records—I choose Klemperer—read Bloch, read Bouilly's story, listen to Beethoven's music. Find it hard to think of the right approach. I imagine dotards, an apocalypse, corpses dropping into black graves—find I have other things to do...

Haven't really done anything yet, so why an opera? In my student days I went to two or three operas, can hardly remember them, everything is grey. I recall how supercilious I was about opera and go back to the music... Astonishing how contentious it is, how charged with emotion, how cathartic: the individual, the captive community, the prisoners' longing for freedom, corruption and travesty alternating with the hope of universal union in one great human family.

First drafts—a few sketches: a black sea of prisoners sloping up as far as the horizon. Men covered with cloths, with heavy blackness like eternal lemurs, but still remembering movement. Above them a barely perceptible pendulum beats out time like a metronome—the pendulum is a ray of light. The slope is broken by a shaft of light at its centre. Leonora steps through the blackness casting a light shadow that divides the rigid blackness with its motion.

The result pleases me—there is a strip right up front, dividing the stage into two; it provides an interface with the spectator where the real story can be unfolded. The strictly symmetrical area to the rear of the slope becomes the realm of the abstract collectives.

Wouldn't be a bad idea to turn the stage into a mirror image of the auditorium; the spectators in rows and facing them anonymous groups of humans just as regularly disposed. The henchmen carry large black knives, their sharp edges pointing ominously towards the public—the knives are black battens with mirrors glued to them. This is the world of domineering power, of Pizarro; no idea for the prison as yet.

Could a white area serve for the final scene?

Keep thinking of large groups of people, of masses. And now the scenery for the prisoners' chorus: to do justice to the euphoria of the song it ought to be the most beautiful, the freest, and yet the narrowest prison in the world. Deceptive hope. The prisoners in grey; angular spikes, grey stakes drop into their midst.

With Lehnhoff look at the various musical complexes—am astonished by his musical expressiveness and the resulting gain in directness. We agree on a division of the stage into an intermediate area/forestage: representation of the individual conflicts; and a slope: the anonymous collective, followed by officers and henchmen, the group of prisoners as Utopia, the liberated collective. We need a large number of extras and voices—at least 120 for the final apotheosis. Develop the idea that everyone on the stage advances into the auditorium in intense brightness—a choreographic intertwining of all the participants.

We come to the narrator now. Should we seat him in the auditorium? Does the minister become the spokesman of the people? The transvestite transformation of Leonora is the subject of lengthy discussion.

Aren't the representatives of the State double-faced: well-disciplined outside, but corrupt within? I am exhausted. Listen to the music again and again. Have invited a friend to join in the next conversation—he was a prisoner for twelve years. Try to discover from him what it feels like to hope without hope. How can the transformation of Fidelio the man into Leonora the woman be reflected in a change of scenery?...

Have our first meeting with the technical management in Bremen—discover that we still lack the scenery for the prison. I should have liked best to show a man in deepest loneliness, his existence split between two oppressive slabs. The stage as a narrow slit between two massive, dark blocks of stone, and between them Florestan.

Discussions in Bremen. Am impressed by the receptiveness of the technical director. We are very optimistic. Speak to Enzensberger about the 1805 première, about Beethoven's period. Europe changed by the idea of the French Revolution. Napoleon glorified—and reviled—as the great unifier. Beethoven, sympathetic to Napoleon, but disappointed by the restoration of the monarchy and Napoleon's self-styled emperorship. The Thermidor—a highly topical theme. I become increasingly identified with this opera.

Visit Enzensberger... We explain our conceptions and hope to convince him.

Enzensberger is increasingly interested, and we agree to meet in my studio in Düsseldorf for further discussions after the model set has been completed.

Translation of a work report: Günther Uecker, 1974.

1974, MILAN   TEATRO ALLA SCALA

Producer: Günther Rennert — Stage designer: Rudolf Heinrich† — Costumes: Rudolf Heinrich† — Conductor: Karl Böhm

When Rudolf Heinrich and I accepted the offer to present *Fidelio* in Milan we knew that, because of an extremely tight budget, it would be impossible to use the traditional scenic approach. Hence it seemed only natural to develop for a picture-frame stage the *Fidelio* conception we had tried out as early as 1970 in the Salzburg Felsenreitschule: a choreography of light, without scenery.

Existing stage material such as rostra and stairs, together with heavy, modern prison-like walls, helped us to create a stage split into several levels on which our conception—the condensation of the opera into a dramatic event unfolded in a single arena—could only be realized with the help of a carefully devised lighting technique. To produce an austere production in this opulent opera-house was our greatest challenge.

Whereas the 1968 Salzburg production (Grosses Festspielhaus) had emphasized the destiny of a community, of a nation, the central element of our Milan performance was the achievement of an individual—Leonora's fight for her husband—as the great hymn to love.

We tried to avoid all expressions of pathos in gesture or habit. We aimed at simple gesticulation, truthfulness of expression, directness in speech and reply, true dialogue instead of rhetoric, and dramatic conviction. Rather than produce a realistic political record, or an ideological allegory, we reached for a poignant and timeless simile, to which the opera had lent itself even in its own day. The timelessness of this interpretation appeals to us much more today than any time-bound political commitment. [Rennert, 1974, p. 98.]

Compiled by Wolfgang Haefeli after an interview with Günther Rennert.

Fidelio

'The courtyard of the state prison. At the back is the main entrance and a high wall overgrown with trees.'

Milan, 1974   Rennert/Heinrich

Salzburg, 1968   Rennert/Heinrich

Vienna, 1970   Schenk/Schneider-Siemssen

Düsseldorf, 1971 Reinhardt/Soherr

Bremen, 1974 Lehnhoff/Uecker

Florence, 1969 Strehler/Frigerio

Florence, 1969   Strehler/Frigerio

Fidelio

'The courtyard of the state prison.'

Düsseldorf, 1971   Reinhardt/Soherr

Milan, 1974   Rennert/Heinrich

Vienna, 1970   Schenk/Schneider-Siemssen

Salzburg, 1968   Rennert/Heinrich

Fidelio

'Parade-ground outside the castle with statue of the king.'

Milan, 1974   Rennert/Heinrich

Bremen, 1974   Lehnhoff/Uecker

Vienna, 1970   Schenk/Schneider-Siemssen

Düsseldorf, 1971   Reinhardt/Soherr

Florence, 1969   Strehler/Frigerio

Salzburg, 1968   Rennert/Heinrich

Il Barbiere di Siviglia *(The Barber of Seville)*

All glitter and fun, bubbling high spirits and flirtatious glances, with just a touch of a storm, formed of irresistible melodic fancies of the purest clarity, with nothing to spoil one's pleasure—*The Barber of Seville* is unadulterated happiness and joy.

Ever since 1816 Rossini's music has afforded grateful audiences light-hearted release. The plot makes use of time-honoured ingredients. A miserly and eccentric old bachelor is set on marrying Rosina, his wealthy ward, and strives to foil the amorous advances of the dashing Count Almaviva, while Figaro, the wily barber, helps the young lovers to attain their ends by resorting to all kinds of tricks and subterfuge.

The theme may be reminiscent of the *commedia dell'arte*—with such stock characters as Pantalone, the Doctor and Harlequin—but the text leaves no room for improvisation and provides a polished comedy crowned by Rossini's masterly score.

The celebrated composer was commissioned to write an opera for the 1816 Carnival, based on Cesare Sterbini's libretto of *Il Barbiere di Siviglia,* a comedy by Beaumarchais. The *Barber* was part of Beaumarchais's Figaro trilogy, the centrepiece of which, *Le Mariage de Figaro,* subtitled 'La Folle Journée', Mozart had set to music and presented in Vienna in 1786, relying on a new version by Lorenzo da Ponte. Long before Rossini, Giovanni Paisiello, too, had used the *Barber* theme, achieving such lasting renown with his own opera that Rossini's later version was greeted with catcalls at its first performance. Soon afterwards, however, Rossini's lovable and cheerful work experienced a meteoric rise, and continues to shine as a favourite star in the operatic sky to this day.

What, if any, are the problems this straightforward comedy poses to the producer and stage designer? One is tempted to say just one: to ensure that the enchantment and virtuosity of the work are fully reflected on the stage. This is not an easy task and offers them untold opportunities for the demonstration of wit and humour.

Doctor Bartolo, physician and apothecary, is a crotchety character who lives in a quiet backwater in Seville—a figure drawn from life and one who, like his Spanish model, might be found to this day in many a small Tuscan town. He is mean and avaricious, but not a really wicked capitalist. Nor is Figaro, his antagonist, a dispossessed revolutionary; on the contrary, as he himself freely declares, he is a prosperous shopkeeper. And the feelings of the loving pair, Rosina and Count Almaviva, are so self-evident that not even the most naïve opera-goer needs to have this point driven home with a sledgehammer.

A culinary delight, then? And why not? The stage offers so many depressing and shocking spectacles that the wary theatre-lover seeks out the *Barber* precisely because it promises him relaxation and amusement. He is resentful when he is told, again and again, that instead of diverting himself, he ought to look to the stage for self-improvement and edification.

Well, this is what the producer, too, might feel, but one would like to beg him sincerely not to rob this gorgeous butterfly of its colours and so change it into a drab and ugly moth. For when all is said and done, the *Barber* is not a ponderous problem play. Its vital elements are spirit and grace, both precious and rare in our time.

Incidentally, Rossini stopped writing music at the age of forty. Having almost as many operas as years to his credit, he felt entitled to devote the more than thirty years remaining to him to the pursuit of culinary pleasures.

Rudolf Hartmann

Scenes

1.1   A street in Seville. At the left is the house of Doctor Bartolo, with a balcony. All the windows are barred.

1.6   A room in Bartolo's house.

1968, SALZBURG FESTIVAL   KLEINES FESTSPIELHAUS

Producer: Jean-Pierre Ponnelle — Stage designer: Jean-Pierre Ponnelle — Costumes: Jean-Pierre Ponnelle — Conductor: Claudio Abbado

For months while working on this opera I was faced with a serious problem—I was uncertain whether one ought to emphasize the artificial element of this type of *opéra comique,* or whether one should use a realistic approach.

Ultimately I decided in favour of the second alternative and tried to give the work the most concrete, credible and realistic background possible. As a result, I was able to bring out its artificial musical structure—or rather, Rossini's special brand of music.

In addition it was important to get away from the operetta style, from a world in which all's well, in which the people are ever so amusing, and in which real problems are glossed over. Instead, I tried to present this opera as a human and realistic comedy in the tradition of Molière or Beaumarchais.

I realized that I could best do justice to this comic opera on a turntable stage, not only because my approach called for very quick changes of scenery, but also because I wanted for musical reasons to fit the movements of the revolve into the appropriate dramatic situations, as in the finale of Act I.

The scenographic conception was dominated by the idea that Bartolo's house must not be shown in complete isolation from its surroundings, but must seem part of a definite landscape: of Seville, with a suggestion of its climate, its social conditions and also, of course, its strict Catholic mores, which explain why Rosina cannot leave her guardian's house.

It was on this basis that I constructed an entire town in perspective round the three main arenas: the square, the barber's shop and Doctor Bartolo's house. The set no doubt reflected my 'romantic touch' and my concern with detail.

It is my considered opinion that the set does not play a decisive role in the staging of the Barber. This explains the fairly monochrome execution of my visual conception.

Jean-Pierre Ponnelle

1970, BERLIN   DEUTSCHE OPER

Producer: Winfried Bauernfeind — Stage designer: Luciano Damiani — Costumes: Luciano Damiani — Conductor: Moshe Atzmon

I decided to produce the *Barber* after lengthy discussions with my then chief, Gustav Rudolf Sellner. I had been conducting a series of experimental productions in various Berlin theatres, and I felt that the opera would provide a splendid counterpoint to these. The stage designer Luciano Damiani had been approached long before, but he had raised objections to all the producers whose names were put to him. Now I was sent to Milan to present myself to the master. Damiani demonstrated what he had in mind with the aid of a finished model: a perfect *opera buffa,* in the spirit of the *commedia dell'arte.* My own ideas were by no means as concrete as his, and I was worried by two purely external factors: the vast stage of the Deutsche Oper is much too large for Rossini; the German language is quite unsuited to the swift *parlando.*

We wanted to attract a broad spectrum of the public and to run this *Barber* for a number of years. The external factors prevented an intimate chamber performance and also led us to forego the *brio* of the Italian original. I discovered the key to the solution in another

of Beaumarchais's works: *The Marriage of Figaro.* In that sequel to the *Barber,* the *buffa* characters have grown into human beings, with Mozart standing godfather to their development.

Damiani and I discovered that we took much the same view of the basic psychological situations, which are so true to life and so appealing in their sensuality, intelligence and amiability. It was a difficult project, but the way in which Damiani outlined what was to him a finished concept, convinced me of his unerring theatrical instinct.

On a functional set of PVC laid on bare boards he proposed to construct two rows of bright façades on a motorized revolve. The front of the façade could be made to open, allowing Figaro to be 'shot' in from the very back of the stage for his *cavatina;* if it was rotated 180 degrees the result was an enclosed room whose high walls emphasized Rosina's isolation and her need to escape from Bartolo's exacting 'prison'. Little Rosina seemed to be growing up; touches of the *Figaro* duchess were beginning to show in her manner. And Figaro, like a mouse in a cheese, kept finding holes in the fortress where she was imprisoned, somehow defying locks and keys, and apparently capable of passing through walls. For his *cavatina* I eschewed all the old *Barber* 'tricks'. Instead he sang it like a *bravura* to an audience of amazed street urchins busily spying on the morning serenade and on Almaviva's unsuccessful cat-burglar's acts. I was able thereby to pour ridicule on the count—a man who could only attain his ends by resorting to bribery.

Bartolo and Basilio, freed from all the chains of the 'tradizione', were presented as serious characters, albeit with human foibles. Precise observation of various types of human beings had produced so many comic stimuli that I could easily dispense with the customary gags. And what touching reactions were introduced by such marginal figures as the amorous old Marcellina!

In the short time left for rehearsals before the première it proved impossible to perfect this comedy of characters. Since then, however, in rehearsals for revivals, I have been able to achieve something approaching the effect I desired.

Winfried Bauernfeind

1973, BASLE   STADTTHEATER

Producer: Martin Markun — Stage designer: Jörg Zimmermann — Costumes: Jörg Zimmermann — Conductor: David Kram

The *Barber,* that Broadway musical of an opera, is also one of the best-constructed pieces of theatre I know, a comic opera *par excellence.* The work has a Mediterranean flavour and, as theatre, it is unbelievably sensual, sparkling and effective. Its music and content make it a spectacular—I use the term without any negative connotations. Rossini's score is naturally light and carefree, with a touch of the indulgently extemporized. This was the overall impression we wanted to convey to the audience.

Starting from the idea of improvisation, we originally intended to stage the opera in a realistic, Italian small-town setting without any special décor. A strolling group of players would arrive, and pitch a tent in the main square. The inhabitants would flock to it, and an improvised play would gradually develop. The juxtapositon of 'real' incidents among the 'spectators', and the incidents portrayed by the actors, would undoubtedly have set up sufficient dramatic tension to generate a tremendous sense of fun. However we realized from the start that this effect could only be achieved on a film set at great expense. In fact, the project foundered because of the enormous technical demands, and the lack of time and finance.

All that remained was the key word 'improvisation'. We decided to make the *commedia dell'arte* our new starting-point; to create a light, playful and obviously 'theatrical' Rossini on a rough-and-ready stage evoking the street theatre.

An essential feature of our project was the deployment of all stage equipment in full view of the public. All the curtains were transparent, forming an integral part of the performance; even the 'famous' change of scenery was fitted into the dramatic development.

In other words, we showed both the way to a situation and the situation itself. For the same reasons, the actors changed and made up on stage.

All the improvisation, however, did not provide the basic elements of the plot.

The play began with bare scaffolding vaguely reminiscent of a circus tent. Before the appearance of the first characters, the spectator would have no idea how a *Barber* could finally emerge from it all. Then the first actors made their entrances. They pulled on various ropes to bring down painted curtains, and a street scene was created. Each singer thus produced his own set out of thin air with just a few gestures.

We consider this scenographic approach of primary importance, believing that a highly realistic or polished *Barber* set tends to turn the spectator into something of an opera tourist. Our approach, by

contrast, invited his direct participation since, by this improvised version, he has to contribute a great deal of fantasy of his own.

He must be able to imagine that four curtains make a street, that a hole in a piece of fabric is a window, and that a 'cloud' of material pulled on by strings is a thunderstorm. In short, the spectator has to co-operate.

All scene-shifts appeared highly disorganized, to stress that the audience was watching a play, and not a true portrayal of real life. This approach helped us meet all the technical demands in the easiest and simplest way, and to add pieces of scenery as we went along.

The continual creation of something half-finished out of nothing was the real fascination of this presentation, particularly since it proved so fitting a complement to a score which, for all its perfection, seems quite casually composed.

Martin Markun
Jörg Zimmermann

1974, SYDNEY   SYDNEY OPERA HOUSE

Producer: John Cox — Stage designer: Roger Butlin — Costumes: Roger Butlin — Conductor: Myer Fredman

The Barber of Seville is an exceptionally elegant work, full of accurate human observation and warmth of sentiment—more, perhaps, in the spirit of Jane Austen and Thomas Love Peacock than Beaumarchais.

My presentation was intended to counter the mistaken view that the opera is merely a farce. In my version it became the elegantly constructed comedy intended by its authors. I chose a stage designer who shared this view, and felt capable of translating it into visual reality.

I proposed to him to set the production in Rossini's own lifetime. I was especially stimulated to do so by the fact that Rossini had often performed for the Prince Regent's court at the Royal Pavilion in Brighton which is, like the opera itself, a brilliantly original product of the early nineteenth-century spirit. Its extravagant yet disciplined fantasy of design provides an accurate parallel to Rossini's musical style, and has the additional advantage, in its imitation of the Moorish style, of conveying a Spanish atmosphere.

The stage of the new Sydney Opera House was renowned for its problems, so we designed a set that was functionally independent of the stage machinery.

When defining the character of the roles and the crucial events in this opera, I eschewed the traditional farcical approach and all exaggerated comic effects.

John Cox

Until quite recently I had only a casual acquaintance with Rossini's *Barber of Seville*. I have seen it, I suppose, about four or five times. Each performance seemed to confirm the impression that it was a rather vulgar and witless pantomime, that it was coarse-grained, self-indulgent and nudging.

Perhaps I was unlucky in what I *saw* but I do know that, when I first *listened* to a performance on records at home, without the distracting vulgarities of the stage, I was astonished at the brilliance, wit, sparkle and great stylishness of the score. Certainly no vulgarity. I seemed to be floating off the ground, smiling at nearly every bar. It bore no resemblance to my experience in the theatre.

Faced with the problem of designing it myself, I wondered how one could externalize Rossini's stylishness visually to provide an ambience for the more than two-dimensional characters he had created. I felt that the scenery should *look* like the music, or the music *sound* like the scenery!

While still researching, I read that Rossini had played for the Prince Regent at the Brighton Pavilion in England. Although this was a comparatively unimportant event in Rossini's life, it set a train of thought going in my mind. I knew the Brighton Pavilion well; it is an extraordinary building—a Moorish chinoiserie extravaganza, an example of architecture *in extremis*—and a very close visual equivalent to Rossini's music. It has wit, elegance and style, and it conveys a Rossini world of its own.

The Brighton Pavilion was a place where people lived—yet so exquisite in its decoration that it takes one's breath away. Exactly like Rossini. I decided therefore on a beautifully built structure—rather like a Victorian mechanical toy—which could provide the right location and geography for the singers *and* place them firmly in a Rossini world. I do not wish to imply that our *Barber* was

set in Toytown but rather that the set must possess the skilled craftsmanship and ingenious engineering common in that era. Updating the period to the date when the piece was written has certain distinct advantages. The costumes of the early nineteenth century, with their elegant line and beautiful detail, have great strength and charm—adjectives one might well use to describe the music.

The attempt was made to create not only a marriage of visual and aural elements, but to create credible music theatre, perhaps approaching the style of an Oscar Wilde comedy of manners.

The set consisted of a white reflective floor and a rear wall of simulated white paving. In the middle were two pavilions on pancake turntables which moved independently or together (see diagram). In front of this a ribbon curtain was suspended which we used as a 'front cloth'. On this were projected the effects for the thunderstorm and, in the same scale as the set, a large blown-up photograph of the Brighton Pavilion.

With these ingredients it was possible to present the whole opera with only one interval, and without any delays for scene changes. The abduction scene was played continuously: the audience saw Figaro and Almaviva climbing up the ladder outside Bartolo's house while the set was revolving to show the interior and their arrival. In the first act it was possible to go from outside Bartolo's house into the interior of Figaro's shop without delay.

This scheme provided a solution to the opera, and it solved some technical problems associated with the Sydney Opera House. The Opera House stage has good depth but little wing space, and a turntable which we were not able to use. The Australian Opera Company tours extensively throughout their country to other theatres which have rather more wing space, but rather less depth. With this in mind, we constructed the set with a built-in mechanism that could operate in any theatre. It would have been good to have explored the dynamics of one particular theatre, but this was not possible in the brief time available.

It was important that the set should look more like a plaster cast of the Brighton Pavilion than like a piece of decorative scenery. Great care was taken with the architectural detail and construction of the set to make it look solid and convincing. We sprayed it with an industrial paint to match the plastic laminate of the floor.

The costumes and the use of colour were, like Rossini's characters, a distilled rather than naturalistic reality. It may sound as if all these ideas were the designer's, but on the contrary they arose, in fact, out of many talks with the director, a lot of listening to Rossini, reading about Rossini and constant reference to contemporary paintings, engravings and architecture of the period in which the *Barber* was written.

Roger Butlin

Salzburg, 1968 Ponnelle/Ponnelle

Basle, 1973 Markun/ Zimmermann

The Barber of Seville

'*A street in Seville. At the left is the house of Doctor Bartolo, with a balcony. All the windows are barred.*'

Sydney, 1974   Cox/Butlin

Basle, 1973   Markun/Zimmermann

Sydney, 1974   Cox/Butlin

The Barber of Seville

'A Room in Bartolo's house.'

Salzburg, 1968   Ponnelle/Ponnelle

Don Pasquale

Gaetano Donizetti wrote almost seventy works for the stage, many in the style of tragic grand opera—among them *Anna Bolena, Lucrezia Borgia* and *Lucia di Lammermoor*—but comic opera seemed much more suited to the lightness of his touch, and earned him his greatest successes with *The Elixir of Love, The Daughter of the Regiment* and *Don Pasquale,* first performed in Paris in 1843.

This amiable work, a late offshoot of Rossini's *Barber,* is something one would like to acknowledge with a gallant obeisance at every encounter, if only to enter into its spirit. In perfect cadences, a pellucid score provides the four main protagonists with a wealth of melodic inspiration, and in its arias and duets not only allows them to display their virtuosity but, more so even than in the *Barber,* to express a wealth of happy sentiment. For all that, the action is based on a tried *buffo* plot, reminiscent of the puppet theatre: the amorous old bachelor, the young lovers, the wily schemer. But here it is lent wings by the grace of the music; quite unexpectedly, the protagonists appear to be genuinely human and familiar. Don Pasquale is not unlike the crotchety Doctor Bartolo, but lacks his wickedness; he is made a dupe like Sir Morosus, but does not become a tragic figure—his fate evokes amused and good-natured smiles that only grow into roars of laughter when the servants mock at the happenings in their charming chorus.

It is said that Donizetti wrote his operas with an uncommon facility and in record time. In the case of *Don Pasquale* producer and stage designer would do well to bear this fact in mind. There are many ways of achieving the right effects, but the *buffo* origins should not be allowed to predominate. The inspired development of a simple theme into one of heart-warming geniality is ably prefigured by the sparkle of the music. There are no coarse jokes; instead we have a plethora of enchanting scenes and finally a gallant obeisance by the delighted audience before the feminine graces of the charming Norina.

Rudolf Hartmann

Scenes

1.1 Don Pasquale's room. Main entrance at the back, two other doors lead to rooms on either side.
1.5 Norina's room.
2.1 Don Pasquale's room.
3.8 Garden of Don Pasquale's house.

1971, SALZBURG   KLEINES FESTSPIELHAUS

Producer: Ladislav Štros — Stage designer: Ladislav Štros — Costumes: Marcel Pokorný — Conductor: Riccardo Muti

Don Pasquale fascinates me because it is so like the typical Italian *buffa,* and yet has all the hallmarks of the *commedia dell'arte.*

The musical invention, no less than the structure, of this Donizetti opera holds out the promise of a most rewarding production based on theatrical effects.

I took the view that the opera had to look improvised, the result of a series of sudden inspirations. The actors were enjoined to be at their most sparkling and light-hearted. To encourage this trend, I deliberately refrained from burdening them with psychological demands; I asked only that they share in the delight of the spectacle.

The highly controversial servants' chorus was made to represent a group of dolls since, in my view, it was intended merely as a prop for the 'ladies and gentlemen' who play the main roles.

My set was steeply raked, and provided with backcloths representing a highly stylized street, a house and garden, and so on. All the symbols of Don Pasquale's house—four-poster bed, dresser, wig-block, grandfather clock, water jug—were represented by photomontage on plain flats. Wires suspended freely across the stage carried simple curtains symbolizing windows, doors or chests of drawers as further indications of a given room or area. These curtains were in five distinct colours used throughout the set and also in all the costumes.

Ladislav Štros

136

2 NORINA

1972, STUTTGART   WÜRTTEMBERGISCHE STAATSTHEATER,
GROSSES HAUS

*Producer: Günther Fleckenstein — Stage designer: Leni Bauer-Ecsy —
Costumes: Leni Bauer-Ecsy — Conductor: Josef Dünnwald*

Opera buffa has been a particular interest of mine for a long time; more than any other form, it grants the producer considerable leeway to develop a specific role.

In Stuttgart I tried to keep to the work rather than the word, on Hans Schweikart's principle that the producer 'may do what he likes if he likes what he should'.

The crucial element of *Don Pasquale* is clearly the traditional form of the Italian *commedia dell'arte,* with its well-known characters. In my conception, Don Pasquale corresponds to Pantalone, Doctor Malatesta to the Dottore, and the notary to Arlecchino: a mixture of ignorance, ingenuity, spirit and grace; a man who is everything except pious.

During the overture a story about the actors is told in pantomime form. The actors make up, put on their costumes and try out their masks. Pasquale is the leader of the troupe. There are private tensions, caused by Norina, the director's daughter, and the rivalry of the actors playing Malatesta and Ernesto, which builds up to a fight that is barely averted at the last moment.

The chorus represents various *commedia* characters, who act in consort, as fellow conspirators of Doctor Malatesta, for example.

Every type was cast precisely in the image of his prototype, so that there were two simultaneous actions or reactions, differing according to character and situation. This was achieved in the closest collaboration with David Sutherland, the chief assistant to John Cranko, director of the Stuttgart Ballet.

Our aim was to present a consistently traditional *commedia dell'arte,* and yet to convey a credible idea of the basic features of *opera buffa* to the modern spectator without making character comedy totally lacking in credibility.

My conception received its visual complement in the sets of Leni Bauer-Ecsy. We started with the kind of *commedia dell'arte* platform that was erected in public squares in the sixteenth to eighteenth centuries, as depicted on a host of contemporary etchings and paintings of harlequinades.

Our platform had two rostra that could be played on simultaneously; it could also be reached from the back so that various heights and depths were available for different choreographic arrangements.

The surrounding area was also included in the action. It was filled with fragments of Roman columns, statues, arches and pine-trees, all reflecting the Mediterranean atmosphere of the opera. Interiors were indicated by appropriately painted curtains that could be raised or pulled sideways before and after use, and by other props and furniture.
Günther Fleckenstein

1973, BRATISLAVA   SLOVENSKÉ NÁRODNÉ DIVADLO

Producer: Július Gyermek — Stage designer: Vladimír Suchánek — Costumes: Ludmila Purkyňová — Conductor: Gerhard Auer

Certain composers attract me while others leave me completely cold: my temperament inclines me more towards *opera seria. Don Pasquale,* a bright, humorous story whose characters are lively, truthful and realistic in their relationships is an exception. This opera lends itself to a production combining entertainment with expressivity. In my production I did not treat the title role with sarcasm or spiteful glee, but tried to combine humour and poetry to present him with a sympathetic smile.

A crucial problem was the adaptation of this opera, which is steeped in nineteenth-century fashions, feelings and conventions, for presentation to a twentieth-century audience by a twentieth-century producer.

Again and again I have had the sad experience that classical operas are either impossible or extremely difficult to adapt to con-

temporary conditions. *Don Pasquale* allows this transposition more readily than most because it contains the basic dramatic element of a modern opera—a dynamic development on several levels. It need not even bore the modern spectator 'spoiled' by television.

I deliberately used an ensemble of outstanding singers with exceptional dramatic skills to produce *Don Pasquale* for an average audience.
Július Gyermek

The production of an opera is always a special event to me, since my work is chiefly in the theatre. My approach is strongly influenced by theatrical considerations, so the result is bound to be a mixture of opera and theatre. In the case of *Don Pasquale,* the combination of these two elements was particularly beneficial in that this opera tells a simple, light-hearted story, making very high musical and mimic demands on the actors.

Because our stage was too large for this kind of intimate opera, I decided to reduce the playing area and to condense the special atmosphere of this story even further, and thereby render it more tangible.

The producer asked for a variable set and unified technical system that would ensure a smooth development.

I designed a classical set on which the required shifts of scenery could be effected with the least possible effort. I tried to emulate the principle of the film cut as closely as possible, and there was a minimal loss of time during the shifts and a minimal dislocation of the dynamic flow.

I endeavoured to create a microcosm of the small man; Don Pasquale was not meant to be an object of derision but rather someone who made the audience smile.
Vladimír Suchánek

1974, BERLIN (DDR)   DEUTSCHE STAATSOPER

Producer: Horst Bonnet — Stage designer: Werner Schulz — Costumes: Werner Schulz — Conductor: Heinz Fricke

We were anxious to present this inherently naive work in a totally fresh way, with amused detachment. We intended to combine *commedia dell'arte* figures with certain elements of the modern musical, which meant giving free rein to comic invention while adding a great deal of polish.

The five young singers were enjoined to keep a light touch, thus demonstrating to the public that the cast was enjoying this chance of presenting a fable to best advantage. Artistry could not, however, become an end in itself—the fable had to stand on its own. The actors' movements had been mapped out most carefully. The singers were allowed to flirt with the audience, the conductor and the prompter. We called it 'keeping your bottom in the action and

"Don Pasquale" Norina und Pasquale

Above: Costumes for *Don Pasquale,* Ladislav Štros, Salzburg, 1971   Below: Costume designs for *Don Pasquale,* Werner Schulz, Berlin, 1974

poking out your head at the audience'. We rehearsed about seven hours a day for ten weeks. Ease with this manner of presentation comes only when the technique can be taken for granted.

The scenery and properties were light in weight, easily moved about by the players themselves. The costumes were reminiscent of the *commedia dell'arte,* though more modern in cut and in a number of details. A small drop-curtain showed a gilded State Opera. Between scenes a 'number girl' carried maxims on cards across the stage, providing headings for the various scenes. At the beginning, during the last bars of the overture, all the participants posed for a group photograph, and the opera closed with a 'happy-ending' snapshot. Beginning and end formed a single tableau.

Werner Schulz, the stage designer, pledged his support at our first discussion. We tested various approaches with the help of sketches or small models. Every solution was the result of joint endeavour. Schulz watched the rehearsals and I was present at fittings. During and after rehearsals we discussed our progress at length with everyone concerned. Our team-work was considered a model of co-operation in professional circles. We all had a great deal of fun.

Horst Bonnet

The plot of Donizetti's *Don Pasquale,* the story of a man who falls into his own trap, has been used in numerous works for both theatre and opera-house, all of them heaping scorn on man and his foibles.

The *commedia dell'arte* has, in a highly artistic way, developed special figures of fun to satisfy this need to ridicule. We decided for this reason to emphasize the links between *Don Pasquale* and the *commedia dell'arte,* and to make use of our experiences of the modern musical.

It goes without saying that producer and stage designer collabo-rated as equal partners, complementing each other and striving to achieve a result that satisfied both. This approach was a hallmark of our long-standing collaboration, during which we have studiously avoided any kind of departmentalism.

By typifying the individual roles, by stressing the playful element, and by coupling humour and irony to achieve a critical aloofness from the story (dusty and dramatically equivocal as it was), we endeavoured to present this work as a theatrical diversion that would meet the demands of a modern opera-goer and maintain his interest.

We were fortunate in having a young ensemble that was ideally suited to our production, perfectly graceful and artistic. It would be one in which the theatrical spirit would enjoy free rein, which would achieve its charming end result through the use of a high degree of deliberate artificiality throughout. Thus when Don Pasquale 'played' the role of the dotard with a stick and a large paunch, his belly was quite obviously made of padding and looked like a theatrical aid. All movements were planned in minute detail. The singers were allowed to flirt with the spectators, the conductor and the prompter, as was noted above.

To emphasize the artificial and playful character even further, we chose a style of costume that reflected the typification we aimed at, while emphasizing our detached, 'theatrical' approach: a methodical recourse to the *commedia dell'arte* but expressed in modern idiom, with modern aloofness, modern techniques.

We adopted white as the basis of all the costumes and set off individuals with the help of only the barest accessories, in various colours, borrowed from the inventory of the *commedia.*

The servants' chorus, for whose appearance in Don Pasquale's house there is little justification in the rest of the work, acted as stage hands, thus helping to focus the play on the avaricious old dotard.

The chorus was dressed alike, the men in black and white, wearing tight breeches with pom-poms down the side, and short, striped waistcoats. The Chaplinesque, black-rimmed eyes in their chalk-white faces were capped by shiny black cloche hats. The women wore crinolines in a black-and-white diamond design, with pom-poms down the seams, and aprons of a gauzy, almost transparent material. They were made up like dolls, with white faces, very long 'fluttering' eyelashes, and small tricorns set on top of short, curly, bobbing white wigs.

In other words, they were not dressed like real servants but in obviously theatrical costumes, made in unmistakable *commedia dell'arte* style.

We used the same principle to dress the soloists. They wore the same costume throughout the opera, except for Norina—she appeared not only in her normal dress but also disguised as a well brought-up convent girl and as a woman of the world.

The set was in keeping with our overall conception. The proscenium arch was framed with painted red drapes, simulating a rung-up curtain, behind which the action took place. A set of steps on either side of the forestage led up to a raked rostrum, rounded in front to resemble a tray on which the opera was 'served up'.

The prompter's box was included in the action, disguised as a golden shell, allowing the prompter to console the sad Don Pasquale, and so on.

At the beginning of the performance the audience saw nothing other than a rostrum on a bare stage, enclosed on three sides by a neutral grey screen. Only after the 'group photograph' for which all the soloists adopt a formal, old-fashioned photographic pose do members of the servants' chorus help to assemble the set for Scene I on the stage.

Small painted walls on rollers served as flats that could be moved very quickly and easily by the singers themselves, who thus created their own scenery. The walls were moved along wires running across the stage and parallel to the footlights at a height of some three and a half metres.

These small blue walls painted in a blue perspective afforded glimpses of a southern sky dotted with clouds. Added, as in a collage, were representations of nineteenth-century objects. By altering the position and combination of the individual tableaux, it was possible to produce all the scenes, each tableau being symmetrical. There were no fixed walls; the same furniture—a few elaborate chairs, a table, a bench, two holly trees on tall pedestals—was used throughout the opera.

In the fourth tableau Norina parades the dresses, hats, fans and jewels she had bought at Don Pasquale's expense. For this scene we placed a number of tailor's dummies with Norina's newly acquired dresses, which bore their price tags, into Don Pasquale's room. He moves dumfounded, like a living tailor's dummy, between these silent witnesses of his wife's extravagance. Norina appears in their midst, dressed in a voluminous black and white striped gown, with her parasol, scarf and gloves all in shocking pink, exulting at the discomfiture of the horrified old man.

The fifth tableau, with its romantic mood and the subsequent *dénouement,* also takes place within movable walls, shaped this time like a terrace, with park railings and statues.

From the gridiron the vague outline of a pavilion is flown in, before which the two lovers sing their nocturne. When the scene threatens to become too lyrical and romantic, the conductor dons a small crown of flowers.

All the singers are masked; the chorus lights up the nocturnal scene with lanterns.

The subsequent dimming is abrupt: the bright lights are ostentatiously turned off, starting with the four large 'gas lanterns' suspended above the stage throughout the opera. A small curtain bearing a gold representation of the State Opera partially blocks the view of individual scene-shifts behind. Some numbers, like the servants' chorus or Ernesto's aria, are played in front of this curtain, outside the actual stage as it were, and hence on neutral territory. Here, the famous servants' chorus can be treated almost as a pantomime in song, and when the curtain rises again, 'the play can go on.'

Our production has been running for three seasons. At fixed intervals we take a critical look at it and experiment with alterations to keep the presentation as fresh as possible.

Werner Schulz

Berlin, 1974   Bonnet/Schulz
Stuttgart, 1972   Fleckenstein/Bauer-Ecsy

Bratislava, 1973
Gyermek/Suchánek

Salzburg, 1971
Štros/Štros

Don Pasquale

'Norina's room.'

◁

Berlin, 1974
Bonnet/Schulz

Stuttgart, 1972
Fleckenstein/Bauer-Ecsy

2 NORINA

Stuttgart, 1972
Fleckenstein/Bauer-Ecsy

Costume, Ladislav Štros, Salzburg 1971

Berlin, 1974   Bonnet/Schulz

Don Pasquale

'Garden of Don Pasquale's house.'

Salzburg, 1971 Štros/Štros
Bratislava, 1973 Gyermek/Suchánek

Don Carlos

Verdi's middle period includes, along with such great successes as *Rigoletto, Il Trovatore* (The Troubadour) and *Un Ballo in Maschera,* (Masked Ball) a work based on a verse drama by the great German poet Friedrich Schiller. That work is *Don Carlos.* When he began composing, Verdi was strongly attracted to Schiller's writings. Among his early operas we find *Giovanna d'Arco* (Joan of Arc), (1845, La Scala, Milan) after Schiller's *Die Jungfrau von Orléans; I Masnadieri* (The Brigands), (1847, London) after Schiller's *Die Räuber;* and *Luisa Miller,* (1849, Naples) after Schiller's *Kabale und Liebe.*

Like *Simone Boccanegra* and *I Vespri Siciliani* (Sicilian Vespers), *Don Carlos* was revised both musically and textually following a lukewarm reception. Seventeen years after the Paris première of 1867 Verdi presented a new score for La Scala, with a revised libretto by Antonio Ghislanzoni, who had proved his worth with *Aida.* The importance of *Don Carlos* was not appreciated until later, and it was only fairly recently that it received due tribute.

The magnificent structure of Schiller's poems, their noble spirit and pathos, their exaltation of individual and political freedom, inspired Verdi to write some of his most glorious arias, duets and ensembles. The musical perfection of all these operas rebuts all those indignant literati who allege that Schiller's poems cannot be 'decomposed', least of all in the Italian manner.

The three early 'Schiller operas' do have an Italian feel, but they also have a strong individual stamp. *Don Carlos,* Verdi's last Schiller opera, is of much greater importance than the others. Here Verdi, forever in search of new ideas, tentatively abandoned the safe scheme of Italian opera for the first time. To the customary arias, duets and choruses he now added scenes of unprecedented dramatic force and urgency—the first intimations of the brilliant style of the master's last period.

King Philip's monologue; his exchange with the Marquis of Posa; the entrance of the blind Grand Inquisitor—these dramatic events are expressed in a new musical language, one that soars above merely euphonious melody. By comparison, the more conventional finale is a considerable disappointment. The unprecedented dramatic structure of the earlier scenes is seen again in *Otello,* and carried to a triumphant climax in *Falstaff.* In the interval came the commissioned opera *Aida,* which may be considered the crowning glory of the great Italian tradition.

The producer encounters *Don Carlos* as a heterogeneous work. He is expected to fuse the exaggerated Italianisms of the first part—including the brilliant *auto-da-fé* finale—with the increasingly tense scenes of the middle section. He must balance the conclusion, which relapses into the voluptuous melodic intoxication of the earlier operas, with the dramatic impact of Philip's meeting with the Inquisitor. This climax should set the tone of the production as a whole, and the choice of style in particular.

The stage designer has an easier task: *Don Carlos* is set in a given time and place. He does face the problem of fusing pure opera with music drama. What little architecture he includes should not stifle the singers—at most it should have an eerie, gloomy effect. The clash between Church and State, the interplay of dominance and submission with its injurious effect on individual destinies, must all help to mould the scenographer's conception.

Rudolf Hartmann

Scenes

Prelude Forest near Fontainebleau. In the far distance below, the castle.

1.1 The cloister of the monastery of San Yuste. Arcades around the quadrangle. The covered way at the back leads from the chapel to the monastery. It is joined by a passage to the arcade in the front in which the tomb of the Emperor Charles V is clearly visible.

1.4 A pleasant landscape outside the monastery. On the horizon the blue mountains of Estremadura. In the background steps leading up to the monastery gate.

2.1 Garden of the palace in Madrid. The garden is terraced; the lowest terrace has an ornamental shrubbery with a marble bench and a statue. A spring rises among the shrubs.

2.7 A large square outside the Church of Our Lady of Atocha. To the right, the church, with a broad flight of steps; to the left, a palace. In the foreground, another flight of steps leading to a second square from the middle of which the tip of a stake can be seen to protrude. Large houses and distant hills enclose the scene at the back.

3.1 The King's study in Madrid.

3.7 A prison. A dark, half-subterranean vault. In the background iron bars through which one can see guards pacing up and down.

4.1 The monastery of San Yuste. Night.

1968, MILAN   TEATRO ALLA SCALA

Producer: Jean-Pierre Ponnelle — Stage designer: Jean-Pierre Ponnelle — Costumes: Jeanne Renucci and Georges Wakhevitch — Conductor: Claudio Abbado

In agreement with the conductor Claudio Abbado, Jean-Pierre

Ponnelle chose the four-act version of *Don Carlos*. Verdi composed this version for the Milan première, omitting the first act of the original version. The highly realistic, 'perspectivist' sets were executed in various shades of black and grey, reminiscent of the darkness in El Greco's paintings.

In this framework of neutral colours, Jean-Pierre Ponnelle produced a most realistic tragedy of fate round the figures of Don Carlos, Elizabeth and Philip. He was extremely careful in the delineation of the individual characters, deliberately aiming at a spiritual vision of this drama.

Today Ponnelle believes that, while this solution was fully justified at the time, any new production must have a 'completely new face'.

Report by Wolfgang Haefeli after
an interview with Jean-Pierre Ponnelle.

1970, VIENNA   STAATSOPER

Producer: Otto Schenk — Stage designer: Jürgen Rose — Costumes: Jürgen Rose — Conductor: Horst Stein

During my preparatory study of *Don Carlos* I discovered that the opera is much more logical and consistent than Schiller's original play. Perhaps the Italian librettist simply swept the entangled plot aside and adopted a simple line instead.

Verdi composed the music with obvious delight, creating a canvas on which, though the power of State and Church is ever present, the passions of the individual characters always take precedence. He drew the stock characters out of the drama, and invested them with special musical colours and themes of their own. And I had the rare privilege of casting a star of international renown for each one of

these characters—and was given to understand that never again would such profligacy be tolerated!

The collaboration of an enthusiastic cast was assured, and the music was as passionate and exciting as anyone could have wished. I felt free to dispense with the ostentatious traditional décor of *Don Carlos*—a form of extravagance I detest.

We designed a simple set, with a series of walls made of translucent burlap. We worked on it with imagination and craftsmanship until it could convey the impression of marble, rough stone walls, or evoke the atmosphere of a garden.

The second essential component of the set was a cross. It was never omitted from any scene, for the cross borne by man—the hypertrophied Catholic cross in particular—is what this work is ultimately about. By shifting the flats we could create a maze of corridors and hiding-places so that even the 'eavesdropping scene' looked credible.

The *auto-da-fé* presents to most producers and stage designers a host of almost insuperable difficulties. We quickly agreed that there was no point in pretending that people were actually being burned on stage; this would happen 'behind the scenes', eliminating the problem of the construction and lighting of a stake. We allowed ourselves to be guided by old etchings of this lurid spectacle being enacted on a church square with the spectators crowded into wooden stands. In our set we omitted the usual church façade—which would have had to be made of papier mâché or a similar make-believe material—and constructed a spectators' stand that fitted smoothly into our world of flats and drops.

The costumes were also made of burlap, treated more lavishly to look like expensive raw silk or brocade. The only really expensive material was Philip's 'simple' dressing-gown; it was made of genuine Indian raw silk—and looked like burlap!

Against this Rembrandtesque background and dressed in their simple costumes, the players were uplifted by their voices to appear as vibrant, passionate human beings.

I made a special effort to stress the desperate love of the ageing Philip for his wife: to present him not as a vindictive man, but as a helpless wretch not equal to his duties.

I had little personal success at the première (I had, so to speak, made myself redundant) but this cast was more widely acclaimed than any other that has ever worked with me, a fact on which I greatly pride myself. It proved that with a properly conceived set it is possible to fuse even the most multinational cast into a satisfactory ensemble.

Otto Schenk

We tried to find a basic approach, a condensed visual frame for the entire action. It seemed impossible to reconstruct all the elements of the historical model—Philip II's Escorial—without being smothered in superficial theatrical junk.

The result was a set of Spartan simplicity. On a raked platform running deep into the rear of the stage, I built a foreshortened series of flats parallel to the footlights, representing walls and ceilings: a stylized area that could serve as both interior and exterior depending on the properties used. The 'interiors' were divided by transparent burlap veils which subdivided the entire depth several times. We gave this space greater substance with realistic doors, and more particularly with appropriate period furniture. The 'exteriors' looked more spacious. They were completed and given atmosphere with such architectural accessories as iron railings, steps, wooden frames, and foliage applied to veils.

The entire structure was set in a most colourful panorama. It was less patent in the interiors, though always detectable through the transparent walls; in the exteriors it served as the horizon after a variation in the lighting. The flats were illuminated with side-lights and several flood battens, which placed the figures, set pieces and props into strong relief.

The stage floor, walls and ceilings were also very colourful, and formed a coherent artistic pattern. Although the individual flats were staggered, they had been treated as a single large painting. The same was true of the architectural accessories, all of which took their colours from those of the walls. The actual base material of our *Carlos* scenery was burlap in a variety of combinations, some denser and some more transparent; the natural dark beige colour of this material was deliberately repeated in the paintwork. The dominant colours were variations of beige, brown, russet and indigo-blue. All doors, furniture and wooden frames were made of pine with the natural grain visible, blending smoothly with the colour of the painted walls.

The style and cut of the costumes were based on historical models. The cloth was adapted to the décor, made of different combinations of burlap with cotton and silk. This produced a very colourful effect, since the natural burlap tones and the reds, blues and blacks we had added provided a picturesque complement to the scenic walls.

Jürgen Rose

1972, DÜSSELDORF   DEUTSCHE OPER AM RHEIN

Producer: Georg Reinhardt — Stage designer: Ruodi Barth — Costumes: Inge Diettrich — Conductor: Alberto Erede

Don Carlos, with its truly magnificent music and taut character exposition, is my favourite Verdi opera. These fascinating aspects provide the reason why I have produced this work so often. Particularly successful, to my mind, was my collaboration a few years ago with the stage designer Heinrich Wendel; it made me feel that we had found the best way of interpreting this work.

I later found it most difficult to come up with an equally convincing and credible solution when I had to adopt a quite different approach. Ruodi Barth, the stage designer, quickly agreed that—as with Heinrich Wendel's presentation—nothing but a stylized form would do. He then had the brilliant idea of creating neutral space which could be split up, recomposed and redefined as the situation demanded by the displacement of countless slender pillars of immense height. It was a most 'eccentric' production of *Don Carlos*—in general, far more lavish and realistic sets are preferred.

But that was the last thing we wanted. We chose this admittedly costly solution, one that captured the atmosphere of the Escorial, of the oppressive Spanish court ceremonial, with unusual sensitivity.

With it, I tried to tell the story of Don Carlos without operatic flourishes and ostentation, and with a very severe—but by no means rigid or forced—stylization. Both solo and chorus scenes were strictly co-ordinated and stripped of all superfluous movements. Reduction to the essentials was the watchword of this production.

Georg Reinhardt

Costume designs for *Don Carlos,* Jürgen Rose, Vienna, 1970

Costume designs for *Don Carlos,* Inge Diettrich, Düsseldorf, 1972

I based my approach to this presentation of *Don Carlos* on my other experiences with Schiller's play and the realization that Verdi liked 'musical blue-prints'.

It is not my view, even with other historical operas, that the stage designer must take on the role of travel guide—in this case through Alcazar Castle. I looked instead for a means of merely suggesting different areas with the help of identical architectural elements.

My starting-point was an old ground plan of Alcazar Palace, on which hundreds of pillars were marked at regular intervals. Elsewhere in Spain I had once seen pillars bunched together in groups of four and connected by struts. Depending on the observer's position, he could look through them in various directions. A closer examination of this type of architecture enabled me to construct scenic elements consisting of five pillars each. With twelve of these structures I was able to develop the several spaces in which this drama of family life—of conflict between generations, and between Church and State—could be enacted without disturbing shifts of scenery. On a black stage these vertical elements were continually rearranged to suit the various situations, the lighting helping to produce countless impressions of rooms, cabinets, passages and galleries within the shifting pattern of pillars.

The pillars were made of hundreds of plastic tubes which, placed end to end, would have been two kilometres long. Treated with primer, they had a cold and stony aspect in the light.

My solution may not have been the simplest or the cheapest but it provided a great deal of variable space and—once erected—proved relatively simple to manipulate.

This treatment of space was totally convincing during performances, and I believe this kind of metaphorical approach can encourage audiences to become consciously involved in the dramatic developments. They see a stage: not a would-be study or a papier-mâché garden, but a world invented for the theatre, changeable and adaptable to any conceivable situation that might arise. Once the tour conductor ceases to spoon-feed them, they can give free rein to their imagination.

Although I do not think of this presentation of *Don Carlos* as my favourite or my best, I consider the scenographic approach I used in it a valid modern attempt to break free from traditional opera conceptions.

Ruodi Barth

1975, SALZBURG   GROSSES FESTSPIELHAUS

Producer: Herbert von Karajan — Stage designer: Günther Schneider-Siemssen — Costumes: Georges Wakhevitch — Conductor: Herbert von Karajan

On the basis of three preliminary sketches, Herbert von Karajan agreed with Günther Schneider-Siemssen that their production would be one of Spartan simplicity. They hoped to recapture the

severity, harshness and frugality of the Spanish court, and to reflect the political background of the plot. An essential constituent of Karajan's conception was a subtle representation of the tragic consequences of the Philip-Elizabeth-Carlos triangle, which did not, however, prevent him from dwelling on the omnipotent power of a State and Church that intervene drastically and remorselessly in the fate of the individual.

The credible presentation of all these ideas on the vast stage of the Great Festival Hall demanded scenic concentration. 'So as not to end up with a mere string of illustrations—which is one of the pitfalls of this opera with its seven scenes—I did not design seven different layouts but tried to achieve a tight scenograph conception by developing a unified ground plan.' [G. Schneider-Siemssen.]

Strict symmetry expressed the Spanish court ceremonial, and aided certain dynamic considerations. Günther Schneider-Siemssen created a geometric set with a platform at the rear and two converging flights of stairs, forming a small playing surface. This construction allowed quick changes of scenery with the simple addition of various set pieces.

'For nothing could be more fatal in *Don Carlos* than long-drawn-out scene changes: many of the scene endings do not admit of breaks but demand a prompt, dynamic continuation of the action.'

Günther Schneider-Siemssen considers this 'Spanish triangle' both a scenic and a symbolic framework. He speaks of the visual symbolization of the Philip-Elizabeth-Carlos triangle, saying that it 'is not driven home with a sledge-hammer, and is perhaps only appreciated by the few artistically sensitive spectators who want to feel as well as see'.

On this triangle the individual scenes were constructed of 'symbolic-realistic drawing-board architecture', meant to achieve a concentration of the scenery towards the centre of the stage, so as to emphasize the truly 'intimate' character of this work.

This concentration meant that even nature—in the scenes representing 'a pleasant landscape outside the monastery' and 'garden of the palace in Madrid'—became part of the sober architecture.

The *auto-da-fé* has always posed a very special problem, which I had failed to solve convincingly during an earlier production in Essen. However, I was just as little convinced by the solutions adopted in other productions, which either placed some sort of glow in the sky, or else dispensed with the whole idea. All such evasions ought to be met with Fritz Kortner's: 'They've been playing truant'.

The execution was intended by the State and the Church as a deterrent, but it also served as a public spectacle, much like a bullfight. This must come across on the stage in all its cruelty. Herbert von Karajan and I plumped for a realistic solution. Inside the 'triangle' a stake was erected and faggots piled up underneath. King Philip, Elizabeth and the royal household sat on the tribune before the palace looking towards the stake; the people faced them downstage, as a continuation of the audience. A canopy spanned the top and rear of the tribune, which enabled us to position some of the musicians advantageously on the stage. While the musicians could see the conductor through the transparent canopy, they could not be seen from the house. With an acoustically sealed area behind the canopy—in the palace so to speak—it was possible to achieve optimum sound effects, to fuse visual and aural impressions into a harmonious whole.

Once we had agreed on a realistic representation, the problem of the fire, too, had to be solved realistically. The ceremony begins at sunset in front of the church, prison and palace. As night falls, the condemned are led to the stake and chained to it. The stake itself stands on a grate through which 'fire-light' can be projected vertically upwards. Two torch-bearers 'light' the faggots, whereupon a combination of special effects conveys the impression of a burning stake:

1. Pulsing glow on metal foil between the faggots;
2. Fluttering of rotating chiffon shreds in front of a spotlight;
3. Special effects of flickering fire-light;
4. Spirit flame in a trough;
5. Smoke and steam rising through the fire-light and completely shrouding the stake;
6. Spreading of fire-light (slide mechanism) to include king, royal household and palace by way of a symbolic indictment.
7. Shortly before the curtain falls, when the last heavenly voice is heard, a tremendous jet flame seven metres high (resin) veils the scene and ends the act.

In this way, team-work between the stage technicians and the lighting designers achieved an astonishing effect.

Report by Wolfgang Haefeli after an
interview with Günther Schneider-Siemssen.

Don Carlos

'The cloister of the monastery of San Yuste. Arcades around the quadrangle. The covered way at the back leads from the chapel to the monastery. It is joined by a passage to the arcade in the front in which the tomb of the Emperor Charles V is clearly visible.'

Düsseldorf, 1972   Reinhardt/Barth

Milan 1968   Ponnelle/Ponnelle

154

Salzburg, 1975   Karajan/Schneider-Siemssen

Vienna, 1970   Schenk/Rose

Düsseldorf, 1972   Reinhardt/Barth

Milan, 1968   Ponnelle/Ponnelle

Don Carlos

*'Garden of the palace in Madrid.
The garden is terraced; the lowest
terrace has an ornamental shrubbery
with a marble bench and a statue. A
spring rises among the shrubs.'*

Vienna, 1970   Schenk/Rose

Salzburg, 1975   Karajan/Schneider-Siemssen

157

Milan, 1968   Ponnelle/Ponnelle

Salzburg, 1975   Karajan/Schneider-Siemssen

Don Carlos

'*A large square outside the Church of Our Lady of Atocha. To the right, the church, with a broad flight of steps; to the left, a palace. In the foreground, another flight of steps leading to a lower square from the middle of which the tip of a stake can be seen to protrude. Large buildings and distant hills enclose the scene at the back.*'

Düsseldorf, 1972   Reinhardt/Barth

Vienna, 1970   Schenk/Rose

Don Carlos

'The King's study in Madrid.'

Düsseldorf, 1972   Reinhardt/Barth

Vienna, 1970   Schenk/Rose

Salzburg, 1975   Karajan/Schneider-Siemssen

Milan, 1968   Ponnelle/Ponnelle

Don Carlos

'A prison. A dark, half-subterranean vault. In the background iron bars through which one can see guards pacing up and down.'

Düsseldorf, 1972
Reinhardt/Barth

Vienna, 1970   Schenk/Rose

162

Salzburg, 1975   Karajan/Schneider-Siemssen
Milan, 1968   Ponnelle/Ponnelle

Die Meistersinger von Nürnberg *(The Mastersingers of Nuremberg)*

In Richard Wagner's 'total theatre', *The Mastersingers* holds a special position. After *Tristan und Isolde* the composer reverted to 'opera', selecting a theme that had preoccupied him ever since 1845. From 1861 to 1867 he completed the libretto and score of a large-scale, humorous work whose chief protagonist was no longer a single hero (Dutchman, Tannhäuser or Lohengrin) but a band of master-singers, representatives of the people, and led by the towering personality of the cobbler Hans Sachs.

Through this figure Wagner expressed his unequalled poetic insight into even the most subtle reverberations of the human soul. The other characters too—Pogner, Kothner, Eva, Stolzing and Beckmesser—are carefully drawn from the real world of familiar events. The church service, the noisy bustle of the apprentices, the blows of the cobbler's hammer, the brawling, the lovers' quest, the wiles and meddling of the women, the colourful procession, the gay festival—are so many known and tried motifs of other operas. But then poetry and music suddenly abandon the solid ground of reality to soar into what has made *The Mastersingers* the imperishable work it is: inspired hymn to art, to the majestic power of the creative intellect. The people, the masters at their head, come to a unanimous decision, and pay homage to the victorious genius. Forgotten are all the petty squabbles, the bigoted rejection of the 'new' approach that appeared so suddenly before them, forgotten is the nocturnal rumpus started by Hans Sachs in Act II, forgotten also the suspicious attitude of the self-assured burghers towards the nobleman in their midst.

The clashes and encounters of the leading characters all culminate in the gay abandon of a festival glorifying art.

The Mastersingers is not a work about social or political conflicts. Interpretations of that type are a recent innovation and quite alien to the basic idea of the opera. The brawling scene is no revolution, and Beckmesser remains an individual, not the embodiment of a hateful civic authority or political party.

The Mastersingers is not *Tristan*. Producer and stage designer will have to think twice before they decide whether to give free rein to their imagination and turn the stage into a no-man's-land of fantasy or whether to dwell on the narrowness of mediaeval life, the familiarity of people crammed side by side in the little streets and the frictions of the daily round, the better to emphasize the unexpected ebullience of the burghers. Historical accuracy—an exact replica of ancient Nuremberg—can of course be dispensed with, for that is not the point, but the liberating splendour of the finale, the large festival meadow with the poetic background of St. John's Night and St. John's Day urgently demand the limitation of space and intent in the previous scenes.

Hans Sachs, inspired by the genius of Walter Stolzing, opens doors and windows in a double sense: personal sentiment is transcended, as is all else that constitutes the normal routine of daily life.

Rudolf Hartmann

Scenes

1.1   The stage represents an oblique section of St. Catherine's Church; only the last few rows of pews in the nave (which is supposed to run from the left to the background) are visible; in the foreground is the open space before the choir; this is afterwards shut off from the nave by a black curtain.

2.1   The foreground represents a street in longitudinal section, intersected by a narrow alley, which winds crookedly towards the back. There are thus two corner houses shown: the richer one on the right is Pogner's, the more modest one on the left is Sachs's. In front of Pogner's house is a linden-tree; before Sachs's house is a lilac. It is a beautiful summer evening; in the course of Scene I night gradually falls.

3.1   In Sachs's workshop (front scene). In the background, the half-open door leading to the street. On the right a chamber door. On the left, the window overlooking the alley, with flowers before it; at the side of it a work-bench. Sachs is sitting in a large armchair at this window, through which the morning sun shines brightly on him; he has a large folio on his lap, and is absorbed in reading it.

3.5   The curtains are drawn up. The scene now shows an open meadow, with the town of Nuremberg in the distance. The Pegnitz winds across the stage, a narrow stream practicable at its nearest point. Gaily decorated boats continually unload newcomers—burghers of the guilds, women and children, all in rich festival array. On the right is a raised platform with chairs and benches on it; it is decked with the banners of the guilds that have already arrived. As the other guilds arrive, the banner-bearers also place their banners round the platform, so that finally they enclose it on three sides. Tents, with drinks and refreshments of all kinds, occupy the sides of the foreground of the stage.

1963, MUNICH   BAYERISCHE STAATSOPER

Producer: Rudolf Hartmann — Stage designer: Helmut Jürgens† —
Costumes: Sophia Schröck — Conductor: Joseph Keilberth

The Mastersingers could not possibly be omitted from the opening
programme of the reconstructed National Theatre in Munich. I
started preparatory work with Helmut Jürgens well in advance. I
have always felt close personal ties to this opera, a work that had its
première in the National Theatre and that, during my formative
years in Nuremberg, provided my first chance to try my hand at
opera production.

I examined all the available historical sources, not least those used
by Wagner. In 1963, after numerous productions abroad and at
home (including Bayreuth in 1951–2), I decided to ignore all that
had been done before and to start again from scratch. Helmut
Jürgens, almost obsessed with this task, insisted on going back to
Nuremberg, to examine the locations and to seek fresh evidence in
the archives. He returned with corroboration of many of our views
and with some new and valuable ideas.

For the model of our church in Act I we did not use St. Catherine's, known to Wagner, but the recognized meeting place of the
guild of mastersingers, St. Martha's, with its almost austere brightness. The hymn, the meeting of the masters, and the appearances of
the apprentices, all reflected a Protestant middle-class background.
Apart from the brief encounter between Eva and Walther, our interpretation was anything but sentimental or passionate. Jürgens's set
for the first act brilliantly solved the problem of the separation of
singing school and nave, and the business of erecting bars and
hanging them with woven mats kept the apprentices suitably occupied during the long David-Walther dialogue.

Act II called for a set that allowed the chorus to be drawn up to
full advantage during the brawling scene, with enough entrances
and exits for the quick development and resolution of the finale.

The houses piled up on top of each other symbolized confinement
and the close proximity of neighbours—a prerequisite for the
tumultuous explosion at the end of the act. For the lyrical encounter
of Sachs, Eva and Walther, romantic details were included in the set
but were not allowed to interfere with the overall impression.

The cobbler's workshop in Act III posed few scenic problems. Its
relatively narrow confines were meant to convey the idea that when
Sachs put his hammer away, inspired poetic thoughts could wing
their way through the encompassing walls.

The open meadow, always a scenic problem, required a large
marquee open only to the rear. Sunlight pouring from the outside
through semi-transparent canvas relieved the uniformity with light-
and-shade effects. The most important innovation, however, was
the arrangement of the masters, Eva and Magdalena on a large
circular rostrum in the centre of the stage, in such a way that any
one of the prize singers had the sought-after goldsmith's daughter
directly in front of him, and so that the people could approach
closely to join in the activities. We dispensed with the castle-and-
town-silhouette in the background: the stock 'Nuremberg ginger-
bread' gibes had to be prevented at all costs. I did not wish to
dispense with the town altogether, and, devised, with Jürgens, a
plastic emblem for every one of the guilds represented, each with a
metallic sheen. When carried at the end of the procession, these
emblems combined to represent a symbolic outline of Nuremberg.

In the meadow scene we were careful to avoid any display of
German chauvinism. Instead we focussed on what is, in the best
sense of the word, the 'democratic' element of the opera—the fact
that the voice of the people is consulted. The people are won over
by Sachs. Against the background of a middle-class town, the inner
destiny of the ageing shoemaker is shaped: his reasoned renuncia-
tion of Eva; his generous admiration of the youthful genius of
Walther von Stolzing—whose path he smooths because, among
other reasons, he recognizes his own limitations. Taking Beckmesser at his malicious word, some producers have seen fit to degrade
Walther from Franconian knight to 'adventurer'. Yet, in Act I the
masters treat him with suspicion precisely because they see him as a
noble knight whose splendid figure runs counter to their bourgeois
preconceptions. Walther's arrogance, increased by his defeat in the
singing school, vanishes in the face of the humane and penetrating
arguments of the shoemaker Hans Sachs, who teaches him respect
for the burghers whose ranks he will enter thanks to his ties with
Eva.

In Act II, ably supported by the conductor Joseph Keilberth, I
made sure that during the brawling scene the various masters did
not leave the stage straight after their entrances, but continued their
individual squabbles in plain view of the audience. Their conten-
tiousness leads to the general tumult. After the excitement of the
singing school they had gone on to the tavern, there to pursue their
arguments over a drink; now they are rudely awakened by the
'noisy behaviour' of their neighbours. The brawl grows into a
riot—short and violent, like a nightmare that can hardly be remembered next morning.

Beckmesser's unfortunate attempt to win the prize may lead to misinterpretation of his character. In Munich it was traditional to treat him as a buffoon—a view that struck me as unjustified quite early on. The Town Clerk is too important a figure in public life to be portrayed as a fool from the outset. His blind love for Eva, his exaggerated need for self-assertion and the sly manipulations of the resourceful shoemaker transform him into a tragi-comic figure. Beckmesser is probably the only one of the masters to know Latin, the only one who can furnish the burghers with legal documents. That is why I decided as early as 1938 (with Clemens Krauss in Munich) to have this role played by the 'character' baritone Heinrich Rehkemper, and later by Karl Schmitt-Walter (Munich and Bayreuth), instead of the customary 'comical' bass.

In the church scene of the first act, I paid careful attention to the direction of the players during the meetings of Eva, Walther, Magdalena and David. Walther, audaciously visiting the church, tries to arrange a meeting with Eva to talk to her undisturbed. Magdalena, guardian of etiquette, keeps stepping between them, until her attention is half-diverted by David's entry. Throughout these proceedings the producer must make sure that Eva and Walther do not stand side by side engaging in 'silent converse'. If they did, there would be no reason for their hurried: 'When shall I see you?'—'This evening, be sure!'

The long first act is likely to give rise to 'positional monotony' if the seating of the masters remains unaltered to the end. Luckily, the action itself suggests a logical re-arrangement: before Walther's 'Prize Song' the apprentices place the chairs of the masters in a semi-circle around the central singing chair. The marker's platform is best located outside the circle, preferably downstage left. Walther is the centre of the scene; several masters half turn their backs on the audience and the admiring apprentices gather around the singing chair. The various groups remain clearly distinct in the turbulent final scene, foreshadowing the arrangement of the players on the festival meadow.

In contrast to the sweeping characterizations he used in his other works, Wagner tried to define the characters of his *Mastersingers* with loving and scrupulous attention to detail. The producer inspired by this should encourage the cast to give a convincing portrayal of all the rich emotions involved. This should be his foremost concern.

Rudolf Hartmann

ded for the picture-frame stage of the court theatre of his century, the late Biedermeier and late Romantic periods.

It is remarkable that one is forced time and again to defend scenic changes in Wagner when such changes have long since been taken for granted with Shakespeare, Mozart and *Fidelio* productions; that is, with all great works. This is probably due to the fact that Wagner wrote many more stage directions than other composers—to him the performance was everything.

I have come to feel that *The Mastersingers* plays a very special intellectual role in the work of Richard Wagner: it is his confrontation with himself, with his own creativity. In other words, *The Mastersingers* has an autobiographical aspect. For that reason, Sachs's workshop strikes me as being the focus of the whole work.

The opera develops the romantic theory of creation—Wagner makes Sachs his own spokesman. In neither his letters nor his autobiography did Wagner show any glimpses of his innermost self, glimpses into his own work. Yet he does this in every one of Sachs's utterances. That is why I consider *The Mastersingers* neither an historical play nor an opera. It is, I repeat, Richard Wagner's confrontation with himself. He states his theory of art for all time, and he wrote a drama on the birth of the work of art.

Translated from: Wieland Wagner, 1963, p. 19.

1963, BAYREUTH   FESTSPIELHAUS

Producer: Wieland Wagner† — Stage designer: Wieland Wagner† — Costumes: Kurt Palm — Conductor: Thomas Schippers

I start from the premise that the score is inviolable, that it records the essential features of the work both for us today and for the future. Richard Wagner's stage directions, by contrast, were inten-

1968, BAYREUTH   FESTSPIELHAUS

Producer: Wolfgang Wagner — Stage designer: Wolfgang Wagner — Costumes: Kurt Palm — Conductor: Karl Böhm

When I took on the production of *The Mastersingers of Nuremberg*, I remembered the various interpretations I had been involved with in the Festspielhaus. My job, I felt, was to re-examine the basic ideas of

the work itself, their significance and expressive force, and then to implement the conclusions.

The set had to suit the special structure of the Festival Hall. This steeply sloping amphitheatrical building introduces special visual relationships, providing an extraordinarily sweeping view of the stage floor. The stage designer ought to bear this fact in mind and treat the stage as an integral part of his set. I developed the vertical components of the scenery from the horizontal dimension of the stage floor in order to mark the tension between the two.

The basic structure was built of half-timbering, modelled on the woodcut illustrations in Hartmann Schedel's *Weltchronik*, published in Nuremberg in 1493. The half-timbering was neither Alemannic nor Franconian; nor was it historically accurate. It was heterogeneous instead, meant to reflect life in a late mediaeval town, the world of the mastersingers, and the reappraisal of values expressed in the conflict of rigid forms with free creativity.

This interpretation was given scenic expression in the multicoloured open surfaces between the half-timbering. With the help of xenon back projection and filters which diffused the light and softened contours, the canvas walls gained a certain transparency. This created an unreal effect, dematerializing space and suggesting the magic atmosphere of Midsummer Eve and the mood of the 'lilac' monologue.

In Acts I and II, the tall, sharply defined areas constituted a solid world of orderly lines, but one that has been thrown out of equilibrium. The dematerialization of space at the end of the two acts was produced by appropriate illumination of the transparent interfaces. The narrowest and brightest space was the cobbler's shop in Act III, treated as a haven of intellectual concentration and knowledge rather than a place of manual work. And then there was the breakthrough, revealing the vast open space of the festival meadow, unadorned with any but the most provisional architectural accessories.

The 'interior of St. Catherine's Church in oblique section' was represented by a set whose near-timeless Gothic elements represented a simple, late mediaeval burghers' church. The stage cloth was patterned in squares of different colours to simulate an inlaid stone

floor; the walls looked like coloured stonework or glass lit from within. The triple-arched entrance to the left of the stage had a functional gallery. It was used at the beginning of the act for the exchanges between Eva and Walther and, during the meeting of the mastersingers, as a spectators' stand for the apprentices.

In Act II, Nuremberg appears as the junction of two narrow streets with tall half-timbered façades and sharply outlined gables. The linden-tree and circular seat in front of Pogner's house with its working oriel window and the lilac bush in front of Sachs's workshop frame the front scene, which is covered with cloth patterns of brown, grey and green. Only a small part of the background between the two rows of houses is visible. House outlines were applied to the front cyclorama—using flat areas of painted plastic, muslin veiling, tulle and other materials of different thicknesses—to produce ever-changing translucent effects. Direct front lighting cast shadows on the painted, second cyclorama, while light from the rear was diffused over a third. The lateral half-timbered surfaces, backed with painted canvas and covered with layers of tulle, also had a floating transparency—they looked almost like illuminated windows.

The visual tension in Act III depends upon the contrast between the destitution of the cobbler's workshop in the first scene to the expansive and gay atmosphere on the open meadow. The cobbler's room is incorporated in the meadow set: Hans Sachs's workshop, sparsely equipped with shoemaker's tools, is set obliquely into a half-timbered façade and constitutes a small section of it. Lights from the gridiron fall directly on to the stylized half-timbering, treated as it was in Act II. The stage cloth represents floor boards. The walls of the workshop are bare; its uncluttered and narrow confines help to concentrate the action.

The meadow is meant to symbolize escape from man-made confinement into the freedom of nature as well as the idealized acceptance of art by the people. Colourful patterns in bright and dark greens, yellows and greys, enliven the stage cloth. At the centre is a disc with an octagonal pattern. Its two halves lie behind the cobbler's shop, in readiness for the transformation of the scene. In the middle of the disc stands a small octagonal platform for the prize singers. Seats for Pogner and Eva—with their backs to the audience—and for Kothner and Sachs, constitute an inner ring on the rostrum. The apprentices are drawn up round the disc in another circle, and the benches for the people form three further rows of circles open to the front. Behind them, a painted wooden frame stands in an open dodecagon; it is embellished with guild emblems. A row of hedges constitutes the next circle. Fully visible this time is the triple cyclorama; the first drop shows a stylized landscape with trees and hills.

The essential factor in the shaping of the open meadow scene is the gradual build-up from the simple, crude and happy utterances of the guild choruses—suggested in part by pantomime—through Beckmesser's professional performance to the climax of Walther's prize song. The Utopian idealization of art is expressed through the democratic device of acclaim by the people—artistically receptive and discriminating people who arrive at a decision that the 'master clique' lacks the acumen to make for itself. This final solution offers one more example of Richard Wagner's Utopian-democratic conception of a people whose identity is based on participation in artistic expression. He saw this ideal implemented in the *polis* and in the theatre of ancient Greece. He devoted a great many of his theoretical reflections to the resurrection of this ideal from which the Bayreuth Festival took its essential impetus.

Richard Wagner preached the ideal of art, not Germanomania. Art standing above nationality—it was this leitmotiv to which I tried to do justice in my production.

Wolfgang Wagner

1974, SALZBURG   GROSSES FESTSPIELHAUS

Producer: Herbert von Karajan — Stage designer: Günther Schneider-Siemssen — Costumes: Georges Wakhevitch — Conductor: Herbert von Karajan

In *The Mastersingers* Wagner seems to turn his back on metaphysics in order to take his stand on the solid ground of reality. It is a popular opera with a very beautiful text and glorious music, a down-to-earth work in which every gable has a substantial wall, every tree a solid trunk and every door a frame.

The work was revolutionary in its own time. Craftsmen—trade unionists, if you like—play the leading roles; there are no courtly gestures, as if the court had disappeared. In the centre stands a town of burghers, artisans, craftsmen, artists, all of them men with men's foibles.

In Salzburg we had several discussions before we agreed how to handle the stage of the Great Festival Hall. I produced three distinct ground plans for the church before looking at the individual scenes in detail: how to seat Eva so that she can see Stolzing, what to do with the apprentices when the masters enter.

I had once designed *Belshazzar* for the Göttingen Festival; the scene was in the church and we did not know where to put the props. Then someone said, 'Stick it all behind the altar!' I remembered this fact, and decided to rotate the axis of the church so that the choir appeared in profile. A curtain could be dropped, allowing the apprentices to pull out choir stalls and benches, and to erect the masters' platform and stalls in a wing of the church.

Karajan attached great importance to sunlight in this scene. The sudden appearance of the sun, or its disappearance behind a cloud, are very noticeable in a dark church. We exploited this fact by allowing the light to pour in from the left and then gradually to creep across to the opposite side, which it reached just as the masters finally arrived.

For the second scene we decided that since we were working on the vast stage of the Great Festival Hall we might as well build a proper town. The centre we made a street, to the left we placed a battlement, to the right the town wall and another battlement. There were nearly fifty windows reaching up as far as the fourth floor, whence all the inhabitants could later look down and pelt the brawlers with refuse, water and anything else that came to hand. There was nothing contrived about our version of the brawling scene, though it was, of course, important to ensure that Sachs could not see the loving couple in Pogner's garden.

Karajan worked hard on the characterization of Beckmesser. He saw him as a highly intelligent man faced with situations that showed him in the worst possible light. He was not meant to look ridiculous. The houses, too, were intended to be genuine, not caricatures: the way they were telescoped together, the sudden emergence of a Spitzwegian atmosphere—all this was quite intentional.

Karajan decided to let Beckmesser disappear unnoticed during the brawl, replacing him with a double who would be thrown into the river. Karajan here showed that he had the courage of his realistic—one can almost say naturalistic—convictions. The light was also very important. It was evening now: the light had to come from the other side. Sunset followed, and then the moon had to rise so that it would shine on Sachs. All these effects had been most carefully planned to be logically consistent. One may recall one of Kortner's sayings, spoken in reply to an actress who had asked him where she should put her fan: 'You have an eagle eye for the inessential.' These details do not escape Karajan.

In the cobbler's workshop it is of course essential to place the table and chair near the window so that they are visible from all sides, and to ensure that the light falls through the window correctly. Sachs's figure must be bathed in morning light. Another important consideration is that the ground plan of the oriel window should correspond with that used in the second act. We achieved this by adding a first floor study to the cobbler's shop; the stage, though reduced to fifteen metres, was large enough. The downstairs room was shown in a muddle; books and cobbler's lasts were jumbled together. We felt the presence of a pillar was important; the singers can lean against it, and it helps the development of, say, the Eva and Stolzing scene. Beckmesser must sneak in through the back door and snoop about; he should not be made to enter from the side.

I made several sketches for the open meadow, the last of which included several awnings—after all, we were portraying a popular festival, with stalls, booths and a screened-off area. The awnings also served as resonators: I took it that the masters themselves would have wanted the best possible acoustic conditions. The awnings were transparent to let in the 'sunlight'. Downstage we placed the platforms, genuine wooden structures in period style. A bridge led to the rear where youths stood about and girls from Fürth waved across as if over the Pegnitz. We dispensed with boats; the stage lacked sufficient depth for the arrival of the guests in a whole fleet. Upstage was the town wall and the gate through which the guilds entered. Because our set involved the reduction of the proscenium arch, we were able to introduce a most striking effect: at the end of the interlude between the two last scenes (cobbler's shop and meadow) the fifteen-metre proscenium arch was lifted out of sight when the curtain rose. The tormentors on either side were drawn back into the wings to reveal the stands on which some of the guilds were already gathered.

Günther Schneider-Siemssen

1975, VIENNA STAATSOPER

Producer: Otto Schenk — Stage designer: Jürgen Rose — Costumes: Jürgen Rose — Conductor: Christoph von Dohnanyi

With *The Mastersingers* one ought not to ask what makes this incomparable opera so fascinating, but rather what *fails* to fascinate. How can anyone involved in the theatre help but enjoy Sachs and his backstairs intrigues? How can any full-blooded producer stage the brawling scene without wishing to join in himself? How can one not be moved by the passion of Eva and Walther, by Sachs's unselfish love, or by Beckmesser's unhappy attachment to Pogner's daughter? Can one help being swayed by the mood of the 'lilac' monologue or being carried away by the procession on the festival meadow, by Walther's glorious Prize Song? Wagner stepped down for once from his dubious pedestal (he himself said, 'Everyone ought to do it once a year') to portray relationships as if he himself had lived through those times. In short, how would it be possible to ignore this mass of human emotion when staging *The Mastersingers*?

I am an avowed opponent of all attempts to explain concepts away. An interpretation that can apparently be compressed into a few sentences is tantamount to a simplification, and I detest simplifications on the stage as much as I do in real life. I am by no means opposed to simplicity in the theatre or opera; only to trivialization, over-simplification or 'intellectualization'. Before I discuss my stage conception of *The Mastersingers,* I must first confess that I originally approached the work with none at all.

It would not be true to say that I followed no guidelines whatsoever. I tried to adhere strictly to Wagner's stage directions, in which I include the music. Almost every step, every glance, every human emotion seems to be most carefully reflected in it. His directions—which often run to half a page in small print—read almost like a scenario. If one follows them and 'reads' his music, the resulting production cannot help being 'realistic'. I did my best to transpose those directions suited to the style of the nineteenth century into our own idiom so as to render them more intelligible.

An opera depicting human weaknesses, which involves a clumsy and ludicrous petty intrigue that achieves good ends, had to be presented convincingly. That meant explaining why the 'new art' of Walther, repudiated by the 'masters' with indignation, should have emerged victorious thanks to Sachs's intervention. I paid very particular attention to shaping the two roles of Sachs and Beckmesser.

Whereas I tried, in my exciting collaboration with Karl Ridderbusch, to bring out some of Sachs's less heroic traits, I also attempted—*pace* Wagner—to lend Beckmesser greater respectability. In Wagner's day malicious expressions of rancour were perhaps more necessary than they are today. In Wagner's interpretation, Beckmesser was something of a dunce—he is allocated the most egregious and cacophonic sounds, and his songs fall flat for the strangest and most ridiculous reasons. I felt, by contrast, that he ought to be treated with some of the respect due to a Town Clerk of his day. In other words, the true motive of his failure—his mistaken and unhappy feelings for Eva—should be brought home to the audience with greater force than is customary.

Beckmesser is not—as is so often asserted—Sachs's antagonist. He is an eligible bachelor whom Eva ought to marry, or at least to reject before all the world by using her veto, thus disgracing the mastersingers by making a mockery of the whole contest. Beckmesser must be someone extremely well-versed in the conventional art of song, someone who can explain it accurately and point out every mistake. What he cannot do is to appreciate the new style represented by Walther. That is precisely how I proposed to characterize him.

Fully conscious of the fact that Wagner's music is too pregnant

Costume designs, Jürgen Rose, Vienna, 1975

with detail to allow a symbolist interpretation, Jürgen Rose devised a set reflecting that wealth of detail and demanding exceptional craftsmanship. The opera devotes a whole evening to the talk of shoemakers, carpenters and tin-smiths, that is, to journeymen and masters, and we should have looked foolish indeed with a set found wanting in craftsmanship. The workshops of the Vienna State Opera excelled on this occasion, and I felt the need to express my thanks to every one of its 'masters' in person.

Apart from this attention to detail, the main characteristic of the stage presentation was its simplicity: an almost completely un-adorned church; instead of a Disneyland Nuremberg full of gables, the simple street we found depicted in old illustrations; on the festival meadow, a tent; and everything done so realistically that it looked ready for immediate occupation.

Otto Schenk

The producer and I agreed that our object must be to present the opera in a plain, unvarnished and realistic setting, studiously avoid-ing any romantic temptations to resurrect mediaeval Nuremberg. We would also eschew any references to the period in which the opera was written.

We wanted to depict the background of the characters in as much detail as we could, to bring home the everyday nature of the action.

We chose lower-middle-class Nuremberg with its artisans and 'pea-sants', rather than the more opulent bourgeois environment depict-ed on so many of Dürer's paintings and drawings. Museums pro-vided us with a wealth of authentic illustrations of life in fifteenth- and sixteenth-century Nuremberg, which influenced me considera-bly.

For the first act I used a sixteenth-century picture of St. Cath-erine's Church—a small, unpretentious Reformation building devoid of all Gothic flourishes. It struck me as just right for *The Mastersingers,* since after the Protestant morning service part of the church is turned into a 'singing-school'.

I constructed a bright set with distempered walls, stone floor and wooden ceiling, stairs and gallery. The centre aisle with wooden pews could be seen through a large archway. The sun could pour in through the tall windows (without stained glass) to create an early morning atmosphere.

I insisted that the fittings and properties be accurate and realistic: the stalls and the marker's box, for instance, were built by crafts-men, to be both dismantled and, in the apprentice scene, properly assembled.

The singers—soloists and chorus—were dressed in individual costumes, the masters and their apprentices in accordance with their respective trades. Some appeared to have arrived straight from work and were dressed differently from those who had attended the morning service. Social distinctions among the masters (between the soap-boiler and the goldsmith, for instance) were reflected in the material and cut of their clothing. I used light-weight cloths throughout, those appropriate to Midsummer Day.

In Act II, instead of an idyllic Nuremberg full of nooks and crannies, with pointed gables and bull's-eye windows, we decided to use half-timbering, shingle roofs, and when possible to show the rear aspect of the buildings with an inner courtyard and adjacent gardens. The town itself was to lie further away. Here, too, my inspiration came from an original illustration of a street in sixteenth-century Nuremberg, the almost English severity of which matched my concept exactly. Every door and window was functional. The half-timbering and the shingles were made of real pine; nothing was imitated or faked.

The cobble-stones were simulated, however—we could not have used real stones in the vast quantities needed. Instead, our workshop produced moulds and used these for polyester casts. The lilac and the linden-tree were not genuine, but had to look as lifelike as possible. Important for the overall atmosphere was the use of a real cart, cobbler's bench, pail, and so on. We found these props in various places on the outskirts of Vienna. As in Act I, the soloists and chorus wore individual costumes—this time in keeping with the nocturnal scene.

When constructing the cobbler's workshop, we considered it most important that the façade of Act II should match the interior of Act III. Doors, windows and ground plan retained the same proportions. The entire workshop was made of pine. The furniture and the cobbler's implements were genuine—Sachs had to be seen to be using his tools properly, with no pretence.

The pavilion in the final festival scene reflected my dissatisfaction with the usual cyclorama. The first three sets having been constructed with unusually realistic materials, it was essential that the fourth be consistent. The 'normal' depth of the stage to the cyclorama was not deep enough if—taking Wagner at his word—we were to allow a large guild procession to pour on to the stage from the rear. I reverted to the old picture-frame principle, erecting a booth over the entire stage, with the back wall open to the back stage and the sides of the stage cut off from view. In this way, I created the illusion that the booth was part of a much wider landscape.

This 'landscape' consisted of a rising, hilly meadow bounded at the rear by plastic foliage and a backcloth of painted trees. The guilds could assemble some thirty-five metres upstage and move forward into the booth, which was built in the traditional way of unpolished pine. For the ceiling I chose natural cheese-cloth which filtered and refracted the intense light from the gridiron, bathing the inside of the booth in an atmosphere of warm summer shade. The 'outside' was made to look all the more brilliant with intense back-lighting directed at the meadow and into the tent entrance.

The costumes displayed bright summery colours in cotton, wool and leather. The individual participants wore different national dress, though members of the various guilds were dressed alike, to emphasize that they were part of a procession.

In the four sets I designed for *The Mastersingers,* symmetry played a decisive part which, though broken from time to time by various details, lent the whole its optical and stylistic cohesion. The sets were well defined and logically lit; the materials were plain and had few illusionist embellishments. In this simple setting the producer was able to concentrate without distraction on the emotions enshrined in the plot.

Jürgen Rose

Bayreuth, 1968   Wolfgang Wagner

Munich, 1963   Hartmann/Jürgens

Vienna, 1975   Schenk/Rose

The Mastersingers

'The stage represents an oblique section of St. Catherine's Church; only the last few rows of pews in the nave (which is supposed to run from the left to the background) are visible; in the foreground is the open space before the choir; this is afterwards shut off from the nave by a black curtain.'

Bayreuth, 1963   Wieland Wagner

Salzburg, 1974   Karajan/Schneider-Siemssen

173

Salzburg, 1974   Karajan/Schneider-Siemssen

Bayreuth, 1968   Wolfgang Wagner

Bayreuth, 1963   Wieland Wagner

174

The Mastersingers

'The foreground represents a street in longitudinal section, intersected in the middle by a narrow alley, which winds crookedly towards the back. There are thus two corner houses shown: the richer one on the right is Pogner's, the more modest one on the left is Sachs's. In front of Pogner's house is a linden-tree; before Sachs's is a lilac. It is a beautiful summer evening: in the course of the first Scene night gradually falls.'

Munich, 1963   Hartmann/Jürgens

Vienna, 1975   Schenk/Rose

Munich, 1963   Hartmann/Jürgens

Bayreuth, 1968   Wolfgang Wagner

Vienna, 1975   Schenk/Rose

The Mastersingers

'In Sachs's workshop. (Front scene.) In the background, the half-open door leading to the street. On the right a chamber door. On the left, the window overlooking the alley, with flowers before it; at the side of it a work-bench.'

Bayreuth, 1963   Wieland Wagner

Salzburg, 1974   Karajan/Schneider-Siemssen

The Mastersingers

'The curtains are drawn up. The scene now shows an open meadow, with the town of Nuremberg in the distance. The Pegnitz winds across the stage, a narrow stream practicable at its nearest point. Gaily decorated boats continually unload newcomers—burghers of the guilds, women and children, all in rich festival array. On the right is a raised platform with chairs and benches on it : it is decked with the banners of the guilds that have already arrived. As the other guilds arrive, the banner-bearers also place their banners round the platform, so that finally they enclose it on three sides. Tents, with drinks and refreshments of all kinds, occupy the sides of the foreground of the stage.'

Vienna, 1975   Schenk/Rose
Bayreuth, 1963   Wieland Wagner

Bayreuth, 1968   Wolfgang Wagner

Munich, 1963 Hartmann/Jürgens

Salzburg, 1974 Karajan/Schneider-Siemssen

Götterdämmerung (The Twilight of the Gods)

'For the end of the godhead draweth now near...' So sings Brünnhilde in her great finale, when she takes leave of all that has been to follow the dead Siegfried.

She inveighs against Wotan, but she knows that the god also longs for death, and salutes him for the last time: 'Rest thou, rest thou, o god!' When she goes on to fling the brand on the wood-pile with: 'So cast I the brand on Walhall's glittering walls,' and chooses death by fire for herself, she is not revenging herself on the gods with bitter irony. She is simply fulfilling what Wotan has decided and decreed: that he—and the myths surrounding all the gods—be destroyed.

Wagner's music is unequivocal. Nevertheless, several recent interpretations of the *Ring,* claiming to have updated the tetralogy by breaking away from the 'mythological fable', have ignored the score and opted for the dubious limelight of sensation mongering. The various justifications of such productions ought to be read with critical attention. It is true that, during the four nights it takes to stage this complex whole, the spectator is offered a wealth of ideas and events that suggests a link with the present. But the question remains: may the interpreter follow his own imagination without hindrance? Is he entitled to run riot with his own interpretations until the work has been completely changed? It would surely be better to provide the poor public, weaned from the habit of forming its own opinion by the constant condescension of the mass media, with an entirely new piece specially written to convey the required message.

Anyone prepared to heed the music and not the libretto alone cannot help but hear certain of Wagner's own opinions. The most intellectual speculations come to nought when the language of the music is not understood. This explains why certain logical experiments, though performed with passion and clearly based on solid research, cannot hope to enjoy lasting success. Perhaps they are necessary phases in a process of crystallization, from which Wagner's work will emerge in an altered form harmonious with his own ideas.

Let us consider the finale of *Götterdämmerung,* as Wagner envisaged it. After Hagen's desperate attempt to seize the ring, after his death in the waters of the Rhine, all the singing stops. Instead the orchestra provides a perfect accompaniment, in a symphonic sweep of sound, for Wagner's precise stage instructions: 'From the ruins of the fallen hall, the men and women, in the greatest agitation, look on the growing fire-light in the heavens. As this at length glows with the greatest brightness, the interior of Walhall is seen, in which gods and heroes sit assembled, as in Waltraute's description in the first act... Bright flames appear to seize on the hall of the gods... As the gods become entirely hidden by the flames, the curtain falls.'

In the last seven bars there rise up once more, in poignant remembrance, the strains of Wotan's wondrous vision from *The Valkyrie,* only to ebb away and die in a solemn and conciliatory D flat major.

The men and women in the ruins of the fallen hall, mentioned expressly on two occasions, have survived the catastrophe and its final notes. They have witnessed, not the end of the world, as so many productions would have us believe, but the dawn of something new, something not yet identifiable. The old gods have destroyed themselves; trembling mankind is about to take the next great unknown step—perhaps towards Christianity.

In this connection, the inclusion of Wagner's last opera, *Parsifal,* as an epilogue of the *Ring,* could well help to give concrete expression to covert intellectual links.

I cannot believe that all Wagner tried to do in the *Ring* was to portray the destruction of an evil capitalist character who called himself Wotan and lost his fight with the even more miserable Alberich. If that were the case he composed badly and would have done better to leave this episode from the Gründerjahre—the period of rapid industrial expansion of Germany in the 1870s and 1880s—to a dramatist like Hermann Sudermann.

A questionable but popular practice these days is the setting of operas in the lifetime of their creators. This is equivalent to declaring that they lacked the wit or imagination to conjure up places, times and events from the past and to shape them through the filter of their intellects into the most perfect works of art. Do we really need these corrections to bring the modern stage up to date? If we do, we merely treat the public as intellectual inferiors whose antiquated ideas must be exorcised and who must be rendered receptive to new interpretations inculcated if necessary by dictatorial decree.

Wagner, the 'eternal revolutionary and innovator', provides the apparent justification for all such stage presentations. Was he truly the man he is said to have been? His youthful outburst in Dresden was directed less against the State than for the freedom of the theatre—the Richard Wagner theatre he had conceived even then. The diary of Cosima Wagner, published in 1976, provides new insights into the attitudes of this fervent admirer of Bismarck, and shows that he took a most positive view of the authority of the State. His life-style was never that of the revolutionary who chooses to starve as a matter of principle. He knew himself to be an artist and an exceptional phenomenon. He needed luxury and ease, and, with the presumption of genius, made heavy demands on the friendship of a generous king.

In view of Wagner's life-style, it seems hardly credible that he should have used the mythology of the *Ring* for a socio-political critique of nineteenth-century life. Many of his statements, as noted down by Cosima, are clear proof of the contrary, of his faith in the *Ring* as a work of art *sui generis.*

Modern producers of that work must of necessity develop new

forms since, like everything else in the theatre, Wagner is not immune to change.

We shall have to wait and see whether or not Bayreuth, now a century old, will come to terms with this task, or whether it will be caught up in speculative experimentation. Nor is Bayreuth the only place where progress in interpretation may be fruitfully wedded to the conservation of the work itself.

In the staging of the *Ring,* the tasks of producer and designer are of unusually great, indeed of crucial importance. After all that has just been said, there is no need to go into further detail.

Rudolf Hartmann

Scenes

Prelude The scene is the same as at the close of the second day, on the Valkyries' rock.

1.1 The Hall of the Gibichungs on the Rhine. This is quite open at the back. The background itself presents an open shore as far as the river; rocky heights enclose the shore.

1.3 The rock, as in the Prelude.

2.1 An open space on the shore in front of the Gibichungs' hall: on the right the open entrance to the hall; on the left the bank of the Rhine, from which, slanting across the stage to the back, rises a rocky height cut by several mountain paths. There Fricka's altar-stone is visible: higher up is a larger one for Wotan and on the side is another for Donner.

3.1 A wild, woody and rocky valley on the Rhine, which flows past a steep cliff in the background.

1965, BAYREUTH   FESTSPIELHAUS

Producer: Wieland Wagner† — Stage designer: Wieland Wagner† — Costumes: Kurt Palm — Conductor: Karl Böhm

In 1965, fourteen years after his first *Ring* in Bayreuth, Wieland Wagner decided to stage a new production. His second *Ring* reflected the experience he had since gained as producer and stage designer. Similar progress could also have been detected by anyone comparing, say, his *Tristan* of 1952 with his presentation of 1962. In both works he had advanced from a statuary, archetypal approach to one much more mobile, more diversified, and more warmly human in conception and expression.

The characters in the *Ring* were given greater individuality and originality than before, though Wieland Wagner tried, as always, to leave their symbolic value unimpaired. This synthesis of the unique, the individual and the general was what made the second wave of his productions such a magnificent experience.

The characters in his second *Ring* cycle should be considered from this double viewpoint. Wotan is the embodiment of the will to power, derived philosophically from Schopenhauer's absolute pessimism. Wieland Wagner saw him also as the guilt-laden politician, whose policies *must* ruin the world. It is not only Alberich or Hagen who long for the gold, but Wotan too; according to Wieland Wagner, Wotan more so than all the rest. He does not consider, even for a moment, the return of the gold to the Rhinedaughters, despite his repeated protestations. When he sends Waltraute to persuade Brünnhilde to part with the ring, he does not intend to restore the disturbed world order by returning the gold to the Rhinedaughters, but only to regain personal possession of it.

This is what Wieland Wagner calls the 'eternal double game of all politicians', of 'all who lust for power'. Wotan is, to him, the main culprit in all the events leading up to Siegmund's death, to Siegfried's death, to Brünnhilde's humiliation—ultimately to the destruction of the world. That destruction is also Wotan's own. This fundamental notion of Richard Wagner is clarified by his grandson, who obviously likens Wotan to an 'antediluvian Adolf Hitler', a man who has 'prepared a more or less heroic suicide', and who 'burns in Valhalla's storm of fire like a guilty criminal'.

The links between Wieland Wagner's second *Ring* and the historical circumstances in which he grew up are made crystal clear.

This process of updating an universal theme was reflected in the scenography. At first Wieland Wagner was only interested in the symbolic meaning of the works. He left the stage almost empty and consigned the shaping of scenic space to the lighting designer.

In the second *Ring*—as in later productions—he turned his back on the absolute emptiness of his original conception. He now tried instead to achieve a synthesis of symbolism and topical action. Needless to say, his was not a return to primitive Bayreuth naturalism. As always, Wieland Wagner worked with light in his second *Ring*. The lighting was no longer directed towards symbolic worlds or philosophies, but rather to clarify that special world in which the story of gods, and heroes transformed into men, could be unfolded.

Antoine Goléa

1970, SALZBURG   GROSSES FESTSPIELHAUS

Producer: Herbert von Karajan — Stage designer: Günther Schneider-Siemssen — Costumes: Georges Wakhevitch — Conductor: Herbert von Karajan

Many people have a latent cosmic awareness. Those who do might look on the Salzburg *Ring* as a process of emergence, a path through cosmic space and time in lyrical or dramatic form.

Wagner's *Ring* comprises creative as well as natural elements. *Rheingold,* the prototype of our planet, is water; *Valkyrie* is fire and rock; *Siegfried* is living nature, *Götterdämmerung* is civilization, constructivism and decline.

Herbert von Karajan's and Günther Schneider-Siemssen's basic scenographic concept is the *Ring*-ellipse. It becomes, in the tetralogy, the symbolic and dramatic bearer of several functions, techniques and lighting methods. In *Rheingold* it appears in its original state. In *Valkyrie* it fuses, divides, dissolves and floats in space. In *Siegfried* it is overgrown by nature. And in *Götterdämmerung* it is a basic structural element. From the *Ring*-ellipse are developed, by the interaction of realistic and symbolic representations, all the necessary scenic and dramatic building blocks. The Salzburg presentation must be considered a visionary *Ring* in which every scene has its own shape predetermined by the music, and executed in light and projection.

All universal works have a special attraction for me— they answer my innermost urge to probe the cosmic realms. Since the Ring demands an extraordinary degree of imagination, technical mastery, ability to create symbol-bearing elements and to cope with sweeping visions—even from the stage designer—I consider this cycle one of the most tremendous tasks I have had to perform, and at the same time one of the greatest challenges.

Although Richard Wagner prescribes many things with extraordinary attention to detail, he nevertheless leaves a great deal to the imagination. For that very reason, I disapprove of the fairly common practice of cutting out difficult parts of his work. I try in such cases to deploy all my creative powers to come up with something in keeping with the contemporary mood, while satisfying Wagner's own demands.

This statement by Günther Schneider-Siemssen constitutes the foundation of all his subsequent work on the *Ring* concept. To determine his general approach to the four works of the cycle he invariably starts with *Götterdämmerung,* which combines all the leitmotivs of the three preceding works. He considers careful analysis of this opera a prerequisite for any attempt to create the necessary accents and relations and to cope with the extremely difficult technical transformations of the tetralogy.

'This mammoth work calls for a designer who—though he must have a pictorial sense and may even have visions—must be chiefly concerned with detailing developments. Otherwise he is bound to founder in the course of the four evenings.'

Because the size of the Salzburg stage favours the representation of infinite cosmic space, Günther Schneider-Siemssen chose a spacious yet severe set, with the *Ring*-ellipse as its symbolic and static expression—a set on which everything appeared governed by cosmic laws.

In this interpretation he attached the greatest importance to light and projection, translating most of the cosmic-elliptical and spiral forms of the structural elements into this medium of theatrical expression.

Lighting and spatial arrangements were adapted to the music and the characterization of the roles. The stage designer believes that individual scenes, and individual acts, must have spatial characteristics of their own.

Report by Wolfgang Haefeli
after an interview with Günther Schneider-Siemssen.

1974, KASSEL   OPERNHAUS

Producer: Ulrich Melchinger — Stage designer: Thomas Richter-Forgách — Costumes: Thomas Richter-Forgách — Conductor: James Lockhart

Our Kassel *Ring,* one of whose essential features was its break with the traditional unity of the tetralogy, certainly helped to change the tone of the Wagner debate that started after Wieland Wagner's death.

In the 1960s many scenographic abstractions of operas culminated in a marked allegorical transparency. The limits of their usefulness became obvious whenever the symbolic simplifications of an imposed aesthetics had no tangible correlates. It was in coping with Wagner's mythology that producers faced the great danger of introducing a 'timeless' factor—generally a euphemism for non-commitment. Mythologization usually went hand in hand with an effectively darkened stage.

We aimed instead at an up-to-date, critical reinterpretation guided by a sharpened historical consciousness. We accepted and gave scenic expression to Wagner's declared abhorrence of all 'domination based on capital, property and exploitation' and tried to advance, beyond the mythological facets that are undoubtedly present in the *Ring,* to a social problem that remains as topical today as when the work was written. It had to be presented with modern means of expression. Richard Wagner's socio-revolutionary attitudes had to be updated with the help of the trappings of modern industrial society. The mythological superstructure, the world of the gods and the giants, was transposed on to a modern plane and presented as Utopian fiction.

Our interpretation was not based on quotations of the master's sacrosanct dicta by his 'disciples' and eulogists but on Wagner's work itself, in which the world of the gods and heroes is shown to be as open to criticism, as questionable and as shabby as the world of the 'villains' Alberich, Mime and Hagen.

Our guideline was the need to demonstrate how these gods and demi-gods—conditioned by the realistic temptation of the gold, by the quest for the ring and for power—become increasingly human, increasingly petty and conventional, while the humans who try to become gods find that their efforts are just as unavailing. We considered the presentation of this decline and this apparent rise which was bound to end in disaster, the revelation of the mechanisms of permanent change, two of our most important tasks. The public could then safely be left to draw up its own balance-sheet.

As part of our basic approach, we tried to show that Wotan is not superior to Alberich. The equivalence of the leading protagonists—an iron law of the classical theatre—was achieved by deliberate emphasis of this dialectical principle both in the text and the music; we treated the leitmotiv as the context of the prose.

There are an astonishingly large number of detailed similarities between these two roles and a host of parallel developments. We carried the argument to extremes: we almost preferred Alberich and Hagen to Wotan. They are absolutely honest from the very start, saying exactly what they want. Wotan, by contrast, veils his ambitions. He quotes pseudo-legal principles and agreements, but uses illegal means to attain his ends, perverting justice and the very order for which he is responsible. Wotan is a hypocrite!

We thought it was essential to offer a consistent justification of the 'humour' by which *Siegfried* is treated as the comedy in the *Ring,* and which Bertold Brecht once defined as a manifestation of the dialectical consciousness.

Wagner was anxious to give spectators a chance to identify themselves with the characters in the *Ring.* That meant he had to evoke their sympathy and their laughter—the two go hand in hand. Because producers have for so long dwelled almost exclusively on the pathos of the *Ring,* people may be forgiven for thinking that it contains few situations likely to release liberating laughter. But these situations are plentiful. As an example, consider the great 'guessing scene' in *Siegfried,* Act I: Wotan—as the more intelligent man and the one who knows in advance how this 'game' will end—deals Mime a tremendous blow. At this point the laughter makes way for a reproachful attitude: Wotan's behaviour is shabby as well as funny; the cheap triumph of the strong over the weak. This negative trait turns the 'god' into a 'man', bringing him close to us. Were he to remain invested in 'divine' remoteness throughout the long work, our interest in him would be bound to flag. . . . .

It should be added that in his brilliant leitmotiv technique, Wagner developed a means of commenting on the dialogue and the plot that is clearly understood by the audience. When a sad plea by Wotan is accompanied by a leitmotiv that betrays his true thoughts, the spectators will often burst into laughter. The score contains such critical commentaries by the hundred, and it is upon them that I have based my own interpretation. They also make me think that the approach which makes our reading of the *Ring* so radically different from all previous interpretations is the right one. [Schaefer, 1974, p. 6.]

The precisely balanced dialogic and dialectical quality of the music demands a very precise style of presentation, one that responds with analytical clarity to its impulses.

This posed a crucial staging problem. Wagner takes his own time to illuminate the plot with his music. The sung dialogue proceeds much more slowly than it would if spoken. What we had to do, therefore, was to develop a form of expression that takes advantage of the disconcerting slowness, and with the aid of a host of gestures clarifies the complex links between scenery, dialogue and music as thoroughly as possible. [*Op.cit.,* p. 12.]

Another feature of our interpretation was the attempt to bring out the stylistic differences of the individual parts of the *Ring.* Our purpose was not, however, to provide an excuse for our own style which revealed, emphasized and even aggravated incongruities. What we aimed at was the construction of a contemporary 'picture', one suited to any particular scene, the better to provide the modern spectator with a vivid and convincing presentation of the *Ring* and all the 'men' and 'women' in it—if necessary at the cost of aesthetic unity.

The décor of our *Ring* presented an artificial and yet 'self-evident' world fit for gods and legendary figures. We designed it specifically to tell this tremendous saga convincingly to modern audiences. We made it visually obvious from the start which aspects of Wagner's work were prognostic, and hence as valid in this century as they would be in the future. To that end, we opened up scenic realms that brought this fictive future—about whose shape we can only guess—into play even now.

Wagner's stage directions were based pragmatically on the technological limitations of his day, and may therefore be freely translated into the vocabulary of the modern stage. This means, of course, that the producer's or designer's individual 'signature' is brought into play. Thomas Richter-Forgách and I do not claim that our achievements in the scenic and visual realms prove that we have found the philosopher's stone. [*Op.cit.*, p. 12.]

To give modern audiences a better understanding of the contents of the *Ring,* every effort was made to stress associative elements. Inconsistencies, ambiguities and anachronisms were pointed out. This syncretic approach allowed us to effect a fusion—or a surrealistic juxtaposition—of the most varied styles and planes of reality: early Germanic ornamentation, bourgeois-romantic realism, pan-Germanic monumentalism, surrealism, and all modern forms from op, pop and kinetic art to the most futuristic science fictions. [Grosse, 1976, p. 3.]

We chose this imaginative composition of trivial art forms for two reasons. First, these forms have become the intellectual property of the modern public. They also lessen the temptation to mythologize the material. Runes, twelfth-century objects, larger-than-life late nineteenth-century cast-iron figures, Albert Speer's 'School of the Nation' in saccharine postcard style, a Führer bunker from the Atlantic wall—these and similar elements were combined with the most modern machinery, the latest materials and science-fiction elements into a vast and chimeric figment of our imagination.

A computer circuit turns out to be the Norns' control room; Alberich's gold smithy proves to be a modern reactor centre. The tree in *Valkyrie* looks vitreous and transparent—it is shaped out of thermoplastic resin. The Manhattan skyline is constructed with gigantic multi-coloured sheets of Plexiglas; the furniture is plastic, and aluminium sheeting covers the entire floor. There are flying machines compounded, after some three hundred drawings, of motor-cycle, submarine or fish-like shapes; mobile bases for the robots; an armchair 3½ metres wide for Wotan which could have been designed by Walt Disney, and dozens of other prominent details.

The costumes with their appliqué machine parts and switchboards reminiscent of robots conformed to this artificial world.

Götterdämmerung ends in a collage reminiscent of Beckett. Two blind dotards grope their way across a gigantic rubbish dump, the midden of two cultures, those of the gods and of the bourgeoisie—or, if you like, across the ruins of all the symbols and relics of the entire *Ring*. These two dotards are Wotan and Alberich, two greedy and treacherous contenders for power, now helpless shadows of their former selves, still in search of the ring that will enable them to master a world long since decayed. A seedy, ignoble conclusion.

It may be that in ten years' time we would have to come up with quite different answers. *The Ring of the Nibelungs* is one of those masterpieces that can never be exhausted by any one interpretation. I believe, however, that our attempt has helped to shake off the yoke of tradition and prejudice. Even so, it cannot be emphasized enough that our interpretation was based on a strict analysis of the work itself. A wave of purely anti-traditional presentations that are based not on the work but on purely subjective theatrical ideas would merely cover up what our analysis and exegesis have tried to bring into the open. [Schaefer, 1974, p. 14.]

Compiled and adapted by Wolfgang Haefeli after a taped interview with Thomas Richter-Forgách, and after the interview between Hans Joachim Schaefer and Ulrich Melchinger which appeared in the Kassel programme.

1976, LEIPZIG   OPERNHAUS AM KARL-MARX-PLATZ

Producer: Joachim Herz — Stage designer: Rudolf Heinrich† — Costumes: Rudolf Heinrich† — Conductor: Gert Bahner

It took us more than four years to elaborate our general approach to the presentation of the *Ring* at the Leipzig Opera. As always with Rudolf Heinrich, we made no attempt to fix the final form of the presentation, and only asked: what is it all about, what is the story? In the summer of 1972 we worked for seven days from early morning till late at night to sketch out our basic concept of the entire cycle and to consider *Rheingold* and *Götterdämmerung* in greater detail. We were greatly helped both by the chief drama adviser of Leipzig—who forced us to engage in heated discussions by giving a running commentary to a description of the plot—and also by two contrasting recordings—only one of which had any real appeal for us.

Once again, it had not been easy to enlist Rudolf Heinrich's collaboration, and once again there was a fruitful tension. Shocked by an early theatrical experience with *Siegfried,* the designer proposed to take a critical stand not only towards the work but also towards the cult surrounding it.

We agreed that there was no need to force open doors: our potential audiences were not hamstrung by their political past, but would see our *Ring* with an open mind, anxious for new experiences. Our task was to decipher the work rather than to present it as an equivocal problem play. Our differences in attitude came to a head when we broached the characterization of Siegfried, but then John Weaving's performance provided a solution that satisfied us both. The critics said rightly that Weaving 'pulled down the hero without harming the man'. And the man was one whose unusual past and upbringing precluded him from coping with the objective circumstances of his life.

Though Wagner was, in fact, portraying the conflicts of typical groupings in his period, these conflicts disturb us even today. Wagner himself saw no concrete solution, but his finale, like that of the *Magic Flute,* is suffused with hope—albeit expressed more instrumentally.

Our basic principle was to reveal the timeless reality underlying Wagner's symbolic characters. We resolutely refused to construct visions of the future; mankind will have to cope with such visions suggested by the work, if it wants to have any kind of future at all.

We placed the figures based on myths squarely into Wagner's own time. Late nineteenth-century architecture, emblems, fashion and art determined the décor and the costumes—in particular the predilection for Nordic references by Wagner's contemporaries and their successors.

Our idea was to tell the story in so fantastic a way that Wagner's artistic speech, and the glosses provided by his music, could fit into it smoothly. The occasional clashes of voices and stage properties were deliberately introduced, not to shock, but to charm with their gay abandon. Alliteration and the alien world of the Nordic sagas served to express the conflicts of Wagner's age. Our task was not to tell the history of the nineteenth century but *a* history with nineteenth-century prototypes, characters who are still of interest today.

A prerequisite of this montage of history and myth was the exposure of the artifice of its production. That is why, even in *Rheingold* (1973), we placed the flood-lights on the stage and also showed the rising, sinking and circling movements of the stage machinery. The spectator had to realize that the theatrical world before him, compounded of history (image) and myth (language), was an absolutely artificial world. He had to relate that world to one that has become history but that nevertheless helped to shape his own situation. The elaboration of each of the four works constituting the *Ring*—based on intensive studies of Wagner's writings, sketches and drafts, of contemporary history and historical analyses—occurred during sev-

eral periods of strict seclusion, first in Leipzig and later, when we had built a model, in Munich.

Because of the shortage of stage hands, we exploited the technical equipment of the New Leipzig Opera to the limit and sometimes, with due explanation, even beyond.

In *Götterdämmerung* the skein spun by the Norns tears and drops down on them. No longer of use to anyone, the Norns are carted out together with the jumbled pile of their unsolved problems. The rocky cavern of Siegfried and Brünnhilde, with a bed of enormous proportions, reflects their encapsulation and the fact that Brünnhilde—now only Siegfried's wife—has abandoned her mission and forgotten why everything had to happen this way. Once the great gate is opened, the fire can be seen blazing in the far distance, just as it did during the Norn scene. Siegfried is shown voyaging down the Rhine. He is the phantom of the Messiah, the hope of the nation—a hope misplaced in one who has no inkling of what is happening in the world, or of why the people should long for a hero. He passes Gunther and Hagen, then the coldly gleaming 'control room' screened off with armour plating, and finally (at Gutrune's entrance with the potion) a delicate winter garden: a new world to which Siegfried succumbs.

For Act II Rudolf Heinrich constructed a dreamland setting for the masses, and for the ending of the conflict. The workshop of Gunther and Hagen was decorated for the wedding, and screened off once more with armour plating for the conspiracy, so effectively that Alberich, who blunders about in it like a belated guest, looks utterly amazed.

Our setting of the banks of the Rhine continued the thread from the theft of the Rhine gold to the dragon's cave in the forest: the water is black, nature violated by man's greed.

'Wer ist's des Gram so voll Emphase tönt'—this lament for the hero was written for Wotan, whose dream it was that a hero should change the world, who had nurtured the dream for two generations and must now carry it into his grave. Standing between the pylons of Valhalla (from *Rheingold*; see illustration), he greets the host of heroes who parade before him in his fevered imagination.

Gutrune's bridal couch becomes the catafalque of her slain husband. Burning torches screen Hagen, who is prepared to intervene up to the last moment and who is eventually forestalled by his own father. Alberich seizes the ring before Loge's fire can swallow it up; as in the other *Ring* performances, the fire is represented by dancers in fiery veils and by Loge's mask.

The hall disappears in the fire. The Rhinemaidens float down the river in the gondolas first seen in *Rheingold*; as they snatch the ring from Alberich, Valhalla suddenly comes into view and begins to burn. Hagen and his vassals are cast into the depths represented by a strobe-light effect, and Valhalla collapses. Men appear from the depths looking with bewilderment at an event whose meaning they are trying to guess. Around them is a white surface, a *tabula rasa*.

After the completion of the *Götterdämmerung* model, Rudolf Heinrich died. His brother designed the costumes in accordance with the sketches; his assistant supervised the translation of the model into the actual set. Many technical problems, particularly the immensely complicated finale, still remained to be solved and their solution had, of course, a profound influence on the quality of the final result. The solution was provided by the Leipzig technical staff and workshops with a drive and application that I can only call exemplary.

Joachim Herz

1976, LONDON   COVENT GARDEN

Producer: Götz Friedrich — Stage designer: Joseph Svoboda — Costumes: Ingrid Rosell — Conductor: Colin Davis

The new *Ring* presentation at Covent Garden opened in September 1974 with *Rheingold* and *Valkyrie*: *Siegfried* came a year later and the cycle was completed with *Götterdämmerung* in September 1976. The first technical discussions between Colin Davis and the producer were held in 1971. At the end of 1972 work was begun with Joseph Svoboda (scenery) and Ingrid Rosell (costumes and masks). The stage conception was based on the following ideas:

The *Ring* is Wagner's most comprehensive work, a product and a document of an entire epoch (much like Aeschylus' *Oresteia* or Shakespeare's royal dramas). Written and composed over a period of almost three decades of the nineteenth century, the cycle makes use of past experiences even while contemplating the future. It is not enough to conjure up the nineteenth century with nostalgia or to make the social contradictions of capitalism the sole and exclusive objects of a socio-critical presentation. The *Ring* is not only a late attempt to sum up the 'intelligence of the age' for the operatic stage, but also one of the most important artistic documents of the entire bourgeois era.

Because of its wealth of ideas and possible—often contradictory—interpretations it seems reasonable to suppose that the *Ring* was conceived for a musical stage. This means that the elaboration and quotation or rejection of ideological structures are not enough for a living performance. These structures must, of course, be studied as part of the preparatory work, and can help to cement mutual understanding.

We aimed at an autonomous theatrical creation, one that would bring all the known, problematical, questioned or fictitious elements into the open and turn them into a play. We hoped that our delight in Wagner's theatrical visions would be a spur to the invention of new, provoking and illuminating scenic representations in keeping with the original.

We believed the world portrayed in the *Ring* is that of the theatre. The fight over the ring and the gold is an intense struggle for power that topples the mighty. The theatre once more becomes the world: the world theatre of bourgeois parable. Mythology itself is not the object of the presentation; it is alienated or alienating material that helps one to shape the *Ring*.

The slice of history told in the *Ring* is best understood as a superposed series of fragments and climaxes of theatrical history. And because the *Ring* speaks of the power game in the language of bourgeois society—gold as the concentration of power, etc.—it must also choose the narrative form of the bourgeois theatre.

Further, both the pre- and post-bourgeois forms of the theatre must be represented. The apparently ideology-proof mystery play with the clear distinction between top, middle and bottom is *Das Rheingold*. The psychological drama in which the music takes over an essential, often unconscious, part of the narrative is *The Valkyrie*. This species of play was to culminate—without music—in the work of Strindberg. The fairy-tale as a black comedy in which nature reveals its alienation and finally explodes into the universe is *Siegfried*. The theatrical variant of Orwell's *1984* completed with Arrabelian intellectual barbarisms and yet, in its very decadence, sometimes endowed with the nobility of an Aeschylus tragedy, this is *Die Götterdämmerung*.

Our aim was an unmasking, a disclosure of the contrasts in the various parts of the work. The London *Ring* acknowledged the existence of *three distinct* works with a single prologue. The inherent contrasts of the work must be logically played out in the representation of the overriding legend, whose main protagonists change: from Wotan through Siegfried to Brünnhilde, always counterpointed by Alberich, Mime and Hagen.

We had to ask ourselves in what period the *Ring* is set. Our reply was: then and now. Wagner's 'then' always meant 'once upon a time' and 'in the future'. His 'now' was the time in which he wrote the work; our 'now' is the date of the performance. In other words, the *Ring* is set in no concrete period to be illustrated with historical examples, but reflects a charming system of overlapping time coordinates, of different historical and artistic spaces. In any case, 'artificial' time.

Das Rheingold is set at the time when Wotan begins to mistrust the 'social contract', symbolized by the runes in his spear, because the lowly Nibelungs, excluded from the agreements, now press their claims with force.

The Valkyrie is set at the time man first steps on to this world theatre, in the form of Hunding. He was treated unsympathetically for decades, probably because people felt that the divine order ought not to be questioned. This is a great misunderstanding, for it is precisely when it comes up against Fricka's plea for Hunding and bourgeois marriage that Wotan's conception of the hero as redeemer founders.

Siegfried is set at all times when persecuted or demented specialists (Mime) move their laboratories to the 'edge of the world'; when knowledge is perverted for the sake of gold and power; when man's lust for power turns him into 'a forest beast'.

Finally *Götterdämmerung* is set at five minutes to twelve—wherever and whenever the inevitable end is fast approaching. Evocations from the recent past (Wilhelminian Germany; Hitler's rule) would only serve to veil the burning actuality of the writing on the wall. The 'time of the action', however, includes tomorrow as well: this work is, above all, a caricature of a late civilization in which decadence surrounds itself with barbaric props and attitudes; a world in which the moving but flawed idol of a Siegfried founders just as surely as the élitist rebel Brünnhilde; a world that destroys the dream of freedom and is fit for nothing but destruction.

Where is the *Ring* set? Certainly not just in Scandinavia during the first millennium A.D., nor just in German lands during the last century. Nor is it set in any specific modern empire, or in outer space. But such speculations are not without their attraction, and so we might take them into account, saying that at its best, the *Ring* is set in the theatre. In our particular case, on the stage of Covent Garden.

It is an old-fashioned theatre with a rectangular aperture, with no side stages and a very small back stage. Its floor is a square consisting of five rostra that can be lowered to open the understage. We were grateful for the opportunity offered by this construction. The practical advantages were associated with a theoretical consideration: the circle, the ring, of all the *Ring* stages during the past few decades has been an emulation of the orchestra of classical tragedy, not a natural expression of the bourgeois theatre. In our view, a square stage is far more in keeping with the *Ring;* particularly when its advantages are fully exploited. By covering the square with boards we were 'quoting' the platform of the mimes, of comedy—the counterpoint to idealist tragedy.

This necessitated a primarily epic narrative approach for the London *Ring*—one that would elucidate and openly communicate with the spectator. The Covent Garden stage owes its astonishing versatility to the genius of engineers and technicians. A hydraulic piston holds and moves the platform in every conceivable direction: it rises and sinks, circles, and tilts at extreme angles. This piston was to us the concrete symbol of vast energy, the energy needed to support and to move this cosmic theatre.

This kinetic principle allowed us to dispense with most conventional décor; we could rely on effects produced with artificial simplicity.

Costumes and masks came fully into their own to play a large part in the visual dramaturgy. In *Rheingold,* the 'people of light'—the gods—appeared in the most varied shades of white; the 'people of night'—the Nibelungs—were in black. Erda was a shadowy figure rising up from the ground. The Rhinemaidens seemed vitreous in their sea of mirrors. The giants, like compliant trade unionists, wore bright overalls and a kind of space helmet, to show that Valhalla lies outside the earth. And the demigod Loge, played by a black tenor, wore a flaming red poncho over his white jeans.

In *Valkyrie* the fabrics ranged from the fur of the 'wolf child' Siegmund and the leather habit of Hunding to the armour-plated and braided uniform of Wotan and the macabre costumes of the Valkyries—in which they appear as combined Amazons, birds of death and sexually aggressive Barbarellas.

The *Siegfried* costumes of Mime, Alberich and the Wanderer have bestial attributes. The actors look like forest creatures, almost dehumanized by their lust for war. This caustic humour culminates in the ostentatious figure of the dragon, moved by twenty dancing extras.

The new characters introduced in *Götterdämmerung* are almost chic: Hagen and the vassals wear the black leather and dark skins of neo-barbarians.

The typical Wagnerian interchange of dramatic and epic structures must be driven home to the spectator by gestures. Stylized immobility now seems merely an excuse for a failure to grasp the meaning of Wagner's characters. They are theatrical forms as well as singing orchestras. The representational mode ranges from alienating gesticulation to emotional identification and the indication of basic attitudes by suggestion.

This variety is both supported and determined by the stylistic differences in the individual works of the cycle. *Rheingold* relies chiefly on epic representation, on revealing actions and attitudes, and repeatedly posts narrators on the forestage. *Valkyrie* relies on psychological identification, a style that can be used either with restraint or schizophrenic abandon. It has a disclosing effect of its own.

Exaggerated use of humour and malice—with lyrical interruptions—presides over the first two acts of *Siegfried*. The third again calls for a concentrated gesture which actions' can dissolve into vivid associations. Wotan is linked with Erda; Siegfried with Brünnhilde.

In *Götterdämmerung* there is a sense of horrible sterility, a caustic satire on grand opera (Act II), a bizarre barbarism coupled to quiet melancholy. The result is a frightening and oppressive end-game atmosphere.

There is no need to dwell on the fact that the producer and his team tried to respect and make full use of the specific and clearly enunciated narrative function of the orchestra. This was and remains one of our most essential duties. Nothing we did is finished; we make corrections year after year. The great adventure of this universal theatre is infinite, not to be marred with modish short-cuts. These, then, were the ideas upon which we based our work with the *Ring*. What follows is a discussion of the work itself.

Rheingold was played without a curtain before a bright cyclorama. As the audience entered, they could see the crucial feature of this performance: a stage covered with boards, the platform of the mimes. It would later rise and fall, circle and halt, respecting the square ground plan even when poised at the steepest slants. It was in this last position that the boards unfolded horizontally to form stairs for the entrance of Erda and the road to Valhalla.

This type of stage does not need the reinforcement of additional décor. We placed sizable scenic elements only on the understage: mirrors for the Rhine scene; red-hot iron sections for Nibelheim; and a tube made of optical glass for Alberich's 'control centre'. The underside of the movable platform was mirrored and, when the stage was tilted and the flaps unfolded, this mirror reflected everything that happened on the Rhine and in Nibelheim.

Our aim was to set off the symphonic passages, which describe natural events, from verbal exchanges between the players. The symphonic passages were always played without a curtain. We projected laser films, specially made [by Siemens] in Erlangen, on to the cyclorama: they depicted elementary nature, its laws and cosmic 'trips'. The dramatic scenes were interrupted and bridged by movements of the platform and by laser films.

To emphasize their stereotyped and pre-human qualities, all the actors wore masks, dominoes, or the exaggerated facial make-up we know from primitive cultures. The soloists were joined by forty children: the army of the Nibelungs, and doubles for the Rhine-daughters, Alberich, Wotan and Loge.

The Valkyrie was played before a dark cyclorama. The boards on the platform have been replaced with a dark red cloth: the earth has been blood-soaked ever since Wotan ordered his Valkyries to unleash a war. The platform was tilted to more extreme positions than in *Rheingold*: geographical 'order' had made way for disorder and chaos. Agitation and fear, horror and death escalate. In emulation of the bourgeois drama, properties were now added to the stage, admittedly only a few, but all on a monumental scale. In Act I we used a tree, a table and a stove; in Act II, two pieces of rock; in Act III, the Valkyries' rock which was a launching pad for the Valkyries' journeys to and from Valhalla.

With laser effects we tried to meet Wagner's wish that, during the entrances or exits of the gods in Acts II and III, the sky should darken, thunder and lightning should strike, and a 'fire glow' should blaze up. These were to be signs that Valhalla had moved far from the earth, that it had become a kind of skylab of the mighty, whence Wotan, longing for death, is impelled towards the earth time and again.

A dark curtain falls between the acts. When he re-enters the house the spectator is once again shown the open stage, this time with a steeply tilted platform. As the music begins, the platform starts to pitch and toss. Amidst flashes of lightning people pursue one another across it: a man-hunt, a persecution. Then, quickly, from a few pieces of scenery, a shelter for the fugitive rises up—Hunding's hut.

Siegmund, Sieglinde and Hunding are 'normally' made-up. The gods, too, have lost their mask-like appearance. Only Fricka carries her *Rheingold* mask, as if refusing to acknowledge the tremendous, world-shaking leap between the two works. Wotan has been 'psychologized'; the greatest character of the cycle, the one whose character is least defined, appears as a tragi-comic cross of Lear and Strindberg's General. The Valkyries, products of Wotan's delusion, wear silvery make-up and red lips: they are blood-sucking, troubling and seductive angels of death.

Siegfried: During the first season we used a 'string cyclorama' resembling the one Joseph Svoboda had developed for his Bayreuth *Tristan*. We subsequently decided in favour of the dark, yet more light-receptive, cyclorama we had used for *The Valkyrie*. The underside of the stage platform was covered with a silvery wire mesh. Under the projection used in the first two acts it was luminous, but in Act III, when seen against the brightly lit cyclorama, it conveyed the cool atmosphere of the 'psychological laboratory' in which the final scenes were played out.

The dense, gloomy forest made way for a bright emptiness; here nature is a vulnerable dramatic element. The forest was simulated in the first two acts by a great number of strips of synthetic material. They also constituted the 'curtain' before every act. They did not behave as passive decorations, but could respond to the movements of the actors and of the platform. Thus the dominant visual element was transformed into a participant in the action. We found this a theatrically attractive process and one, moreover, which affirms that nature has ceased to be a romantic ideal; nature has become serviceable, vulnerable to men and their political interests.

The forest is indeed injured and manipulated in many ways. 'At the edge of the world', Mime builds his smithy; he proposes to forge the sword for Siegfried. The mechanical bowels of this smithy were attached to the understage—reminders of Nibelheim. The forest above served as camouflage.

In Act II synthetic strips marked the path along which the monstrous dragon Fafner heaves himself to the source. Meanwhile the Nibelung, Alberich, waits on the understage for some swaggering knight who might kill the greedy monster, a symptom of the fundamental law of capitalist accumulation.

The platform, fixed in just one position during Act I, took four positions in Act II. It began to teeter as soon as Siegfried engaged the dragon in mortal battle. Thereafter, the front edge flaps opened so that the fight between Mime and Alberich could be played like a clowning scene on a raised-up rostrum of the understage. When Siegfried rolled the dead dragon back into the cave, the platform returned to the position it occupied at the beginning of Act II. The movements of the stage invariably set off changes in the strip 'forest'.

The events portrayed in Act III were epically highlighted by five positions. The Wanderer waits on a steeply down-tilted slope. Then the platform tilted up: Wotan appears below and so does Erda, in a confusion of strips beside the hydraulic piston. Then the platform returned to almost the same tilt with which the Act had opened and the Wanderer meets Siegfried. Siegfried's path to the Valkyries' rock leads him across the sharply tipping platform and through the understage which, by reflection, multiplies the passage through the fire. For the last scene the platform rose straight out of the Valkyries' rock.

Every act began (as in *The Valkyrie*) without a curtain. Between and behind the strips appeared the three who wait motionlessly, everlastingly. Mime waits for the moment when Siegfried will be strong enough to play his allotted role. Alberich waits for the hero whom, like his brother, he can use and then deceive and destroy. And in Act II the Wanderer waits for the one who slew the dragon.

Waiting is the basic attitude of the prologues but, in contrast to *Parsifal,* it is a waiting for a doomed redemption. The basic situations reflect the difficulties inherent in the creation of heroes.

We should not fear that Siegfried will be considered a Nazi idol. He, better than any other figure, demonstrates the vanity of all ideologies; a champion—compounded of Punch, 'Unlucky Jack', Tolstoyan peasant and Caucasian Mohammed Ali—who runs amok in pursuit of absolute individual freedom. His fate is to be destroyed by a world that, even while collapsing, still has the terrible strength to turn revolutionaries and rebels into mere 'characters'. The pain of the funeral march in *Götterdämmerung* is our own.

Götterdämmerung develops the legendary and visual material of the preceding parts of the cycle, completes it with new elements and finally leads up to a conclusion that poses the problem of a new beginning. At the end the platform reaches the same position it occupied at the beginning of *Rheingold*—an offer of a new play, an invitation to new inventions in the 'world theatre'.

The steeply down-tilted platform provided the audience on entering with a view of something like a 'world wall' or a 'wailing wall'. As the orchestra began to play, the front edge rose for the Norn scene, clearly differentiated from the Valkyries' rock. The position and material of the set created a parallel with Erda's entry in *Siegfried:* the Norns rising from the understage were mirrored in the undersurface of the tilted platform; the 'rope' was tied to the hydraulic piston in the middle by a confusion of other strips, ropes and wires—an archaic computer system through which the Norns grope, when the rope snaps, before finally sinking down.

The Valkyries' rock was the same one used in the last scene of *Siegfried*. The cyclorama darkens when Siegfried takes his leave. Brünnhilde breaks down in despair when he rushes off.

We used no curtain during the Rhine journey. The tone of the scherzo suggested an apparently naive picture: we projected water on to the tilted platform, creating 'Rhine' and boat together. Siegfried appeared on the rear edge with a large oar, then stepped boldly forward; this was the last pretence of wholeness by one who had set out to learn fear, only to lose his identity in the world of the Gibichungs.

For the 'hall', the platform returned to a normal stage surface while various large sections of optical glass were flown in. These archaic bits of architecture gave a glassy effect reminiscent of the Manhattan sky-line. Behind the lenses the figures were distorted: they grew and shrank, and often seemed to be standing on their heads. The result was total confusion, the most terrifying human alienation; as soon as Siegfried entered, he, too, was distorted.

At the end of the Gibichung scene Hagen sat down on the forestage to keep watch. He remained in full view of the audience when the open stage changed back into the Valkyries' rock, when Waltraute came to Brünnhilde (here we quoted the 'airborne steeds' from *Valkyrie* with laser beams) and when Siegfried entered in Gunther's form. Siegfried had once awakened the sleeper with his kiss; he now made her suffer the deepest humiliation. All this took place as if it were manipulated in Hagen's brain.

Throughout Act II the platform—with additional stairs—remained in a fixed, tilted position. The variable glass scenery and critical lighting made it possible to use and develop scenic montage, emphasizing the transformation of external action into internal process. The grand-opera tableau was meant to convey a large-scale projection of the alienation of individual destinies.

Alberich rose up from the understage to meet Hagen, who was still on the forestage, as in Act I. The rear of the stage remained in darkness. Siegfried appeared behind a lens as if by magic; with the aid of the Tarn helmet he had hurried ahead of Brünnhilde and Gunther. When Hagen called up the vassals, the whole stage suddenly lit up. The forestage remained the plane of epic representation and fragmentation: for Hagen's grim parody of religion; and for Brünnhilde's cry, 'Holy gods, ye heavenly rulers'. A shaft of light on the darkening stage showed up the trio as the reflection of an inner process until, with the last sound of the voices, bright light suddenly flooded the stage once more, revealing men, women and priests assembled for the wedding procession. Wagner's principle of sudden explosions from inner into outer reality was varied by us in the manner of the finales to Acts I and II of *Tristan and Isolde*.

III,1: The platform was in the same position it had occupied during the Rhine scene at the beginning of *Rheingold*. The ageing Rhinedaughters were repeatedly mirrored by the lower edge of the platform and by the reinforced metal foil on which they were frolicking. Our Rhine was 'polluted'; all living matter seemed to have vanished from this 'aquarium'. Siegfried appeared on the front flap of the unfolded platform and then moved down to the forestage.

III,2: As the horns were sounded, the stage changed into the basic position of Siegfried, Act II. The forest of strips had formed huge encrustations, four mighty trunks symbolizing Siegfried's imprisonment. The place in which he now told his story was the same as that in which he had tried to probe into his dark origins in Act II. Everyone had left the stage after his murder. No one raised him up. No man or god came near him. Slowly, the tree-trunks lifted into the air. On an empty stage lay the lonely corpse. Criticism of those who had tried to make him a hero or victim was balanced by sentimental compassion. Instead: *Ecce homo*.

At the end of the funeral march, the glassy architecture descended to transport the corpse into the world of the Gibichungs. ('You see my son, here time makes way for space,' says Gurnemanz to Parsifal.) For a time the dead man remained hidden from Brünnhilde and Guthrun, who were stumbling through glass walls. Only when

Hagen sings, 'T'is a boar's ill-fated victim', does Siegfried's body become visible.

When Brünnhilde lit the wood-pile—spot-lights and metal foil—the fleeing men and women strayed, in the reflected light of the fire, through the glassy cage of their burning civilization. Brünnhilde mistook one of the fleeing shadows for her horse Grane. It was Hagen, searching for his spear. Rigid and helpless he suffered Brünnhilde's endearments, which were for Grane. When his reaction finally came, it was too late—Brünnhilde had surrendered herself to the fire.

Our portrayal of the last stages of the ruin was in fairly close agreement with Wagner's stage instructions: 'The men and women press to the front in terror... as the whole space of the stage seems filled with fire.' No one remained; everyone had fled. The platform was set into violent motion. The lenses and other pieces of glass vanished; the world of the Gibichungs became Nothing. The Rhinedaughters appeared. Water projections chased across the platform. Hagen plummeted from the upper edge into the understage. The Rhinemaidens (doubled by children after they have regained the ring) danced gaily across the stage.

On the cyclorama Valhalla appeared with seated gods, heroes and Valkyries. We used a montage of film sequences and of still and moving projections. Alberich stepped on to the forestage. He watched the fires consume Valhalla and the gods, and disappeared into the wings as soon as the last motif was sounded. The platform returned to the position with which we opened the cycle.

The cycle was completed.

Translation of an adapted version by the author: Götz Friedrich, 1976

1976, MUNICH   BAYERISCHE STAATSOPER

Producer: Günther Rennert — Stage designer: Jan Brazda — Costumes: Jan Brazda — Conductor: Wolfgang Sawallisch

After a long era of predilection for philosophical drama at New-Bayreuth, the Wagner stage has recently developed in the opposite direction. The designer and the producer have come to attach increasing importance to concrete facts—though admittedly, with the aim of reshaping the *Ring* into a social parable. A case in point was *The Perfect Wagnerite*, Bernard Shaw's socialist *Ring* interpretation of 1898. We started from quite different premises:

First, the socialist parable does not work because its real hero Siegfried turns out to be a failure. I take a completely negative view of Siegfried. He is not the 'new man' with whom Wotan intended to oust the aristocracy of the gods. Siegfried does not translate Wotan's nature into the essence of a free humanity; he drifts into anarchy, as do most socio-romantic idealists. It was not until *Parsifal* that the new man attained the ethical power needed to redeem the world through compassion.

We also believed that all deliberately modernizing, sociological interpretations ignore the mythological dimension of Wagner's music, or at best degrade the music into some arbitrary medium of contrast.

To me the *Ring* is primarily a musical cosmos. Its dramaturgy is developed in accordance with musical laws, and its conflicts and similes are primarily the visions of a musician—even the libretto was written for primarily musical reasons. In the words of Thomas Mann, it is a case of 'seeing with the ears, hearing with the eyes'.

The *Ring* is governed by the 'principle of interdependence', the basic tension between man and woman or, more simply, by Wotan's and Siegfried's failure in love. In our interpretation of these two figures we tried to show that their selfish lust for life is such that they do not shrink from any misdeed, thus preventing the advent of a freedom rooted in ethics. In Siegfried's unbounded individuality, the 1848 socio-romantic Utopia of a 'free, happy man' is consistently converted into its opposite, into anarchy and inhumanity. The highly personalized basic tension between man and woman (Wotan-Erda; Siegfried-Brünnhilde) is the starting-point of all the complex conflicts portrayed in the *Ring*.

In this way I affirmed the current tendency to express the action in concrete form and to show that it is the result of intense psychological conflicts. Wagner's stage directions contain much that is psychologically apt, and one ought to take him strictly at his word. To my mind the realism so much in vogue among Wagnerians ought to be expressed in the psychological realm. We ought to find associations with individuals, not solely or primarily with social conflicts. For the rest, it can be left to the spectator to associate social conflicts with the individual conflicts we present on the stage.

On another level I took pains to include the irrational mythological events underlying the real action. This symbolic dimension is best expressed on the stage by the presentation of certain scenes, in contrast to others, in a wide-angle perspective. For instance, in *Valkyrie*, Act I: a typical bourgeois interior unfolds into the cosmos; and in Act II: Wotan's intervention explodes the natural space. The justification for such changes of perspective is Wagner's mythological fusion of dramatic narrative with lyrical preludes and epilogues.

Similar principles apply to the appearance of the stage. We deliberately used the techniques of the contemporary illusionist theatre. The real playing areas—the hut, the ash-tree, the mountain pass and Brünnhilde's rock—were suggested cryptically, concisely and stylized like formulae. At the same time we introduced unreal, constantly changing arenas corresponding to the dynamic mood-changes of the music: they were deliberately made to look ambiguous, intricate and disguised. To achieve this effect we used a number of novel projection mechanisms. I tried in this way to render visible the continuous evolutionary developments corresponding to Wagner's world of sound. I am fully aware of, and welcome, the fact that everyone understands something different by this term.

Günther Rennert

1976, BAYREUTH   FESTSPIELHAUS

Producer: Patrice Chéreau — Stage designer: Richard Peduzzi — Costumes: Jacques Schmidt — Conductor: Pierre Boulez

These photographs are of *Götterdämmerung,* the fourth part of the *Ring,* which I produced in Bayreuth in 1976. The pictures are mean-

ingful only if considered in conjunction with the earlier ones. Our presentation was a deliberately anachronistic mixture of mythology and nineteenth-century ideology. We tried to highlight the deep contradictions of the work. *Götterdämmerung,* the end of the cycle, represents a more fictional and at the same time more modern world than the rest, a world in which the myth no longer holds sway and in which the mythological characters, Siegfried and Brünnhilde, are lost in the world of men.

Patrice Chéreau

Bayreuth, 1976   Chéreau/Peduzzi

Munich, 1976   Rennert/Brazda

Kassel, 1974   Melchinger/Richter-Forgách

Götterdämmerung

'*The Hall of the Gibichungs on the Rhine. This is quite open at the back. The background itself presents an open shore as far as the river; rocky heights enclose the shore.*'

London, 1976   Friedrich/Svoboda

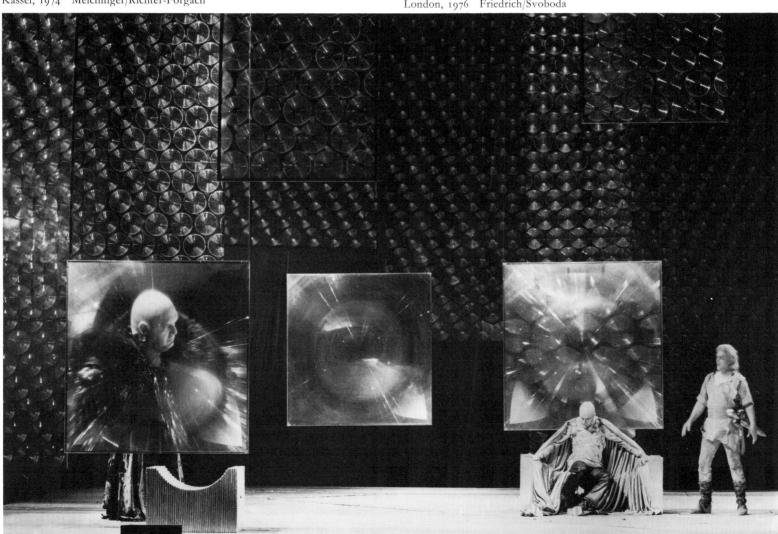

Leipzig, 1976   Herz/Heinrich

Bayreuth, 1965   Wieland Wagner

Salzburg, 1970   Karajan/Schneider-Siemssen

193

Götterdämmerung

'*The Rock.*'

Munich, 1976   Rennert/Brazda

Bayreuth, 1976   Chéreau/Peduzzi

Kassel, 1974   Melchinger/Richter-Forgách

Leipzig, 1976   Herz/Heinrich

Salzburg, 1970   Karajan/Schneider-Siemssen

London, 1976   Friedrich/Svoboda

Götterdämmerung

'*An open space on the shore in front of the Gibichungs'
hall: on the right the open entrance to the hall, on the left the
bank of the Rhine, from which, slanting across the stage to
the back, rises a rocky height cut by several mountain paths.
There Fricka's altar-stone is visible: higher up is a larger
one for Wotan and on the side is another for Donner.*'

London, 1976   Friedrich/Svoboda

Leipzig, 1976   Herz/Heinrich

Bayreuth, 1976   Chéreau/Peduzzi

Kassel, 1974   Melchinger/Richter-Forgách

Munich, 1976   Rennert/Brazda

Bayreuth, 1965   Wieland Wagner

Salzburg, 1970   Karajan/Schneider-Siemssen

197

Götterdämmerung

'A wild, woody and rocky valley on the Rhine, which flows past a steep cliff in the background.'

London, 1976   Friedrich/Svoboda

Leipzig, 1976   Herz/Heinrich

Kassel, 1974   Melchinger/Richter-Forgách

Bayreuth, 1976   Chéreau/Peduzzi

Salzburg, 1970   Karajan/Schneider-Siemssen

Bayreuth, 1965   Wieland Wagner

Les Contes d'Hoffmann *(The Tales of Hoffmann)*

What a gift for producers and stage designers! In these loosely assembled scenes, the theatrical imagination can be given full rein, to revel in the sheer joy of play-acting, strange events and bizarre characters. There is nothing in the least 'edifying' about this opera; it is pure theatre and, as such, a dramatic challenge.

The French playwright, Jules Barbier, wrote the libretto based on his own play, *Les Contes d'Hoffmann,* first published in 1851. The main character is the German poet, E.T.A. Hoffmann, acting out his own tales which, in rambling sequence, recall his unrequited love for a celebrated opera star in a series of grotesque scenes. The very titles of the short stories from which the individual scenes were derived are capable of thrilling the dramatic imagination: 'Fantasie-Stücke in Callots Manier' (Fantasies after Callot); 'Nachtstücke in Callots Manier' (Nocturnes after Callot); 'Abenteuer der Silvester-nacht' (Adventures on New Year's Eve); and 'Die Serapionsbrüder' (The Serapion Brethren). Hoffmann was a romantic and a strange mixture—painter, musician, poet and Prussian judge all rolled into one—and the theatre held him enthralled. For almost seven years he was *Kapellmeister* in baroque Bamberg, composing, conducting, designing theatres and, as if that were not enough, producing a large number of paintings and drawings. His rooms in the narrow house facing the theatre were as strange as his predilection for the tower of Altenburg Castle, high above the rooftops of the town. It was in these romantic surroundings that his opera, *Aurora,* was first performed, and the basic ideas for his *Undine* were born.

The series of episodes in Hoffmann's life, as dramatized by Barbier, fascinated the composer Jacques Offenbach who had previously created the style of the French operetta and was known for his caustic musical wit. It is not at all clear whether Offenbach wrote this tragic opera to fulfil a secret, life-long ambition to enter the ranks of 'serious' composers; in any case Offenbach did not live to see its première. It took place in 1881 in the Opéra-Comique in Paris, and the stage presentation was inconsistent. The original arbitrary scene-shifts, cuts and additions were, however, retained for a long time, the public responding warily to the ambiguous result, so that the opera failed to make an impact. Gradually the confusion was remedied, and, in its more comprehensible form, partly based on Hoffmann's own legacy, and, of course, with Offenbach's music, applauded from the start, the work has had a lasting success.

At the première Offenbach intended to have the four feminine roles played by a single singer. The soprano, Adèle Isaac, seems to have possessed the right vocal range, though the entire second act had to be omitted. To achieve the best artistic effect it is probably better to use four different artists, rather than to overstretch the vocal powers of one singer. The part of Stella, the heroine, requires powerful acting abilities. The close resemblance of the four characters to one another, which is essential to the clear exposition of the plot, can be achieved convincingly with the help of wigs, pieces of jewelry, ribbons or the like. As for the male roles, the same singer can be used in the different scenes without difficulty. The stage must reflect the fictional and improvised character of the successive tales, and, if possible, present them in sharp contrast to the real world of Lutter's tavern in the prologue and epilogue. The over-romantic, sentimental finale with the entrance of the Muse is usually omitted—to the advantage of the work as a whole.

The shift from the real world to the intoxicated day-dreams of the poet calls for an appropriate scenic response. Projections through layers of veils, and the optimum use of lighting equipment greatly facilitate this task. In Act II, with the famous Barcarole, the waters of Venice must sparkle and reflect the light, mysteriously beckoning like Giulietta, spectrally sombre like the adventurous figure of Dapertutto. The other two acts pose equally stimulating problems, but it is essential not to allow the stage effects to run away with themselves, and to observe strictly all matters of form. The temptations of scenic invention once even ensnared the great Max Reinhardt, whose Berlin *Hoffmann* overflowed into a romantic super-revue lasting four hours and yet proved a flop.

Jacques Offenbach was in perfect control of the balance of his stage creations, as his one-act works and operettas prove so convincingly. It is regrettable that, in this case, he was no longer able to do what had always been his custom: to attend the rehearsals and to intervene whenever it seemed necessary. His inspired score has earned him immortal fame and the clarity of its exposition should be the producer's guide with restrained fantasy as his motto.

Rudolf Hartmann

Scenes

Prologue	In Lutter's tavern.
Act I	In Spalanzani's physical cabinet. Performing dolls are standing about. A feast is being prepared.
Act II	In Giulietta's palace in Venice. View of the lagoon in moonlight.
Act III	Simple room in Crespel's house.
Epilogue	In Lutter's tavern, as in the Prologue.

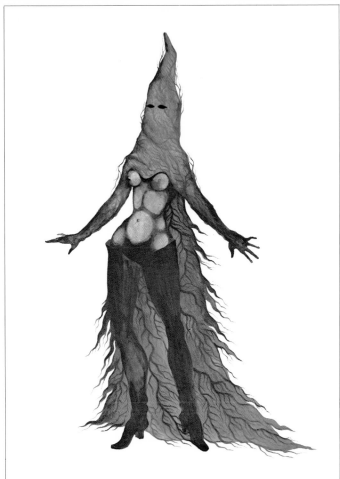

Costume designs,
Pet Halmen,
Düsseldorf, 1969

201

1969, DÜSSELDORF   DEUTSCHE OPER AM RHEIN

Producer: Bohumil Herlischka — Stage designer: Hermann Soherr — Costumes: Pet Halmen — Conductor: Günther Wich

Lutter's tavern, the visual framework of the *Tales,* lends a demonic tone to the whole work: a tall, spare 'backstage' room with an iron door and gallery, a grotesquely overladen table in the centre; the traditional cellars deliberately omitted.

The mysterious non-reality of a world of robots characterizes the Olympia scene. The stage is dominated by a black bellows of an oversize folding camera with laminae of various materials, terminating in a gigantic lens just where Olympia is standing. The bellows was also conceived as a bit of street theatre; the entire structure revolved around a central axis and was equipped with farcical wheels, cogs, cranks and transmission belts. Its exaggerated mobility had an irritating effect: it made nonsense of the scenic space.

Giuletta's world is shown to be in the process of moral decay: the miasma rises up tangibly from the canals. Polyhedral, dark, rotting, corroded, mobile towers surround the playing area with a shiny translucence. At a height of some four metres they are crowned with exaggerated elements of Venetian design: architectural features; dingy mouldings; figures.

Movable *barocchetto* props with proliferating ornamentations in large glass spheres (diameter 2.5 metres) stand on the floor like so many air bubbles in the mud of the lagoon.

The Antonia story is played out in a transparent, colourless room, visible only in outline, and with a high narrow rake that runs to the back in perspective. The only furniture standing on its black parquet floor is a pianoforte. Bare willow branches with innumerable candles convey the shadowy impression of a cemetery—a symbol of approaching death. When the 'voice of Antonia's mother' is heard, an overburdened catafalque looms into sight at the far end of the rake.

Hermann Soherr

1971, PRAGUE   NÁRODNÍ DIVADLO, TYLOVO DIVADLO

Producer: Ladislav Štros — Stage designer: Ladislav Štros — Costumes: Marcel Pokorný — Conductor: Hans Hus Tichy

I staged this operatic fantasy first in Prague, and three years later in Karlsruhe.

It captured my imagination as had no other work: most of its scenes are set in an unreal, barely comprehensible world, a world without standards, without a beginning or an end. The opera placed no limit on our inventiveness: it challenged our imagination to the extreme and perhaps overstretched it.

In Prague as in Karlsruhe I combined the roles of Nicklausse and the Muse, as joint attributes of the poet. I also wrote a prologue for the Muse, so that the epilogue no longer appeared as an unwarranted 'appendix' to the work.

Hoffmann has dreams and spins fantasies. As if in a delirium, he relives the events of his unhappy love life, which follows him into the brutal reality of Lutter's tavern. The figures of his day-dream dance past him, each as incomprehensible as the world in which it lives. Hoffmann is unable to capture love, it eludes him time and again, as it will ultimately in the real world as well.

This interpretation called for unusually fast entrances and scene-shifts, and I felt that I could best meet these demands in a 'black theatre'—a stage lined completely in black.

In the foreground, this setting was surrounded by a constant frame—in the style of an old suburban café. It served as a bridge between prologue and epilogue, and brought the 'reality' of the tavern home to the audience throughout the performance.

The scenery for the various tales was created with very few drops, representing real and imaginary subjects; and with just a few essential properties that impeded the actors no more than the opera itself sets limits to the interpreters' imagination.

Ladislav Štros

1973, WUPPERTAL   STÄDTISCHE BÜHNEN

Producer: Kurt Horres — Stage designer: Jürgen Dreier — Costumes: Edith Biskup — Conductor: Janoš Kulka

The task of producing Offenbach's *Hoffmann* stimulates, disturbs, and reveals interpretative difficulties. One does well to recall Heinrich Heine's view of E.T.A. Hoffmann: '... all nature now seemed an uneven mirror in which, distorted a thousandfold, he could behold nothing but his death mask. His works are nothing less than a hideous scream of terror in twenty volumes.'

I am fascinated by this individual's desperate longing for fulfilment in love, his enslavement to blind fate; by this genius—for that is how I see him—wrestling for his life, delivered over to passions that cannot always be recaptured.

In our production we tried to eliminate personal prejudice and all preconceived optical ideas. We read each other the libretto in turn, and discovered very quickly that the stage presentation must evolve on two levels. On the tangible world of Lutter's tavern; and the surrealist dream world of Antonia, Giuletta and Olympia.

I was chiefly interested—and so, incidentally, was Jürgen Dreier—in the surrealist world of Hoffmann's day-dreams. I proposed a special study of Paul Delvaux, the Belgian artist whose style is akin to my own. Many of his paintings depict a lonely man walking through the countryside, who attracts curious looks wherever he goes. He returns the glances, but one has the impression that he is not really looking. To my mind, this man is the image of Hoffmann.

Jürgen Dreier and I told the story as if it were a surrealist death dance, for which purpose he quoted surrealist elements with a bearing on the action.

My production was about an 'Orpheus'—Hoffmann, a poet in a state of irate resignation. His tales became a drama, the lament of a rejected lover, a brilliant outsider, a great individualist out of his depths. Like a stroke of lightning, Offenbach's music leaps to complement these visions.

It is a work about spoken silence, full of the loneliness endured by a dauntless, talented man; I find it beautiful and distressing all at once.

Kurt Horres

A marked personal affinity with the romanticism of the early nineteenth century and with the poet Jean Paul were essential factors in my concern with the theme and author of this work.

Moreover, the fine intelligence of Offenbach's music—which, though distinct, is nevertheless in tune with the web of E.T.A. Hoffmann's tales—demands the loving attention to detail that I have always found to be most stimulating.

For that reason, however, the dramatic events must be clarified by optical simplification. Surrender to a wild fantasy world would do justice neither to the music nor to the narrative of this extraordinary work. Here the slogan, 'Art is precision', must be unreservedly applied.

'Magical realism' was the hallmark of our interpretation. It implies the consistent implementation of precise ideas, the construction of a coherent vocabulary, and close adherence to its rules.

Kurt Horres and I began to imagine ourselves in Hoffmann's world, one more precise and autonomous than reality: it is bright, vigilant and thoroughly planned.

Our conception involved the portrayal of two distinct levels of reality. The first is the realistic and tangible world of Hoffmann, set in an artist's bar shown in relief, in which the customers are jammed tightly together and the walls covered up to the ceiling with countless photographs of artists, theatres, ensembles and play-bills. The scenes set here were depicted in the narrative style of film realism.

The second level is the magical dream world, the place of the surreal and sometimes incomprehensible. Despite its insubstantiality, it is full of particularly intense impressions.

The 'Olympia' scene is set in a dark red studio, built in relief and floating in a dream landscape. It has a glass roof and an iron framework reminiscent of early factory buildings.

The 'Antonia' scene is set between two tall, violet, disc-like walls that seem to compress the events. The set is open to the rear: a dream-landscape peers in. There are strange doors that might have been borrowed from a conservatory or a gloomy concert hall. A shrouded chandelier on the ceiling and a spinet resembling a coffin create an oppressive atmosphere.

In the 'Giuletta' scene the landscape is one of petrified waves, the stage a petrified sea. Above it two façades with luminous glass windows are ominously suspended and there are two projections reminiscent of early railway-station architecture. The dream has turned into a nightmare.

The awakening in the dim of the closing tavern scene leads back into fatal realism: it is worse than the worst dreams that preceded it.

Jürgen Dreier

1974, SYDNEY   SYDNEY OPERA HOUSE

Producer: Tito Capobianco — Stage designer: José Varona — Costumes: José Varona — Conductor: Richard Bonynge

The Tales of Hoffmann is an extremely powerful opera. Though its

music is perhaps rather uneven, it contains dramatic elements of sufficient force to stimulate the producer to 'flights of fancy', and to exercise a substantial influence on the production.

The composer and librettist themselves call for a 'fantastic', eerie and oppressive atmosphere for Hoffmann's three love affairs.

Surrealistically, almost farcically, the events pass Hoffmann by; he is powerless, unable to alter his fate. As one 'great love' after another slips out of his grasp, he is left to face the pains of a miserable reality.

It was clear to us from the outset that we had to treat *The Tales of Hoffmann* not as a recounting of real events, but as the product of a twisted mind. Using a form of film flash-back technique, we turned Hoffmann's three adventures in love into an extravaganza of sorts. With due respect for the composer and librettist, we tried above all to address a contemporary audience, to acquaint them with an intelligible version of the work.

Tito Capobianco

I have designed three productions of *The Tales of Hoffmann* in three different countries. This opera so appeals to me that I could happily start a fourth one as if it were a new piece. *The Tales of Hoffmann* is, as far as I am concerned, a true masterpiece. Unfortunately it has been categorized as a blown-up operetta by a superficial composer, a work that cannot be considered grand opera in its real sense. But though its music does have a few light touches here and there, it breathes profound inspiration. Was not Brahms in awe of Johann Strauss as a musician?

It is neither the music nor the story that makes *Hoffmann* a masterpiece. It deserves that title as total piece of theatre, albeit it is unfinished and more patchy than any other opera I can think of in the standard repertoire. Considering the period in which it was created it is a very unusual work. *The Tales of Hoffmann* contains such a wealth of modern ideas that it is more relevant today than it

was in the nineteenth century. It was never properly appreciated in its own time, and musical and stage authorities have underestimated this opera ever since.

Now, a hundred years later, its values are evident. Let us consider the possibilities that this piece offers to a modern stage director: the obsessive, frustrated career of the protagonist, more like a character from Kafka than from Goethe in the projection of failure; the symbolism, the fascination of its stories with their multiple variations on the themes of evil, love and servility; the incredible discovery of the flash-back, fifty years before it was discovered by film makers; the real action taking place in the tavern of the prologue and epilogue, while the middle scenes are a dramatization of Hoffmann's reveries and self-delusions. What a haunting, beautiful story!

My feeling for this work, needless to say, brought zest to my drawing-board, as did the fact that Richard Bonynge, the conductor, wanted a production as close to Offenbach's original idea as possible. His musical version, the outcome of years of study of the subject, resulted in what might be the version closest to the composer's idea that this opera has seen.

Gone were the mediocre recitatives, added after Offenbach's death. The musical numbers were restored to the right scenes and characters, carefully interwoven with spoken dialogue. Some scenes were changed considerably, like the Venice story at the end of which Giuletta dies of poisoned wine.

Since the music is faithful to the story, the designer can follow either and remain fair to the whole. All along I personally kept in mind both the story and the music. I didn't find it difficult to separate them because, as I have said before, the value of this opera lies in the overall effect. The music is bold in the tavern scene, somewhat sarcastic in the Olympia sequence, wrapped in mystery in the Venice episode, and bursting with romantic feeling in the Antonia story—providing more than accurate guidelines for a visual approach.

In the case of the Australian project, our production had to be fitted to the problem-ridden stage of the new Sydney Opera House. As the shortcomings of this striking architectural conception merit a longer discussion, I will just say that the production had to be one of great technical simplicity.

We decided with Mr. Capobianco, the director, to have one basic platform for the entire production and different elements that were flown or glided in on casters. There was also a black cyclorama with irregular vertical strips of plastic mylar mirrors, that remained throughout the spectacle. Towards the front of the stage a portal which was part of the tavern also remained through the different scenes, a constant reminder of the place where the stories were being told.

The tavern scene was the most realistic, executed with wooden beams and stained-glass windows. Most of the students wore the German uniforms typical of the period.

The scenes depicting Hoffmann's stories were not realistic. They formed a sharp contrast to reality of the tavern. I used metallic mesh and steel piping as the main building elements. With added lighting and the use of projections each scene could become eerie or magical, according to mood.

The Olympia scene was a rather pompous mixture of bourgeois splendour, with the wheels and gears of Spalanzani's madness. Olympia appeared from a small glass pavilion. The costumes in this scene were caricatures of the Biedermeier period, and as a social satire, the guests appeared to be artificial. At times the director endowed them with movements even more doll-like than those of the heroine of the story.

The Giulietta scene took place on the terrace of a palace. The vertical mirror strips of the cyclorama blended with the verticality of the piping to create the architecture of this scene. All this suggested the reflection from water. There were many lanterns and no gondola—only a sumptuous couch, so much more suitable for love-making purposes! The idea of using a gondola on stage derives from the famous barcarole, a type of song reminiscent of the gentle movements of a barge on the water. This does not mean, of course, that one must have the actual barge on stage. Nor does a soprano, when she attacks a cabaletta, necessarily have to ride a horse.

The Antonia scene was ghost-like with the white, dusty house of the sick heroine. In this scene the structure was metallic, and the curtains and wall coverings were made out of metallic mesh. It was a particularly effective scene.

José Varona

1974, PARIS   THÉÂTRE DE L'OPÉRA

Producer: Patrice Chéreau — Stage designer: Richard Peduzzi — Costumes: Jacques Schmidt — Conductor: Georges Prêtre

Our 1974 production of *Tales of Hoffmann* was an attempt to return to Hoffmann. I was anxious to have another encounter with this German spinner of fantasies. A large town was constructed against a background of piercing cold—to some extent reminiscent of German romanticism—where processions and funerals could take place, where memories could be rekindled.

The prologue in Lutter's tavern was played before the curtain of the Paris Opéra, which then became transparent to reveal people, dreams and Hoffmann's intoxicated inspirations. Next came the nightmare of waking, three times in succession: the same town in the north looking like a frozen picture, each time more desolate, more hostile.

Patrice Chéreau

The Tales of Hoffmann

'In Lutter's tavern.'

Wuppertal, 1973   Horres/Dreier

Düsseldorf, 1969   Herlischka/Soherr

Paris, 1974   Chéreau/Peduzzi

Sydney, 1974   Capobianco/Varona

Prague, 1971   Štros/Štros

Prague, 1971 Štros/Štros

Düsseldorf, 1969 Herlischka/Soherr

Paris, 1974 Chéreau/Peduzzi

The Tales of Hoffmann

'In Spalanzani's physical cabinet. Performing dolls are standing about.'

Wuppertal, 1973   Horres/Dreier

Sydney, 1974   Capobianco/Varona

Düsseldorf, 1969   Herlischka/Soherr
Paris, 1974   Chéreau/Peduzzi

The Tales of Hoffmann

'In Giulietta's palace in Venice. View of the lagoon in moonlight.'

Wuppertal, 1973   Horres/Dreier

Sydney, 1974   Capobianco/Varona

211

The Tales of Hoffmann

*'Simple room in
Crespel's house.'*

Sydney, 1974   Capobianco/Varona

Paris, 1974   Chéreau/Peduzzi

Wuppertal, 1973
Horres/Dreier

Prague, 1971   Štros/Štros

Pelléas et Mélisande *(Pelléas and Mélisande)*

All that is written about this nocturne of passions should be set down in silver letters on midnight blue, for it is night that presides over the scene, even though afternoon and evening precede it. The dense forests round the Castle of Allemonde admit no ray of the sun; swirling mists and a pale moon bathe tower, cave and well in milky unreality—the characters appear like visions from a dream, as intangible as the objects through which they move. Mélisande, an enigmatic creature, steps mysteriously out of the dark; love and tortured jealousy entangle her until her life ends silently and, gently, she disappears.

In 1893 the Flemish writer, Maurice Maeterlinck, strongly influenced by the mystical symbolists, took this fine-spun fable and turned it into poetic speech, but not into a 'drama', as it is called in the sub-title. Debussy, after a frantic search for a new path, away from conventional opera and dramatic sonorities, was profoundly moved by Maeterlinck's work and felt that it was eminently suited to the realization of his own ideal: the ethereal union of words and music.

In early youth he had fallen under the magnetic spell of Wagner, but soon afterwards he began to search for other modes of expression, for escape from exaggerated pathos. He wanted a poet 'who leaves things half-unspoken and allows me to add my own musical poetry to his verses, who creates timeless figures, and does not set his scenes too rigidly, but leaves me free... to complete his work.'

The first draft of *Pelléas and Mélisande* was ready early in 1895, but the composer worked on, rejecting here and changing there, so that it was not until April 1902 that the work was first performed in the Opéra-Comique, Paris. The première was a failure, to which public and press alike paid scant attention; only a handful of the more discerning appreciated the epoch-making importance of a work that was a deliberate attempt to stem the pervasive influence of Wagner. In the years that followed, however, the opera gradually prevailed and became a milestone of a new, typically French style that came to be known as 'musical impressionism'. Debussy achieved his effects with remarkable skill. Throughout the opera poetry enjoys pride of place, the music underscoring the text and reflecting its varied moods in a scintillating texture of sound. Even the accents remain subdued echoes from an intangible dream world. The sombre climax, the murder of Pelléas by his fiercely jealous brother Golaud, is no searing flash of lightning—rather is it like the timid glow of the moon before the plunge back into eerie night.

The views of Debussy mentioned above afford the producer and stage designer a wide choice of exciting solutions, but also face them with many pitfalls. They cannot hope to achieve a satisfactory scenic effect with conventional techniques; the fifteen scenes demand a delicate touch and the most careful restraint. If they treat this opera simply as an *art nouveau* piece, they will, at best, arrive at a dubious and contrived product. Their chief concern must be to maintain the flowing transparency and smooth continuity of the whole, avoiding all breaks or disenchanting shifts of scenery. For the producer the child Yniold's spying on the lovers, or Mélisande's letting down of her long hair at the castle window, are so many perilous rocks on which the spectator's credence may founder. Avoidance of cheap sentimentality or of unintended hilarity is an exceedingly difficult task and calls for a great deal of creative imagination.

'Art nouveau' or 'Jugendstil' and 'impressionism', concepts borrowed from art and architecture, are the three labels most frequently attached to *Pelléas and Mélisande*. We must leave it an open question how far they are justified. This opera is a signpost on the road to timelessness, which was Debussy's great dream. If the music can be called impressionistic, this is only because it is reminiscent of a pointillist pastel—stippled in silver on a backcloth as dark as night.

Rudolf Hartmann

1 A forest.
2 A room in the castle; six months later.
3 Before the castle; next evening.
4 A fountain in the park; noon.
5 Golaud's room; evening of the same day.
6 Before a grotto; following night.
8 The vault of the castle; afternoon.
9 A terrace before the castle; afternoon.
10 Tower with Mélisande's chamber; same evening.
11 A room in the castle; morning.
12 As Scene 11.
13 A fountain in the park; same evening.
14 As Scene 13; later that night.
15 Mélisande's chamber; late autumn evening.

1962, VIENNA   STAATSOPER

Producer: Herbert von Karajan — Stage designer: Günther Schneider-Siemssen — Costumes: Georges Wakhevitch — Conductor: Herbert von Karajan

It may be due to my innermost feelings that I persistently attempt to interpret music visually, a basic attitude that I naturally applied to *Pelléas*. I had been asked to design a set for *Il Trovatore (The Troubadour), La Bohème* or *Pelléas*. I did not know *Pelléas,* but I was told

that its music was extremely transparent. I then made a close study of the score and sensed that it was full of hints for the stage designer, hints at transparency, vitrescence and translucence. These, and the interplay of colours in the music, drew me to *Pelléas*.

It was my first collaboration with von Karajan. I brought along some tentative sketches; von Karajan put forward the very precise idea of a sort of cylindrical set, representing the imprisoned destinies of Pelléas, Mélisande and Golaud. The cylinder would be transparent, to reflect the colourless transparency of the music.

The resulting gauzy structure was closed to the front and to the rear. Through openings on either side the necessary scenic elements could be introduced or withdrawn: drooping branches, gates, the sea-wall and balcony for the hair-combing scene. When the model was completed, the stage hands went on strike and the whole production appeared to be in jeopardy. When Karajan said he could see no way around the situation, I suggested the use of projection and the omission of all large scenic sections.

An emergency solution can sometimes have great artistic merit: the production proved the most dream-like von Karajan has ever staged.

The essential feature was projection: on to the gauze cylinder at various angles; and on to the proscenium veil in front of it. That demanded frontal projection from the auditorium; projection on to the veil from the towers; and back projection on to a screen from the bridge. Projection from a mirror at the top was also required, on to the raked, round disc on which the gauze seemed to be stretched.

The tremendously subtle lighting thus achieved made all the architectural and natural elements appear so transparent and vitreous that the human figures were revealed as the essential ingredients. There were but three chief characters, and nothing was allowed to deflect attention from them. In this subtle form, I believe, we achieved the first genuine 'light-production'.

Günther Schneider-Siemssen

1966, SPOLETO
1973, MILAN   TEATRO ALLA SCALA

Producer: Gian-Carlo Menotti — Stage designer: Rouben Ter-Arutunian — Costumes: Rouben Ter-Arutunian — Conductor: (in Spoleto): Werner Torkanowsky; (in Milan): Georges Prêtre

Quite independently, Gian-Carlo Menotti and I approached this work with the same visual idea: to use the new art forms developed at the time *Pelléas* was written and to try to solve the dramatic and historical problems in that way, deliberately rejecting an historicism based on present-day ideas and interpretations of the libretto.

The stage was a steeply raked box with a changeable back wall and corresponding light slit.

Except during the last scene, the stage was lined totally in black. Inside this claustrophobic area with its impression of invisibility, successive layers of veils were freely suspended, painted in various colours to suggest plants, rocks or the elements. These veils were combined with a variety of imaginary architectural fragments to produce a radiant centre of colour that floated in boundlessness, as it were, sucked out of the surrounding blackness.

The incorporation of brightly coloured surfaces in the plainly impressionist and transparent veils was meant to set off the strict lines of the architectural fragments, whose shapes were influenced by art nouveau ideas. Even the costumes were reminiscent of the Pre-Raphaelites, William Morris, Edward Burne-Jones and especially Odilon Redon.

In the last scene—Mélisande's death—the black stage made way for a structural equivalent: total white. In the centre floated a bluish, vacuum-tube-like oval, into which shadowy figures made their entrances. On its left edge stood Mélisande's crib-like, up-tilted bed; on the other side was a lighted window with curtains, and a unilateral, liana-like frame winding upwards.

During the musical interludes, and the various changes of scenery, a bright and sometimes transparent veil was brought down. The ends of its irregular fringes were 'animated' by a slowly moving beam of light, to produce the impression of falling rain.

Rouben Ter-Arutunian

1972, NEW YORK   METROPOLITAN OPERA HOUSE

Producer: Paul-Emile Deiber – Stage designer: Desmond Heeley — Costumes: Desmond Heeley — Conductor: Colin Davis

We gladly accepted Rudolf Bing's invitation to stage *Pelléas and Mélisande* at the Metropolitan. We were excited about using a large stage for the presentation of a chamber opera that was first performed in the confined space of the Opéra-Comique, a work whose musical and intellectual grandeur are reminiscent of Monteverdi's *Orfeo*.

We have always been impressed by the perfect harmony of words and music in this work; it seems almost inconceivable that Debussy did not work in direct collaboration with Maeterlinck. Maeterlinck's text would probably be considered too precious and dramatically unconvincing for our age. Debussy corrected these shortcomings with his music, which reveals the deepest feelings of the characters, the stirrings of their souls. It has often been said that Debussy lent meaning and clarity to Maeterlinck's most obscure utterances. That was certainly not the case. The meaning was Maeterlinck's own; Debussy simply illuminated the underlying psychological processes.

In our analysis of the work, we kept coming up against double meanings with almost every phrase. Consider, for instance, the character of old King Arkel. He is physically blind, but he is also blind to Pelléas, Mélisande and Golaud, since he cannot 'see' the awful catastrophe conjured up by these three.

We thus paid close attention to the possible interpretation of the symbolisms in which the work abounds. Take the scene at the beginning of the opera, when Mélisande watches her crown glittering in the water and exclaims, 'This is the crown he gave to me. It dropped because of my tears.' When Golaud proposes to bring it up out of the water, Mélisande reacts with a startled, 'No, no; I want no crown; sooner I'd meet my death, here on this very spot.' Why does she respond in this strange manner? She is prepared to explain why the crown has dropped into the water, but unwilling to speak about her origins. Her past lies at the bottom of the well; we, the spectators, will never learn anything about it.

The same is true of the first scene between Pelléas and Mélisande at the fountain of the blind. Maeterlinck no doubt chose this very setting because in the past—this is stated explicitly—the eyes of the blind were opened by the fountain. Since King Arkel has been going blind, people have ceased to come here, with the exception of Pelléas and Mélisande. Why? They are not blind, not dependent on the healing powers of the fountain, nor do they seek clarity in their relationship.

In the same scene Mélisande toys most expressively with her ring. She knows that she is playing with her fate, with Golaud's love. The ring glitters in the sun and falls into the water; she senses that something has suddenly gone wrong and asks Pelléas what she should tell Golaud when he asks about his gift.

The scale of emotions expressed in this work, and its intimate characterizations, seemed at first sight quite unsuited to the setting of the Metropolitan Opera. Our chief problem was the creation of a visual world that would be faithful to Debussy's music and yet give full expression to the tender emotions of the roles. To present *Pelléas* in a realistic setting is quite impossible; the stage must appear part of a dream world—ultimately the world of the theatre.

We revised our ideas until we found what we thought was the best approach: the 'rediscovery of impressionism'. The designs looked like paintings by Claude Monet, which we then translated to the stage as 'pictures without frames', conveying the impression of infinite distances, boundless space. We broke down the stage into different levels; net curtains treated with a plastic substance that becomes transparent when it dries, together with suitable lighting projection effects and essential properties, produced a series of illusory locations.

Special care was taken with the lighting design. Throughout the work there are references to 'noon' and 'midnight', the two fateful hours. Light and shade, sun and moon had all to be incorporated into the lighting plan. Scene-shifting was accomplished in full view of the audience, under subdued, mainly projected, light. It was difficult to see exactly what was happening on stage during a change of scenery; one could tell only that something had changed. The trees in the first forest scene turned gradually into castle arcades. And there was an intermingling of different projections throughout the performance.

Realism was studiously avoided, the outline of the scenery left blurred. The characters stood out all the more sharply. Pelléas and Mélisande are young, artless, and almost primitive in their actions, swayed by 'instinct'. They fall in love at first sight, although not consciously, as one might be tempted to assume.

It is said that Mélisande is out to catch Pelléas in her meshes, a woman who lies even from her death-bed. We did not take this view. When Golaud, alone with Mélisande, asks her whether she has loved Pelléas she replies directly 'Of course! I did love him. Where is he?' Mélisande's ingenuous answer is totally convincing.

Golaud's tragedy is that he does not believe her and that he shows all the signs of pathological jealousy—just like Othello. Othello kills himself, but Golaud lives on after Mélisande's death, tortured by doubts.

Golaud is not wicked. He is a strong man who has come to the end of his tether, knowing that he will be wracked with doubts until the bitter end. In the finale he cries out in deep anguish: 'T'was not my fault!'

Pelléas is the least interesting character in this work. For all that, he is allotted several wonderfully lyrical sequences. Mélisande is a much more striking role. She is a person of mysterious origins, so pure and radiantly innocent that she seems to scorch like the sun. Geneviève is the voice of wisdom and humanity; a woman who has lived, who understands everything and says little.

The singers' movements must not interfere with Debussy's music, which needs no choreographic emphasis. It would have been wrong for us to impinge more forcefully on the spectators' eyes than Debussy impinged on their ears.

Paul-Emile Deiber

1973, MUNICH   BAYERISCHE STAATSOPER

Producer: Jean-Pierre Ponnelle — Stage designer: Jean-Pierre Ponnelle — Costumes: Jean-Pierre Ponnelle — Conductor: Reynald Giovaninetti

The stage presentation of *Pelléas et Mélisande* poses the textual problem of the relationship between an object and the reason for

its inclusion, for instance the legendary fountain that can cure blindness, and will now open the eyes of the blind lovers; and between the libretto, with its double meaning, and the music.

Debussy's work is a symbolist reaction against both 'academic sterility' and naturalism. Under the pressure of political and social events, the intelligentsia escapes from reality into myth, into aristocratic affectation and aestheticism. [Giovaninetti and Ponnelle, 1973, p. 57.]

I was fascinated by the music, which is anything but pastel-coloured. The work strikes me as being powerfully masculine, even brutal. Its music, libretto and language are of equal importance; this fact alone almost compelled me to pass the story not only through the filter of the music, but also through that of the dialogue. My attempt to place Debussy's music in the context of his period—that is, in close association with Maeterlinck who was, though not a giant of world literature, a writer of renown in his own day—was an essential facet of my interpretation. I took a long and sober look at Maeterlinck's play in an attempt to dispel the diffident, Flemish, 'poetic' mist.

No matter what one's attitude to this poetry, the dialectical interplay of word and music is of primary importance on the stage. In other words, expression of the double meaning of the poetry, and of the nature of the music, is far more important than the revelation of the author's intentions, or the clarification of the text… [*Op.cit.,* p. 127.]

My own starting-point was the moment of Mélisande's death, during which the film of her life is, as it were, being played back to her. To intensify that impression, I kept showing Mélisande returning to her death-bed from her almost childlike wanderings through the scenery. The other roles also mark out her feverish fantasies. Arkel and Geneviève are like silent shadows, bearing the heavy burden of fate with bowed heads and drooping shoulders.

Pelléas is one of the few operas that has allowed me to form a clear scenic picture in my mind while still elaborating the overall character of the production—something that does not usually happen to me. The basic feature of this presentation was not the simple flash-back or the attempt to overdramatize the story, but a scenic technique that I consider particularly suited to the deeper logic of the work.

While I was working, I was suddenly struck by the frequent references to nature's prolificacy, in the most various connections—architecture, landscape, cosmos. This persuaded me to allow the action to unfold around a tree. In the eyes of the dying Mélisande, it conjures up memories of a childhood holiday; but with the help of special light effects and a few scenic elements, it can also turn into a tower, a fountain and other objects.

I am convinced that this type of interpretation will help audiences not familiar with the French language to a better understanding of the work.

Compiled by Wolfgang Haefeli after an interview with Jean-Pierre Ponnelle.

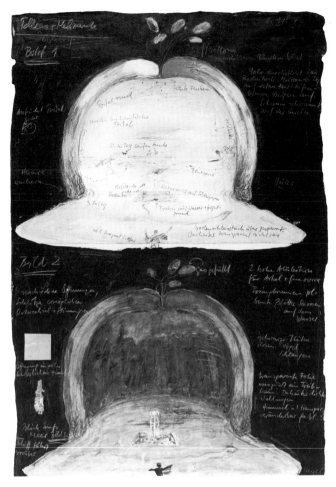

Producer: Hans Neugebauer — Stage designer: Achim Freyer — Costumes: Achim Freyer — Conductor: Gerd Albrecht

Our presentation may well have reflected our rejection of the customary idea that this unworldly Flemish legend—half dream and half reality—must be 'Wagnerized' into a beautifully sad and mystifying spectacle.

This first of all literary operas is suffused with musical realism and completely dispenses with operatic pathos. Its thirteen brief scenes tell the very real story of the tragic love of two children and their vain struggle for fulfilment. This story, seen from the child's colourful, vibrant, erotically fresh viewpoint, reflects a most delicate and spiritual attitude to life and its demands.

This production was designed to release the work's dramatic force in an anti-illusionist manner. The stage was Golaud's palace—a glass-house, a transparent prison for Mélisande—which closed behind her, only to open upon her death. The oppressive vaults held the crowded, pipe-lined heating plant of this hothouse, filled with proliferating, colourful and moist vegetation. Outside the glass walls—through which a remorseless Mediterranean sun almost always beats—dogs run about, children play, and the polite world passes by indifferently.

In this glass pavilion of an imaginary 'belle époque', Mélisande's balcony and Yniold's playthings are glistening ladders, painted swings. We deliberately introduced anachronisms: a light touch of irony in Maeterlinck's vision of pessimism and fatalism. Ibsen and Strindberg stood godfather to the entangled relationships of the characters. The stage presentation of the many optical layers of meaning, of the right balance between ear and eye, did not emerge until after long discussions with Achim Freyer.

A stay in Japan had influenced me greatly: I placed King Arkel and Geneviève on long ladders, as in Far Eastern puppet plays. From these sumptuous and presumptuous monuments to themselves, they made oracular pronouncements about childish behaviour, unwinding long silk scrolls with bloody letters. Pitiable wax mummies, these élitist relics of an epoch reflected what Romain Rolland called the weariness of 'Europe's intellectual aristocracy' with life.

The physician, half-heartedly trying to cure Mélisande, is close to the high-ranking personages. To the 'children', Golaud is an unsympathetic, faltering brother who indulges his vicious temper until he approaches madness. He wears a larger than life-size sword, and inflicts larger than life-size wounds, covering the whole stage with blood. The young lovers were to be presented in all the poetic delicacy and ingenuity of their emotions: the infantile boy in a sailor's suit with lace trimmings; and the girl, all arabesque, a monosyllabic mermaid cast ashore as an object of pleasure for the world of men. We were careful not to endow this hothouse nightmare with even the slightest pseudo-impressionist shade of meaning.

I worked in such close association with Achim Freyer that the question 'which is whose?' can no longer be answered unequivocally. The issue ultimately does not matter. The whole conception could only have worked with him and through him. This is something I cannot emphasize enough.

Hans Neugebauer

It is impossible, after more than a year, to reconstruct the reasoning behind a production that would, no doubt, surprise and astonish me were I to see it again. How can I possibly recall past dreams and efforts? My entire approach has changed; I have read and listened a great deal, studied interpretations and ideas which remain alien to me. Were I to re-read *Pelléas,* I would have to remodel my set.

These preliminary remarks reflect my conviction that the essential cannot be recaptured in words; it has, like history, passed through the filter of my experiences, my nature. The set—the creative act of my design—is unrepeatable.

The form and content of the music, the changing historical and social dimensions, modern production techniques, my own receptivity and ability—all these combine to determine the optical and sensual expression of the set. What volumes, what spaces are to be conjured up before the ear? Against what scale must the events be seen, in what masses and movements are the figures translated in musical space? Where does the libretto form part of the music, where does it have an independent impact—why and how?

I encounter a work and it has a certain feel, like a first impression. I come to know it better, I ask questions, the picture begins to gel; I want to describe it, to convey it to others. Yet even the punctuation marks produce new associations of ideas, new answers, new questions—even at the end, there is no end! Always the exchange of feelings and ideas with everyone engaged in the production. At last it all begins to make sense, to come into focus; the picture can no longer be smudged by minor changes.

For many years I had felt the urge to try my hand at Debussy's music, at the kind of composition that dissects an object, dissolves in it, allowing of new musical structures of the utmost rigour, to express its unique psychological content in all clarity.

Surprisingly, Maeterlinck's language lent itself to a convincing optical presentation of *Pelléas,* even though the music is more condensed than any anecdotal description of the action could hope to be.

The subject matter—an élitist and introspective microcosm—is reified in the composition and magnified by the regularities of the musical dimension without distorting its almost chamber-musical form. This demands a relatively small stage. In our production its depth was no more than six metres, and its acoustics were designed so that the small ensemble of singers could produce the requisite volume and yet appear in proportion to the set. The orchestra pit was covered with a transparent sheet (shades of Wagner) so that the musical action seemed to 'shine through' the tangible action on stage.

Two phosphorescent snakes, four phallic symbols, constituted the proscenium through which the first scene appeared: a spacious, bright room; 'nature' outside; hounds following the bloody tracks of a boar. The stage cloth was made of layered transparent and iridescent materials; Mélisande was caught up in it, an integral part of nature, her thighs two mounds between which a silvery fountain fed a well covered with water-lilies. Golaud, while hunting, frees Mélisande and pierces the cloth with his sword; bubbles rise up, a gaping red wound is left in the landscape.

The following scenes represent the inner world of male power, male privilege, isolation from real life, oppression, artificial nature: a hothouse.

Geneviève and Arkel, larger than life, are immobile on ladders; the air stands still. Mysterious woods encompass the castle, darkening or lightening the psychological space.

The basic background can variously represent inner and outer, above and below, wide and narrow, without destroying the ideal effect, the hermetic élitism, so that minimal changes convincingly suggest new settings and developments.

Mélisande, uprooted, finds her freedom only in death, in a return to the world, to nature; an open window once again reveals a clear autumn sky (Ill. 1) with bitterly cold spectral colours and vaginal, mouth-shaped structures. The oppressive atmosphere has made way for the freedom of expanding space.

Achim Freyer

Milan, 1973
Menotti/Ter-Arutunian

Cologne, 1974
Neugebauer/Freyer

Pelléas and Mélisande

'A room in the castle.'

Munich, 1973   Ponnelle/Ponnelle

Vienna, 1962   Karajan/Schneider-Siemssen

Pelléas and Mélisande

'*Fountain in the park.*'

Munich, 1973
Ponnelle/Ponnelle

Vienna, 1962
Karajan/Schneider-Siemssen

Milan, 1973 Menotti/Ter-Arutunian
New York, 1972 Deiber/Heeley

Pelléas and Mélisande

'Entrance to the grotto.'

Cologne, 1974   Neugebauer/Freyer

New York, 1972   Deiber/Heeley

Vienna, 1962
Karajan/Schneider-Siemssen

Munich, 1973
Ponnelle/Ponnelle

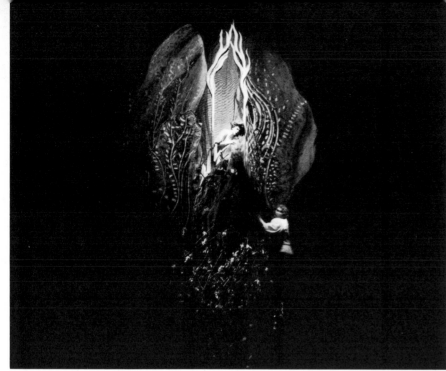

Pelléas and Mélisande

'Tower with Mélisande's chamber.'

Milan, 1973   Menotti/Ter-Arutunian
Cologne, 1974   Neugebauer/Freyer

Munich, 1973
Ponnelle/Ponnelle

Vienna, 1962
Karajan/Schneider-Siemssen

227

Munich, 1973 Ponnelle/Ponnelle

Milan, 1973 Menotti/Ter-Arutunian

Costume design, Georges Wakhevitch, Vienna, 1962

Pelléas and Mélisande

'*A terrace before the castle.*'

Vienna, 1962   Karajan/Schneider-Siemssen

Die Frau ohne Schatten *(The Woman without a Shadow)*

To the end of his life Richard Strauss felt a special love for this work, despite much worry and pain. His previous operas—*Salome, Electra, Rosenkavalier*—had all been successful, but *Die Frau ohne Schatten* was given such a bad reception at its 1919 Vienna première that Strauss never recovered from his disappointment. He blamed its failure on the economic circumstances prevailing immediately after the First World War: the State Opera could no longer afford the lavish production Strauss would have liked. The composer, spoilt by success, was dealt a grave psychological blow: decades later he refused to sanction the première of *Die Liebe der Danae* (The Love of Danae). He had allowed the staging of *Capriccio* in 1942, only because he believed that it called for very little scenery or expense—and in any case he did not expect to attract large audiences with this musical *conversazione* on the theme of 'word and tone'. He was mistaken: *Capriccio* became an oft-repeated success.

Die Frau ohne Schatten made very slow headway after the première. Even when the general economic situation had improved, only a few large houses presented the opera. In retrospect it seems that the highly symbolic libretto which Hugo von Hofmannsthal wrote is exceptionally demanding on the audience. Richard Strauss, who had always reacted strongly to the stimulus of words, responded to this poetic work and found a wealth of musical inspirations in it. Poet and composer, both at the peak of their creative lives, pooled their skills to produce a masterpiece that plumbed the most intimate of human relationships: the relationship between man and woman. This theme will be topical as long as there are humans left in this world. Hence Strauss's opera is a timeless morality play.

Strauss's score is a fusion of all his previous creations, including *Ariadne auf Naxos* (Adriadne on Naxos). The perfect control of the orchestra and of its relationship with the singers made for a work of great maturity and superb craftsmanship.

Perhaps the year 1919 was unsuited to the deep inwardness of *Die Frau ohne Schatten*. It is remarkable that a work solely concerned with individual human problems should have become a spectacular success immediately after the ravages of the Second World War. Munich opened its rebuilt National Theatre with *Die Frau ohne Schatten,* New York used it to inaugurate the new Metropolitan Opera, and the restored Vienna State Opera gave pride of place to the Strauss opera that had had its première there. The work has been performed in England, Belgium, France and Austria, and in opera-houses throughout the world.

Opera lovers had not become more sensitive after the Second World War. Modern stage developments had thrown up so many textual and musical problems that the structure of *Die Frau ohne Schatten* no longer prevented the acceptance of this intimately interwoven dream of poet and composer.

The basic theme is actually of a compelling simplicity. Barak's deep longing for children of his own dominates his every thought and action. The fertility of his beloved wife, symbolized by her 'shadow', is the only meaning of his life. Barak is the central figure of the action; around him the lives of his wife and the empress revolve. Caught between them, and impelled by demonic unrest, the nurse casts her magic spells, betraying everybody and finally destroying herself. The emperor remains trapped in his misanthropic, petrified world until he too opens himself to human emotions.

It is the producer's task to make sense of the many symbols and apparitions without destroying important meanings by unjustified cuts. The director's chief concern should be the theatrical communications of the two couples; another is to ensure that the finale does not degenerate into an operatic apotheosis. Cuts in Act II are advisable, provided they are approved by the conductor.

The stage designer has an imaginative and rewarding task: he must apply theatrical techniques with virtuosity but never allow them to obtrude; he must clearly set off the realistic plane (the dyer's world) from the exalted (imperial scenes) and the fantastic (Keikobad's kingdom), and yet preserve the overall unity of the presentation.

The love Richard Strauss bore his work has clear religious overtones, a fact reflected in his greatest melodic inspirations. The other-worldly realm of the invisible godhead was the deepest symbol of his own universal faith, of his firm belief in the survival of the spirit. Producer and stage designer will discover that surrender to the music is the key to the problems of interpretation.

Rudolf Hartmann

Scenes

Act I   On a flat roof above the Imperial Gardens. At the side, the entrance to the chambers, dimly lit.

In the dyer's hut. A bare room serving as both workshop and living quarters. Upstage left is a bed; upstage right the only door. Downstage is a hearth; the entire set conveys an impression of oriental shabbiness. Dyed cloths are drying on poles; the room is littered with troughs, buckets, tubs, vats hanging from chains, large ladles, stirrers, mortars, mills, bunches of dried flowers and herbs hung up on strings or heaped along the walls; there are pools of dye on the clay floor, and dark blue and dark yellow stains here and there.

The dyer's hut makes way for the interior of a resplendent pavilion: it is the chamber of a princess. The floor seems to be covered with a carpet in the most glorious colours;

the impression is produced by slave girls in colourful gowns.

The scene changes back to the dyer's hut.

Act II   The dyer's hut.

The imperial falcon-house in a lonely forest.

The dyer's hut.

The Empress's bedchamber in the falcon-house.

The wall of the chamber disappears to reveal a large cave with an opening. Dim lamps here and there cast a dull light over ancient tombstones hewn into the basalt. To the right an iron door leading to the interior of the mountain.

The dyer's hut.

Act III   Subterranean vault, divided into two rooms by a thick wall down the middle.

The vault sinks into the earth. Clouds appear, divide and reveal a rock terrace of the kind that appeared to the Empress in her dreams. Stone steps lead up to a temple at the entrance to the mountain. Facing it flows a dark river, cut into the rock.

The interior of a temple-like room is lit gradually but not fully.

A niche in its centre is draped.

A charming, steeply rising, landscape appears. In its midst a golden waterfall cascades down a gorge.

1964, BERLIN   DEUTSCHE OPER

Producer: Gustav Rudolf Sellner — Stage designer: Jörg Zimmermann — Costumes: Jörg Zimmermann — Conductor: Karl Böhm

Opera producers enjoy the challenge of conducting the public, as if by magic, safely through a maze of plot and scenery. Explaining is part of their work, though their chances of doing so are fewer than people believe. The job of disentanglement and clarification is so intriguing that many producers feel drawn to works that are mysterious and hermetic or, rather, 'encoded'. *Die Frau ohne Schatten* is one of the most complex operas, and for that reason one of the most fascinating.

Conceived in a *fin de siècle* ivory tower, it makes demands on the audience that are apparently quite beyond the capacities of modern opera-going public. The enthusiasm for this work of opera lovers in general and of Strauss fans in particular was always based on understanding and knowledge, or perhaps it was fostered by the nostalgic atmosphere that prevailed at the beginning of this century, during the First World War and throughout the Twenties. Perhaps it was a much more emotional approach than many believe today. In any case, *Die Frau ohne Schatten* was undoubtedly then—as now—a difficult work and one that was not performed very often. It is a unique product of the Hofmannsthal-Strauss partnership, strange and artificial, an exotic fruit.

It developed amidst the shattered dreams of a hapless generation. The longing for new forms of life, for richer emotions, inspired a turning to the East even before the turn of the century. And Hugo von Hofmannsthal's fable, *Die Frau ohne Schatten,* undoubtedly bears witness to a fascinated concern with the East, with its religious, philosophic and magical influences. Set somewhere between the Himalayas and Indo-China, it is a compound of oriental myths, restrained by language on an even higher plane than Hofmannsthal normally attained.

The book he sent to Richard Strauss as a draft for the opera already contained most of the elements of the prose poem Strauss was to set to music. We who re-created it are fortunate in being able to read the original fable as a commentary on and a guide to the meaning of the complicated symbolism, the reality of the fairy-tale.

That was all that the 1964 Berlin presentation aimed at. Its scenic pillars were Jörg Zimmermann's imaginative yet topographically accurate sets. Though they did not attempt to imitate Asia, they had an Asiatic 'feel' to which the public was quick to respond.

The Emperor's world: golden cupolas on transparent buildings. Indian and Thai elements were present, but not the sort that arouses any wish to travel. Sombre skies, a bluish confusion of rocks: a landscape made for ghosts, a world of the subconscious. The Emperor himself appears more as a Parsifal than as a representative of his class. His egocentrism is partly unconscious: part social gesture, part youth. He is made to experience hell, the most drastic process of individuation. His fate is more visible and comprehensive than the other transformations to which men are subjected in this opera.

The Emperor's falcon-house is also the Empress's meeting place with destiny. Reminiscent of an oriental hermitage, it clings to an incline in the rocky forest, a lonely place of meditation, a bridge between the spirit world and man. The Emperor's entry into the mysterious openings of the rocks presages the existence of gigantic vaults, the meditative landscape of Act III, which evokes the atmosphere of Asiatic shrines.

We did not deny the esoteric nature of the work and took its parapsychological facets seriously. For how can one possibly read a fairy-tale without taking the existence of the fairy for granted?

All the pictorial elements were intended as similes; every 'external' event was a mirror of an 'internal' situation. This parallel was continued right down to the solid foundations of the story—to the dyer's world on the jungle banks of the delta, at the clammy, stinking edge of a tropical town. It is here that the leading characters are at home; tangible actions can be performed. Here lives Barak on his little piece of ground, by a river running with the dye of skins and cloths, in poverty and despair.

This bit of reality is the solid ground of the fairy-tale. Here man is visited by the supernatural; here in this lowly region, extra-terrestrial visitors discover the holes through which they can slip into man's world of shadows. It is on the 'dyer's world' that the opera rests.

With incomparable genius Strauss sketches its temperaments and characters, blending his music with myths, and stirring up psychic anxieties. Religious sentiments flourish, from the humble faith of the folksong to the noble expressions of the oratorio-like ensembles. Barak is invested with a musical cloak that makes him the most poignant figure of the whole opera. Strauss makes him the chief victim and leading role; through ingenious treatment of that role he renders him comprehensible and transparent. The significance of his several trials is shown to be man's victory over the powers of darkness.

Even the nurse—at first the unequivocal messenger of Keikobad, King of the Spirits, who remains in the dark—experiences a transformation in the wake of her contacts with earthly creatures. In the end she betrays the realm from which she has come. Though she is a lowly creature, she plays the part of goblin, capable of producing any transformation in the world of men. Care should be taken not to portray her as a witch, but rather to leave her with the demonic aspects of a 'hybrid creature'. Evil is less her nature than her whim; she can nevertheless respond to tragedy.

The Empress, with her strange 'falcon's fate', has become half man, half spirit. She can no longer escape her humanity, for she has tasted love. She may be considered the positive side of escape from the kingdom of the spirits. The difficulty of the role stems less from the need for a consistent characterization than from the fact that, in her yielding and delicacy, the Empress is reminiscent of 'Constance', though her role was composed for a highly dramatic voice.

The dyer's wife, after Barak the most important figure of the opera, seems rather uninteresting because she poses no riddles. Her drab life is characteristic of the miserable world she inhabits. Her resentment at humiliation and slavery only becomes virulent as a result of her childlessness. Birth and prenatal life are dominant concerns of the spirit world in Hofmannsthal's fable. This concern is frequently expressed by symbolic or magic rituals—like the episode of the 'little fishes'—but its full significance is embodied only in the figure of the dyer's wife.

I can say very little about the characters without illuminating the environment in which they were to become human. That environment accordingly played a special role in our production: it was a visual composition. Jörg Zimmermann succeeded in changing the scenery with gigantic roll-up pictures before an open curtain, enabling me to keep nature in constant flow. The various realms could thereby be mingled in the interludes, and the dream spun further.

The last act was based on the 'Sacred Mountain' of ancient Chinese dramas—the abode of enlightenment and earthly satisfaction, of solution and fusion. We succeeded in visually excoriating Keikobad's spirit realm from that of the mountain chain, whose presence behind the transparent background could be suspected throughout the performance. We were unable to discover any symbols for this loneliest of lonely spots. This will always be a difficult problem: the Magic Flute elements of the opera become difficult to deal with at this point.

As we know, Richard Strauss himself was dissatisfied with the conclusion. He found it too academic. Perhaps he felt too close to Hofmannsthal's esoteric flights of fancy to transform them satisfactorily into earthly reality.

If our Berlin production had any value at all it should be recorded that it was deeply influenced, night after night, by Karl Böhm.

Gustav Rudolf Sellner

My introduction to *Die Frau ohne Schatten* was provided by Karl Böhm's recording of the score. There was no other standard of comparison for our Berlin production.

The music had an exceptionally powerful effect on me. It is music that allows—that demands—visual expression. It is descriptive, graphic and very colourful. Hofmannsthal's book also calls for an optical elucidation of the various realms and situations it conjures up.

To me the crucial aspect of the work is its setting in an invented, exemplary world. Even the reality of the dyer's world is deceptive. The fairy-tale character of the music and the plot call for a transparency that allows reality to be continuously questioned. Nothing is immobile or immutable. Every scene represents several states of being. Even the reality of the dyer's hut is undermined by apparitions: servant-maids; a youth; a watchman. In these elements the different worlds of this opera are visibly confounded.

The stage development of the opera is immensely complicated. There are many changes of scene, and the musical interludes vary markedly in tempo. It is probably because of the insoluble problems these many changes pose that this work was neglected before the Berlin production.

My work with Gustav Rudolf Sellner made it clear that the complex and sweeping action must not be interrupted by shifts of scenery behind a closed curtain. Long musical interludes would have made it too difficult for the audience to follow the twisted thread of the story. We decided to link successive scenes in the same way as the music links individual situations.

In the Berlin presentation we introduced several basic innovations; Sellner made a number of most beneficial cuts. The presentation was intended to be clear and concise; to my mind, however, this opera will always retain its mystery.

Jörg Zimmermann

1966, NEW YORK   METROPOLITAN OPERA HOUSE

Producer: Nathaniel Merrill — Stage designer: Robert O'Hearn — Costumes: Robert O'Hearn — Conductor: Karl Böhm

I believe the most important aspect of Strauss-Hofmannsthal's *Die Frau ohne Schatten* is its universal appeal. Even if we dwell on the obvious parallels between the characters, and on the constant and dramatic transfer of human values among them, the most significant factor of *Die Frau ohne Schatten* remains the shadow and its symbolic meaning.

I do not normally believe that psychological theories lend themselves to adequate operatic treatment. In this case, however, the shadow is a crucial symbol whose deeper significance for all the participants depends on their individual intelligence and emotional maturity. This was the basic idea of my production and the challenge it posed for me: building a dramatic framework from which no possible interpretation of the shadow would be excluded. The cleaning lady in the balcony who sighs, 'Isn't it lovely, she'll have a baby after all'; the intellectual to whom the shadow signifies human understanding acquired through suffering; the psychologist who advances specific theories to support his view—all of them ought to be given an opera they could approach on their own terms.

It was this universality that persuaded us to rule out all specific architectural elements, lest they tie us down to traditional attitudes. We felt vast enthusiasm as we envisaged an entire stage without a single door, wall or other element from any identifiable cultural period! The only exception we allowed was a series of vaguely Siamese-Indian domes, geometric representations of terrestrial elements on the Emperor's terrace in the opening scene. This departure was justified since the point at issue had been left equally vague and undefined by Hofmannsthal: a terrace across a lake on the Eastern Islands.

This production was the only German work out of four operas chosen for the opening of the new Metropolitan Opera House in New York's Lincoln Center. One of the largest contributions to the new house had been a gift of $2,500,000 from the West German government for stage equipment; it seemed only fitting that *Die Frau ohne Schatten* should be the first work for which this equipment was used. I must stress, however, that the decision to use any particular piece of machinery was dictated only by the needs of the production, not by a desire to show off our technical marvels.

During a joint study of the work, producer and stage designer agreed that the scenery must satisfy the following demands: in Act I the scene-shift from the Emperor's terrace to Barak's hut must be made in full view of the audience, for it is during the musical interlude accompanying this change that the Empress, the nurse and Barak's three contentious brothers were obviously intended to make their entrances. In Act II the scenes are not in sequence despite the seamless interludes; in other words the durations of the various scenes overlap. For that reason a light curtain must be dropped to 'fade' one scene into the next, while obscuring the change itself. The Empress's dream requires the same scenery as Act III: steps leading to a gate in the rocks, through which the Emperor enters the temple. At the end of this act, when the shadow leaves the dyer's wife and the Empress orders it back, the messenger from the spirit world must appear to summon all to Keikobad; and Barak's hut with the irascible brothers must disappear at a stroke, leaving an empty stage on which the boat appears to carry the Empress and the nurse away for Act III. The music allows thirty-five seconds for all this: another challenge for the stage designer.

Scene changes in the first two acts were effected with the help of the elevator stage. The Emperor's realm was constructed on the upper floor, Barak's hut on the lower. When we raised the elevator in Act I Barak's hut appeared as the Emperor's terrace rose out of sight. At the end of Act II the hut quickly drops below stage level and the waiting boat comes into view.

All the scenes in Act III are set in the same 'realm', so scenery could be changed without the use of curtains. We used the rear wagon stage, which has a revolve that can slide forwards and backwards. The flight of stone stairs used here was identical with the setting for the Empress's dream in Act I. It moved in vague, dreamy rotations some forty metres forward and back again, as soon as the Emperor had entered the temple.

The set allowed of great fluidity of motion. I tried to co-ordinate the movements of the singers around the shifting scenery so that the effects would invariably satisfy the dramatic demands of the music without assuming the character of a vaudeville stage.

It is interesting to note that because of a technical failure, two versions of this production had to be put on. Thus the revolve, a disc eighteen metres in diameter but only fifteen centimetres thick, had been designed to carry a weight of 28,000 pounds. The steel frame was hopelessly twisted when, in Franco Zeffirelli's *Antony and Cleopatra,* some two hundred Roman soldiers (weighing close on 40,000 pounds) had marched across it. This meant that we had to replan Act III—all the stairs and pylons had to be placed on casters and pivoted with a winch and cable; only the final 180-degree rotation had to be omitted. During our first season the last set was rolled in most unspectacularly on a side-stage wagon. At the final orchestral rehearsal the elevators did not work properly—some of the struts had been bent and it was no longer possible to raise and lower the scenery.

Once again we had to replan the first two acts: the scenery was rolled in from the side. Luckily the elevators were repaired in time for the first night. The production was widely acclaimed as the greatest musical and dramatic event of this, the Metropolitan Opera's first season in the Lincoln Center, but it was only three years later, after the revolve had been completely rebuilt, that *Die Frau ohne Schatten* was performed for the first time as we had planned it originally.

A few additional remarks: when the leading artists arrived for rehearsals some four weeks before the première, all knew their parts from previous productions in Vienna and elsewhere. We often heard complaints like, 'Why should we start rehearsing so long before the first night when all of us have sung our roles throughout Europe? We still don't understand the opera properly, but how can an *American* producer teach us anything new?' Our answer was a series of rehearsals during which I refused to offer an unequivocal definition of any character. Rather, I did my utmost to draw the lines beyond which, I felt, the opera could not be extended. Every member of the cast was forced to read his own meaning into the production and its problems. I can state, with particular satisfaction, that every one of us discovered his private shadow during our year of shared experiences.

Nathaniel Merrill

The difficulty of *Die Frau ohne Schatten* stems from its setting in three distinct realms: Keikobad's spirit kingdom; the dyer Barak's earthly world; and the indefinable in-between dominion of the imperial couple. Underlying this complex story is the theme of humanization, as symbolized by the shadow of fertility.

In my presentation I was particularly anxious to bring out the visual links between Barak's terrestrial province and the imperial world. I therefore constructed Barak's earthbound hut beneath the flat roof of the royal gardens. At the end of the first scene the gardens disappeared upwards and the dyer's hut rose from the depths of the earth, lit by a hearth in earthy tones of brown and red, like the inside of an earthenware jug. The Empress's realm by contrast was a vitreous blue, filled with precious stones, conveying an icy atmosphere. The spirit kingdom was a world of black and silver, of iridescent rocks and large pennate shapes. This was dominated by an enormous flight of stone stairs, mounted on a revolve that could be rotated as the narrative demanded.

I discovered that the action and the mood of Act II lead from light into darkness, while Act III leads from darkness to light. For the latter I designed a rainbow-like progression of colours. Starting

with the black and purple of the vault, I added blues and greens, then a yellow-green and finally a golden yellow: a flash of daylight and of humanity.

I withstood the temptation of Siamese and Indian temples, choosing instead the magnificent forms of microscopic organisms, minerals and precious stones. The background was a batik simulating an accidental organic effect, perhaps as a reminder of Barak, who is after all a dyer.

To superimpose the various scenic effects I used numerous abstract projections, but I did not try to shape a final 'picture' with them. The projections often corresponded with the flats, but gave life to them and a more mysterious aspect.

I did not settle on any particular country or period, thus complicating the work of the costume designer. The costumes were abstract and simple in effect: hand-painted cloths that incorporated the style of the batik used for the flats, together with iridescent pieces of material.

Robert O'Hearn

1970, STUTTGART

WÜRTTEMBERGISCHES STAATSTHEATER, GROSSES HAUS

Producer: Ernst Poettgen — Stage designer: Leni Bauer-Ecsy — Costumes: Gaby Bauer-Ecsy — Conductor: Siegfried Köhler

It took me quite some time to become involved in *Die Frau ohne Schatten*. The impetus came from Wieland Wagner, whom I admire tremendously, and his oft-repeated 'great interest' in the work. Wondering what aspects of the opera could have fascinated him so much, I kept probing until I eventually found my way to Strauss *via* Hofmannsthal.

Since I had no further opportunity to speak to Wieland Wagner about *Die Frau ohne Schatten,* let alone about his own ideas for its presentation, I tried to imagine how he would have tackled this 'monstrous spectacle', how he would have rid it of the odium that had attached to it for so long. I arrived at the following conclusions:

Ultimately the work is about the victory of love over death, and about the projection of that victory into the future. The developing relations between spirits and spirits and between humans and humans, no less than the entanglement of the two spheres, had to be set off as clearly as possible. The important thing was to clarify their interdependence without distracting the audience with the décor, the 'outer spectacle'.

However theatrically effective the nurse may be she is no more than a catalyst in the dramatic development of the four leading characters. The empress, the daughter of Keikobad, becomes a compassionate and loving wife ready for any sacrifice. The emperor develops from swaggering huntsman into an adult and truly loving man thanks to his wife's love. Simple Barak, purged by dire distress, blossoms into love. His wife, after much temptation and seduction, recognizes her own ego as a loving woman.

In the discussion of the stage design, there was no doubt where the work had to be set. We started from the assumption that the higher reality—the surreality, as it were—must comprise the symbolic content of the dramatic situation. In other words, there was no need to trouble about décor in the conventional sense.

The basic design element was an oval—conceived as primitive space—from which the somewhat hyaline imperial scenes of the first two acts and the four scenes set in the dyer's hut were to be developed in a dense, palpable 'haze' of work, meals, and sordid quarrels.

The dyer's scenes were given 'concrete' expression with large pieces of dyed cloth hung out to dry. All the scenery was easily shifted or quickly removed—as in the complete 'dissolution' of space at the end of Act II, when Barak and his wife become the prisoners of their own fate.

This primitive oval space proved its 'load-carrying capacity' particularly in Act III. From the captive dyer couple the scene gradually 'condenses' into the temple set with the well and the petrified emperor, a culminating scene that claims the centre of the stage. During all these transitions the dyer and his wife stray about, seeking and fleeing each other.

The oval also provided a setting for the final quartet. I felt that the usual placing of the couples on different levels was not nearly as convincing as the presentation of a very simple human phenomenon—the love of man and woman—on a single plane.

Ernst Poettgen

1972, PARIS   THÉÂTRE DE L'OPÉRA
1975, STOCKHOLM   KUNIGLA OPERAN

Producer: Nikolaus Lehnhoff — Stage designer: Jörg Zimmermann — Costumes: Jörg Zimmermann — Conductor (in Paris): Karl Böhm; (in Stockholm): Berislav Klobucar

Die Frau ohne Schatten is a fairy-tale for grown-ups, a 'twentieth-century *Magic Flute*'. In contrast to Mozart's and Schikaneder's opera—whose fairy-tale world is understood by young and old alike—Hofmannsthal's complicated and deeply symbolic fable is not directly accessible to the ingenuous spectator.

The various planes of the opera—the world of Barak, the dyer; the realm of the Emperor and Keikobad's spirit kingdom—must be clearly distinguished from one another. Their respective visual symbols must not be allowed to complicate the events further.

In our very close collaboration in Paris and Stockholm, Jörg Zimmermann and I were determined to dispense with excessive symbolism in favour of clarity. I discovered to my delight that Zimmermann had the knack of giving precise graphic expression to mythological ideas.

The human world is depicted in extremes. On the one hand the Emperor, ruler of a rootless world whose shadowless, vitreous aspect also hints at the spiritual existence of the Empress. On the other hand, the commonplace and oppressive world of the people whose prototype is the dyer Barak.

The Emperor's pavilion floats above the cupolas, in a lunar landscape whose bluish-silver, mother-of-pearl sheen reflects the petrifaction of human emotions. It resembles a cage in which the Emperor hides his wife as one might a precious, exotic bird.

Barak, too, locks up his wife—albeit unconsciously—in a miserable, sun-blighted, torrid cave. Its centre—a fire-place with a gigantic pan, surrounded by straw mattresses—reflects the almost bestial greed of this world.

Contrasted with these conflicting human planes is Keikobad's unreal spirit kingdom, the world of trials and of judgment: a dark, severe temple-realm that makes way for radiant open meadow during the sweeping hymnody of the finale.

The imprisonment of Empress and dyer's wife, the two antagonists of the opera, is expressed in their cage-like dwellings. Both try, for their own reasons, to escape from their worlds. A shadow—symbol of fertility—is desired by the Empress but despised by the dyer's wife. Neither the Emperor nor Barak is aware of his wife's moodiness; neither is capable of untying her 'heart's knot'.

The central element of this fairy-tale is the gradual development of the Empress from an Undine into an ethical human being. The intermediate stations of her pilgrimage are the great turning-point in her attitude, demanding the producer's very special attention lest the passivity imposed upon her during these important scenes cause the audience to forget her existence. The bargain in the dyer's hut is struck by the nurse acting on her own initiative. The Empress merely listens and watches as she gradually changes from greedy purchaser ('Ich will den Schatten küssen, den sie wirft.'—'I long to kiss the shadow cast by her.') to one beset with guilt and prepared to dispense with the shadow ('Ich will nicht den Schatten, auf ihm ist Blut.'—'Away with the shadow; it flows with blood.').

Her encounter with Barak in Act II initiates the gradual change in the Empress's selfish attitude. Barak's goodness fills her with a sense of compassion for mankind, and in the course of this scene she becomes increasingly human. Helpfully following the dyer, she hands him dried cloths. She treats Barak's friends to a sumptuous dinner. Her maternal instinct appears when she places her arms protectively around a child who has slipped while trying to escape

from the dyer's wife. Reluctantly and with averted face she hands Barak the sleeping-draught for the nurse, and hovers near him when the dyer's wife and the nurse leave for a journey to the town. The magic mirror—symbol of the nurse's deception—slips out of her hands as she throws herself at Barak's feet, begging forgiveness ('Ich, deine Dienerin.'—'I am thy servant.').

The producer must, in Strauss's words, depict an Empress with 'red blood corpuscles' in these decisive scenes. He must not, however, make the dyer's wife seem over-emotional; he must show the real human impulses that sway her.

Her longing for freedom, glamour and beauty has very specific causes. To make these clear, the tension between dyer and wife, particularly in the first scene set in Barak's hut, must be clearly expressed. Barak's wife is an essentially good-natured soul. She is frustrated with a life confined to 'bed and trough', with playing her role in nearly bestial conditions. Barak's brothers mock her cruelly: 'Tramp that you are, daughter of beggars, you dance to our brother's every whim.' She bleeds to death spiritually, longing for respect

and human warmth, an anguish that Barak is neither able nor willing to recognize. He ruthlessly dismisses all her reproaches and complaints, meeting her grumbles with the impersonal kindness he bestows on all mankind.

The three deformed brothers—symbols of human waste—mock her and threaten her physically. Their parasitic way of life, characterized by indolence and gluttony, is tolerated by the 'Big Father', whose good-heartedness allowed it to develop. The producer must stress the negative aspects of Barak's indiscriminate goodwill to render the frustration of the dyer's wife comprehensible.

The final apotheosis remains a problem. Its spiritual and moral tenor is so high that one can dispense with all theatrical embellishments. It conjures up an atmosphere akin to that of *Fidelio* and the *Magic Flute*. Through these final scenes, beginning with the Empress's acquisition of a shadow, blows the 'breath of academic coldness' which Strauss sensed and feared. His poem culminates in a literary glorification of feminine fertility that is nearly as bloodless as a propaganda speech. Cuts are recommended here.

I tried to strip the mystery of the quaternity at the end, in which the original unity is restored, of its rigid, oratorical pose. The social barriers between the worlds of the imperial and proletarian couples have been torn down. As the voices of the unborn children sing the promise of maternal happiness in the finale, both couples move towards Utopia, the new city that is slowly rising out of the golden mist in the distance.

Nikolaus Lehnhoff

In our Stockholm production, Dr. Lehnhoff and I tried to present the work in full, including marginal episodes and arabesque symbolisms. I built a transparent and changeable set. With changes in the lighting, it could be adapted to the particular situation, real, semi-real or unreal, and made to mirror the variable character of the music and plot.

The architecture of the individual sections was more personal, more original, designed to enhance the unity of music and scenery. The stage was bounded by lateral mirror walls which allowed a changing but always full coloration. The whole stage could be flooded with light by back projection, so that Keikobad's kingdom in Act III, with its severe black and white lines, could be set off with great clarity.

This visual and technical solution allowed of scene-shifts that gave the opera a kaleidoscopic quality: one realm made way for another in the manner of a film dissolve. The result was a fusion of music, plot and scenery.

Jörg Zimmermann

Producer: Günther Rennert — Stage designer: Günther Schneider-Siemssen — Costumes: Bernd Müller and Jörg Neumann — Conductor: Karl Böhm

The object of every production of *Die Frau ohne Schatten* seems to be the weaving of the threads of Hofmannsthal's picturesque fable into a single and scenically visible whole. Description is needed, not rationalization; the symbolic expression of the magical-cum-mythical, not an intellectual analysis leading at best to allegory. It is only in the context of their interrelationships that the characters become endowed with life and meaning. Each one must follow his own path and confront another's world before there can be a fusion of opposites in the final scene. [Rennert/Siemssen, 1974, p. 24.]

In our interpretation we concentrated on the human crux of the opera, treating its 'trial' element as an elucidation of the learning process. The aim of that process is to overcome human weaknesses that can be traced back to psychological predispositions, and that can, in turn, lead to dissatisfaction and unhappiness, or to despair. These problems must be posed by anyone who searches this extremely intricate emotional fable for hints as to a scenic interpretation.

The starting-points of any production of this intricate simile must be the visual symbols that evoke the spectator's powers of association. Hofmannsthal set his fairy-tale in the 'most populous town of the South Eastern Islands'. The stage version is

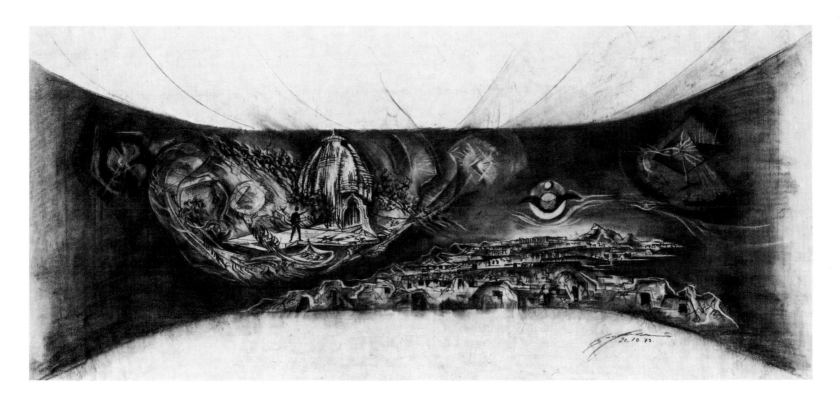

based on Indian and Arabian legends and reveals a multi-layered world that is reflected in a simultaneous set construction. We were fortunate in being able to exploit the unique possibilities of the vast Salzburg stage, where we could, at times, provide a simultaneous display of the three planes of this opera: the real world of the dyer, the imaginary realm of the royal couple and the intangible realm of Keikobad. [*Op. cit.*, p. 24.]

Both the complex individual actions and the dramatic function of the musical interludes demand a consistent visual approach that separates the different planes while fusing them into a convincing visual whole.

We started with the construction of models (scale 1:25) on which the work could be tested against the score. There was still a great deal of sifting: redundant parts were cut out; spaces, depths, heights and presentation details were fixed precisely in accordance with our basic plan. During prolonged building experiments on stage we put agreed ideas to the test and tried out various changes of scenery. We also made several electro-acoustic experiments for the spirit choruses, and tried out projections, optical prisms and films—in short, we examined all the technical possibilities available today.

It was left to the stage designer to adapt the vast and complex lighting system and a host of new instruments to the special demands of this opera. Unfortunately, we were so short of time that we could not, until the second season, give practical expression to all our ideas. For the 'downfall' of Barak's hut at the end of Act II we used concurrent films and optical prisms. While the entire dyer's world was being 'swallowed up', pencils of light were projected to simulate masses of water which seemed to pour in simultaneously from the auditorium and the backstage.

The central figures of the opera are the dyer and his wife, who must appear larger than life. Their personal shortcomings and differences in temperament are shared by most people and preoccupy all mankind. The Emperor and Empress are far less close to us: they are allegorical figures, and provide a means of highlighting the dyer's world. Despite their aloof appearance, they have to undergo the same trial as the dyer couple, albeit on a higher plane. Even more remote is Keikobad's spirit kingdom: a spherical cosmos.

The intellectual construction of the opera suggests that the dyer's world should be placed on the earth—the stage floor—which turns the proletarian plane into the realistic centre of the whole. The imperial couple must be placed in a more elevated fairy-tale region, some three to four metres above the stage. The kingdom of the spirits should be located in an unapproachable region whose existence can only be suspected: we placed it on the elevated rear stage.

These three playing areas were made to encroach upon one another in full view of the audience. We used the full (30 m.) width of the stage and a side stage just as wide but relatively shallow in depth. It was important to make the architectural representation of the three levels seem optically convincing and consistent with the dramatic flow of the story.

The dyer's story was lent greater dramatic intensity by cramming the many tools of the dyer's trade into the oppressively low living and working space of an Indian mud hut.

For the town in the background, we relied largely on Max Ernst's surrealist painting, *The City*. Above the earth floated the Emperor's realm. It resembled an Indian stupa, but one that has been stylistically neutralized to symbolize the fragility and inconstancy of the Empress. The gardens with the falcon-house formed a surrealist plant world. Their formal arrangement suggested a realm of extra-terrestrial vegetation, serving as a cosmic extension of consciousness and providing a bridge to the third plane of the opera—the world of spirits.

At first, that world loomed up as a distant vision, one that slowly grows larger in the Empress's dreams; the world of Keikobad was conceived as the power and wisdom of cruel nature. Only after the two lower planes have touched and intermingled, after the dyer's world has been swallowed up, does the spirit world appear as a dominant world of inorganic organisms. The various conflicts (Act III) are resolved in a fantastic mountain landscape. [*Op. cit.*, p. 24.]

This is true symbolic poetry, in which reality holds sway in a metaphorical sense only. To drive this point home, Act III must tear open an entirely new dimension, spatially no less than stylistically. That dimension, though it might have been sensed in the preceding acts, could not yet be directly experienced. In particular, Keikobad's omnipotent authority must be allowed to dominate much more openly here than during the apparition of the messenger in Act I. All this demands the elaboration of scenically convincing representations for such symbols as the 'water of life' and 'petrifaction'. There must be no naturalistic simplifications!

We experimented with combinations of crystal prisms and diffracted pencils of stroboscopic light to represent the 'water of life' and tried to increase the effect even further during the second run in 1975. The Empress's 'climb to ever greater heights' was simulated with several hydraulically shifted stairways. We tried to express the intensification of space, infinity and unapproachability. To that end, we created a surrealist 'dissolve' in which the stage machinery was not allowed to obtrude in any way.

In the final quartet of Act III the dyer's and the Emperor's worlds are in equilibrium: both couples have reached the same stage of ethical development. We showed a bridge taking shape out of the shadow of the dyer's wife, on which she then went out to meet her husband; at the same time the royal couple rode up from the rear stage to form a square with Barak and his wife. Both planes were still distinct, but their contents had become intertwined. The composer allotted the leading voices in this final hymn to the Emperor and Empress: this too had to be given visual expression. In Mozart/Schikaneder we can read: 'The stage is transformed into a sun.' Something very similar happens here: as the voices of the unborn ebb away, the sun is transformed into a fertility symbol.

For the realms of the Emperor and the spirits we used the full expanse of the stage, the full system of baroque drops and all the modern hydraulics.

The architectural and ornamental forms used were exclusively derived from the Orient. These we mixed with stylistic elements based on the work of Paul Klee and Max Ernst, whose surrealistic and metaphysical approach is very similar to that expressed in this opera. It was from the world of personal experience, out of his own cosmic longing, that Max Ernst created his suns, moons, circles and elliptical forms as particular ciphers of this world.

Paul Klee was the second painter with strong poetic links to *Die Frau ohne Schatten*. The concept of the Empress as a gazelle, fragile and transparent, might come from Paul Klee's fragile world of plants, fishes and other creatures.

Colours helped us to distinguish between the various planes. The dyer's world was painted in the warm shades of the earth; the Emperor's realm and the kingdom of the spirits were in cold hues of green and blue. Where these worlds touch, the colours, too, blend into one another.

The barge carrying the nurse and Empress to the temple was, like the interior of the temple, borrowed from oriental demonology. It was shaped like one of those fabulous creatures whose power holds prisoner all those who surrender to their spell. [*Op. cit.*, p. 24.]

The several roles involved in the Emperor's and dyer's dramas had to be differentiated by specific styles and expressions, while the nurse had to be fitted into the great army of ambitious tempters, mockers and losers. The individual world of each character was used to construct a dramatic field of tension: the entry of figures from the spirit kingdom into Barak's world made that world seem transparent, and the contrast between the two relative rather than complete.

Compiled by Wolfgang Haefeli after an interview with Günther Rennert and Günther Schneider-Siemssen.

New York, 1966   Merrill/O'Hearn

Berlin, 1964   Sellner/Zimmermann

Stuttgart, 1970   Poettgen/Bauer-Ecsy

Die Frau ohne Schatten

'On a flat roof above the Imperial Gardens.
At the side, the entrance to the chambers,
dimly lit.'

Salzburg, 1974   Rennert/Schneider-Siemssen

Stockholm, 1975   Lehnhoff/Zimmermann

New York, 1966   Merrill/O'Hearn

Die Frau ohne Schatten

'In the dyer's hut. A bare room serving as both workshop and living quarters. Upstage left is a bed; upstage right the only door. Downstage is a hearth; the entire set conveys an impression of oriental shabbiness. Dyed cloths are drying on poles; the room is littered with troughs, buckets, tubs, vats hanging from chains, large ladles, stirrers, mortars, mills, bunches of dried flowers and herbs hung up on strings or heaped along the walls; there are pools of dye on the clay floor, and dark blue and dark yellow stains here and there.'

Stockholm, 1975   Lehnhoff/Zimmermann

Stuttgart, 1970   Poettgen/Bauer-Ecsy

Salzburg, 1974 Rennert/Schneider-Siemssen

Berlin, 1964 Sellner/Zimmermann

Die Frau ohne Schatten

'The imperial falcon-house in a lonely forest.'

Costume designs, Robert O'Hearn, New York, 1966

Berlin, 1964   Sellner/Zimmermann

Salzburg, 1974   Rennert/Schneider-Siemssen

Stockholm, 1975   Lehnhoff/Zimmermann

'The interior of a temple-like room is lit gradually but not yet completely.—A niche in its centre is draped.'

Stockholm, 1975   Lehnhoff/Zimmermann

Salzburg, 1974   Rennert/Schneider-Siemssen

Costume design, Robert O'Hearn, New York, 1966

Costumes, Bernd Müller and Jörg Neumann, Salzburg, 1974

New York, 1966   Merrill/O'Hearn

247

Die Frau ohne Schatten

'*A charming, steeply rising landscape appears. In its midst a golden waterfall cascades down a gorge.*'

Stuttgart, 1970   Poettgen/Bauer-Ecsy

New York, 1966   Merrill/O'Hearn

Berlin, 1964   Sellner/Zimmermann

Salzburg, 1974   Renner/Schneider-Siemssen

Stockholm, 1975   Lehnhoff/Zimmermann

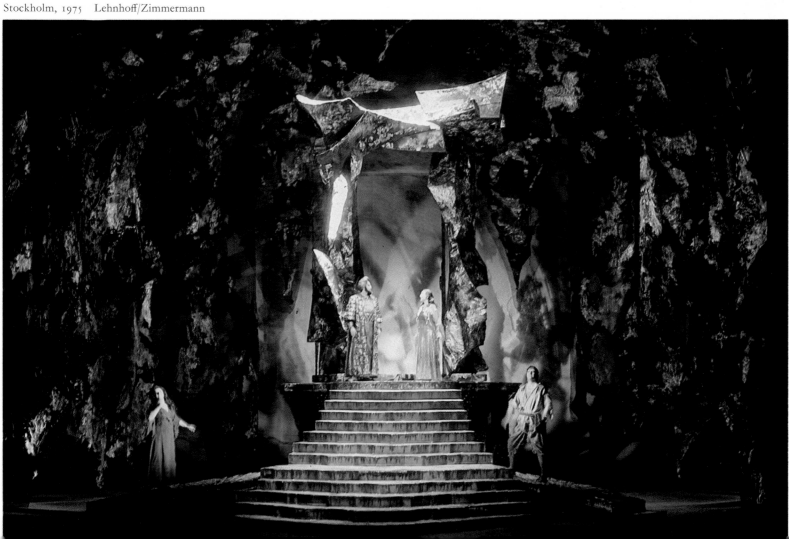

Appendices

AUGSBURG: STÄDTISCHE BÜHNEN

The Stadttheater was destroyed in February 1944 and rebuilt in 1954–6. Seats: 1010. Width of stage: 24.50 m.; depth: 16 m. Width of side stage: 15.80 m.; depth: 7.10 m. Width of rear stage: 25 m.; depth: 15.50 m. Hydraulic lift: 16.85 m. by 2.90 m. Height of proscenium arch: 8.50 m. (maximum); 5.50 m. (minimum). Switchgear: Siemens magneto system, 4 presets, 200 controls, VHF transmitter; 4 large projectors; 85 spot-lights of various makes and output. Interesting technical features: proscenium can be moved through 2.90 m., and cyclorama altered accordingly. Two hydraulic lifts, each measuring 17 m. by 2 m. 14.80 m. revolve. Forty-five hand lines. Orchestra: 3 elevators with room for 65 musicians.

BASLE: BASLER THEATER

The old Stadttheater (1150 seats) was founded in 1834, rebuilt in 1873–5, and reopened on 20 September 1909, after the fire of 1909. Width of stage: 20 m.; depth: 15 m. Width of proscenium arch: 9.20 m.; height 6.50 m. Interesting technical features: cyclorama, wagon stage; portal bridge with 10 spot-lights. Ten projectors. Switchboard with 144 ways (Strand Electric). Operating voltage: 220 V. A.C. Width of orchestra pit: 20 m.; depth: 5 m.

BAYREUTH: RICHARD-WAGNER-FESTSPIELHAUS

The theatre was built in 1872, opened in 1876 and has 1925 seats. A.C. and D.C.; operating voltage: 220 V. Width of stage: 32 m.; depth: 23 m. Width of proscenium arch: 13 m.; height: 12 m. Rake: 2.5%. Overall width of understage: 43.20 m.; depth: 13 m.; height 14 m. Flying systems: 60 cloth hoists, 30 electric point hoists; 3 cyc hoists; 3 electrically operated grave traps. Wagons of all sizes, hand and mechanically operated as required. Lighting bridge. Siemens Sitralux B switchboard, 200 ways; xenon switchboard with 30 variable circuits for discharge tubes. Ten 4–kW HMI projectors; 12 2–kW projectors with halogen quartz lamps; 26 2–kW and 1–kW projectors for moving effects. Orchestra pit: depth 11 m.; width 15 m.

BERLIN: DEUTSCHE OPER

Destroyed during the war; reopened on 24 September 1961. From 1945 to 1961 the Städtische Oper performed in the former Theater des Westens, Kantstrasse. The new house, designed by Fritz Bornemann, seats 1903. Stage, workshops and stores were almost completely rebuilt, though some of the surviving architectural structures were incorporated. Width of proscenium arch: 14.50 m.; height: 8 m. Width of stage: 28 m; depth: 19 m.; height: 27.50 m.; depth of rear stage: 23 m. Technical equipment: 4 lifts; 2 double-storey lifts; 2 side stage wagons; 1 rear stage wagon with 17 m. revolve; 6 electrical point hoists; 2 movable perches; 1 movable portal bridge; 30 electrical cloth hoists; 31 double purchase counterweights; 6 general hoists; 2 electrical cyc hoists. Lighting: 100 spot-lights on the perches, and lighting bridge; forestage: 78 spots, 50 projectors, 2 2000–V xenon projectors; three-phase current; 220/380 V; operating voltage: 220 V. Switchboard with 240 ways and 4 memory facilities, electro-mechanical and punchcard controls. The switchboard is on the left side of the stage. Television system for observation of the conductor consisting of 2 cameras, 2 control desks and 11 monitors. Various other stage controls and radio equipment, HF lighting control system, 2 'light-boards', acoustic and optical wardrobe calls, production talk-back, (inductive) deaf-aid system. Orchestra pit: 4 electrical double-storey elevators; pluggable orchestral desks (Augsburg system). Pit laid out for 120 musicians.

BERLIN (DDR): DEUTSCHE STAATSOPER

Main stage: width of proscenium arch: 12 m.; height: 7.20 m. Width of stage: 15 m.; height: *ca.* 16 m.; depth: 17.80 m. Width of rear stage: 15 m.; depth: 11.70 m.; height: 10.60 m. Six elevators: 1) −0.50/+9.33 m.; 2) −3.00/+2.50 m.; 3) and 4) −2.50/+3.00 m.; 5) −0.50/+9.00 m.; 6) −0.50/+4.00 m. Sixteen electric point hoists, 26 mechanical hoists, 33 hand hoists, 2 cycs.

BRATISLAVA: SLOVENSKÉ NÁRODNÉ DIVADLO

Capacity: 623 seats. Width of stage: 19 m.; length: 19.50 m.; playing area: 16 m. by 18 m. Width of proscenium arch: 10.50 m.; height: 7 m. Width of orchestra pit: 5.60 m.; length: 7 m. Interesting technical features: 13 m. revolve; 50 counterweights, including 30 with motor drive (variable speeds). Lighting (manual): 1 main control, 1 cross fade, 2 presets, 120 circuits. Data storage: 2 memories, 1 cross fade, 1 electronic timer for cross fade. Two hundred forty memory facilities, 120 circuits.

BREMEN: THEATER AM GOETHEPLATZ

Theatre opened on 27 August 1950, on the site of the Bremer Schauspielhaus, destroyed during the war. Capacity: 989 seats. The orchestra pit has two adjustable lifts. The stage house holds wardrobes, rehearsal rooms, workshops and stores. The theatre is used for plays, operas, musicals and dances. Three-phase current 380/220 V. Width of proscenium arch: 9 m.; height: 7 m. Width of stage: 18 m.; depth: 18 m. Interesting technical features: cyclorama, revolve with interchangeable lifts, hydraulically operated double-storey portal bridge and safety installations. Thyristor switchboard: 200 variable circuits of 5 and 10 kW. Programming for cross fade and intensity by punchcards (1–600 secs.). Side stage: 340 sq.m.; rear stage: 220 sq.m. Cloth store with DEMAG mechanical hoists.

COLOGNE: NEUES OPERNHAUS

Opened on 18 May 1957. Capacity: 1364 seats. Width of proscenium arch: 13 m.; height: 7.80 m. Width of stage: 26 m.; depth: 22 m. Main stage with rear stage: 42 m. 2 side stages with wagons. Cyclorama. Orchestra pit: 110 sq.m.; two movable double-storey lifts for some 100 musicians.

DÜSSELDORF: OPERNHAUS

The Opernhaus was built in 1875, completely rebuilt in 1906, largely destroyed in 1943, and reopened after extensive repairs in 1944, with 1041 seats. Closed for reconstruction in 1954–5. Reopened on 22 April 1956. New capacity: 1342 seats. Width of proscenium arch: 11.40 m.; height: 7 m. Width of stage: 22.50 m.; depth: 14.75 m.; height: 21 m. Forestage, side stage (left) and playable rear stage. Rear stage wagon with built-in revolve (9.80 m.). Five hydraulic grave traps. Five lifts (size 2.50 m. by 14 m.) infinitely variable from −3 to +3 m.; electric rack and pinion; lifts can be slanted in all directions. Thirty cloth hoists with infinitely variable speeds from 0.05 to 2 m./sec. and with a maximum load for 300 kg.; movable singly or in groups. Ten hoists for heavy loads (up to 500 kg.). Movable portal bridge and fixed perches with spot-lights and projectors (including 10-kW projector and xenons). Switchboard (with magneto system) and memory bank. Electro-acoustic

system. Three-phase current, 220/380 V. Orchestra lifts hold ca. 108 musicians.

FLORENCE: TEATRO COMUNALE DI FIRENZE

Width of proscenium arch: 17.20 m.; height: ca. 10 m.; width of stage: 21.30 m.; depth: 17.30 m. (without forestage); height: 9.72–6.20 m. Understage: height 3.99–4.49 m. One cyclorama.

KASSEL: STAATSTHEATER

Capacity of large hall: 953 seats; of small hall: 540 or 580 seats. Architects: Paul Bode and Ernst Brundig. Opened on 12 September 1959. Two side stages and 1 rear stage. Width of proscenium arch: 8–16 m.; height: 5–7.5 m. Width of stage: 25 m.; depth: 14 m. Interesting technical features: cyclorama, wagon stage, portal bridge with spot-lights, 33 electrical hoists, 4 lifts 15 m. by 3 m. (+3, −3). Three flying systems. Projection. Revolve. Operating voltage: 220/380 V. A.C. Orchestral pit: ca. 95 sq.m.

LONDON: ROYAL OPERA HOUSE, COVENT GARDEN

The present theatre was built within 6 months in 1856, after fire had destroyed the old building. Architect: Sir Edward Barry. Capacity: 2158 seats. Height of proscenium arch: 8.69 m.; width: 13.49 m. Width of stage (between fly rails): 21.34 m.; depth: 23.42 m. (without forestage). Depth of forestage: 2.13 m. Height of stage: 21.95 m.; 9.14 m. under galleries. Machinery: 52 counterweight flying sets. Lighting: switchboard with 240 ways, 14 memory presets, 40 groups, 4 following spots (xenons with reflectors). Orchestra pit: 95–113 sq.m.

MILAN: TEATRO ALLA SCALA

Built in 1778. 3600 seats. Width of prosce-

nium arch: 10–16 m.; height: 6.60–9.50 m. Width of stage: 20.50 m.; depth: 20 m. (without forestage). Rake: 5%. The main stage is divided into 6 lifts. Rear stage: width 17 m., depth 15.50 m., height 9.20 m. 179 hoists. Cyclorama.

MUNICH: BAYERISCHE STAATS-OPER IM NATIONALTHEATER

Capacity: 2100 seats. Built in 1811 by Karl von Fischer. Rebuilt in 1823–5 (after a fire) by Karl von Klenze. Destroyed in 1943; rebuilt in 1959–63 by Gerhard Graubner and Karl Fischer. Opened on 21 November 1963 with *Die Frau ohne Schatten*, on 23 November 1963 with *The Mastersingers*. Width of proscenium arch: 16 m.; height: up to 13.50 m. Two side stages, 1 rear stage. Three lifts 20 m. by 6 m. Seven wagons, each 6 m. by 20 m. with diagonal displacement. Three-phase current, 220/380 V. Orchestra pit: 105.5–146.4 sq.m. for 120 musicians.

NEW YORK: METROPOLITAN OPERA HOUSE

Built in 1966. Capacity: 3824 seats. Standing room: 253. Width of proscenium arch: 16.50 m.; height: 16.50 m. Width of stage: 30.50 m.; depth: 24 m.; height: 34 m. Width of rear stage: 30.50 m.; depth: 21 m. Understage: height 13 m. Interesting technical features: rear stage wagon with built-in revolve (17 m. diameter). One rear and 2 lateral working areas off-stage are equipped with wagons that can be loaded with stage equipment to a height of 10 m. Two cycloramas, for projection, back projection and background can be rolled up vertically by remote control. Orchestral pit: 222 sq.m. for 110 musicians.

PARIS: THÉÂTRE DE L'OPÉRA

Built in 1862–74 to the design of Charles Garnier. Opened in 1875, restored and modernized in 1936–7. Capacity: 2167 seats.

Width of proscenium arch: 15.15 m.; height: 14.60 m.; depth; 25.30 m. Width of stage: 52 m.; height: 60 m.; depth (inclusive of rear stage): 37 m.

PRAGUE: TYLOVO DIVADLO (FORMERLY STÄNDETHEATER)

Built in 1781–3 to the plans of Antonin Haffenecker. Extended in 1881 to the plans of Achill Wolf. Opened on 21 April 1783 with *Emilia Galotti*. World première of Mozart's *Don Giovanni* in 1787. Originally built for the German nobility, the theatre added Czech to its repertoire in 1812. Handed to the State in 1920 and affiliated to the National Theatre. In 1949, renamed Tyl-Theatre, in honour of Josef Kajetán Tyl, the Czech playwright. Specializes in drama and Mozart operas. Capacity: 600 seats.

SALZBURG: GROSSES FESTSPIELHAUS

Built in 1955–60. Architect: Dr. Clemens Holzmeister. Opened on 26 July 1960 under the direction of Herbert von Karajan with *Der Rosenkavalier*. Width of stage: 74.5 m.; depth: 25 m. Width of proscenium arch: 14–30 m.; height: 9 m. Interesting technical features: 2 cycloramas, wagon stage, portal bridge with spot-lights. Projection equipment: 24 instruments. Switchboard with 300 ways (Siemens). Operating voltage 220 V. A.C.: Orchestra pit for 120 musicians, 4 elevators –3 to ±0 m.

SALZBURG: KLEINES FESTSPIELHAUS

Built in 1925–6. Architects: Hütter and Holzmeister. Opened on 13 August 1927 under the direction of Franz Schalk with *Fidelio*. Restored in 1963. Capacity: 1383 seats. Depth of stage: 26 m. Width of proscenium arch: 12 m.; height: 9 m. Side stage: width 15 m.; depth 15 m. Cut sloat. Interesting technical features: angled cyclorama.

Collapsible revolve; diameter: 18 m.; height: 0.25 m. Operating voltage: 220 V. A.C. Orchestra pit holds 90 musicians.

STOCKHOLM: KUNGLIGA OPERAN

The first Gustavian opera-house, built to the design of C.F. Adelcrantz, stood on the site of the modern building. It was opened in 1782, demolished in 1892 and replaced by the Oscarian house (designed by Axel Anderberg). Various renovations since 1955. Rebuilding scheme in nine stages begun in 1968. Completion due in 1983. Capacity: 1169 seats. Width of proscenium arch: 10.70 m.; height: 9 m. Width of stage: 20.50 m.; depth: 17.50 m. Rake: 4%. No side or rear stages. Fifteen lifts of 10 sq.m. each, adjustable and computer-guided (+2.4 to –6 m.; maximum rake 15%). Bridges at intervals of 2.4 m. Cycloramas. Seventy-five fly bars. Lighting: Siemens switchboard with punchcards. Two hundred ways. Forty projectors. TV installation. Orchestra pit: 2 lifts; total area: 81.75 sq. m.

STUTTGART: WÜRTTEMBERGISCHE STAATSTHEATER

The Kammertheater on the third floor of the Grosses Haus (completed on 15 September 1912), was opened for public performances on 22 December 1946. The Grosse Haus has 1400 seats. One main, 1 back and 2 side stages. Width of proscenium arch: 11.20 m.; height: 7.50 m. Width of stage: 17.50 m.; depth: 19 m. Interesting technical features: cyclorama, wagon stage; portal bridge with spot-lights. Six projectors. Current: three-phase, 220/380 V. A.C. Orchestra pit: lift; floor space 74 sq.m.

SYDNEY: OPERA HOUSE

Capacity: 1547 seats. Width of proscenium arch: 12 m.; height: 7 m. (adjustable). Overall stage area *ca.* 437 sq.m.; area of main

stage: *ca.* 316 sq.m. Rear stage: 102 sq.m. Interesting technical features: revolve, 14.25 m. diameter, on main stage. Two built-in lifts, 10.70 m. by 3.60 m. for changes of scenery between stage and workshop level. Two lifts on rear stage. Two balancing lifts. Seventy-eight hoists; 40 downlights; 2 lighting bridges. Switchboard with 200 dimmers. Fourteen additional controls for regulating fluorescent lighting of cyclorama. Orchestra pit: double lift, self-levelling at any desired height from 11–13.50 m. Holds 75 musicians.

VIENNA: STAATSOPER

Foundation stone laid on 20 May 1863. Architects: Eduard van der Nüll and Siccard von Siccardsburg. Opened on 25 May 1869 with *Don Giovanni*. Destroyed on 12 March 1945 but Ringstrasse tract with the main approach, the vestibule and the loggia preserved. Rebuilt and reopened on 5 November 1955 with *Fidelio*. Capacity: 1642 seats; standing room for 567. Width of proscenium arch: 13 m.; height: 12 m. Width of stage: 27.50 m.; depth: 22.50 m. Rear stage: 19.50 m. by 21 m. Side stage 20 m. by 10.50 m. Interesting technical features: cyclorama, revolve, wagon stage, portal bridge with spot-lights. Five-kW and 10-kW projectors. Switchboard: 270 ways; Siemens-Bordoni system. A.C./D.C. Operating voltage: 380/220 = 110 V. Orchestra pit holds 120 musicians.

WUPPERTAL: OPERNHAUS

Opened on 14 October 1956 with *Matthias the Painter*. Capacity: 851 seats. Width of proscenium arch: 9–11.50 m.; height: 5–8 m. Width of stage: 16 m.; depth: 13.50 m. Rear stage: 12 m. by 12 m. Interesting technical features: lift, portal bridge with spot-lights; projection system with 16 instruments. A.C. Operating voltage 220/380 V. Orchestra pit 85 sq.m., holding 60 musicians.

RUODI BARTH

Born in 1921; awarded a diploma in graphic arts at a technical school in Basle, followed by one year as graphic artist in a printers'; then spent one year with Herbert Leupin. Devoted two years to the illustration of books, and for two years collaborated in designing the Swiss pavilion at international fairs. 1950: stage designer at the Stadttheater, Basle; 1953–63: at the Staatstheater, Wiesbaden. Since 1973: permanent appointment at the Staatstheater, Darmstadt. Visiting appointments at the Burgtheater in Vienna, Munich, Hamburg, Stuttgart, Düsseldorf.

LENI BAUER-ECSY

Born in Hamburg; studied at the Staatliche Hochschule für bildende Künste, Hamburg. Spent three years at the Deutsche Schauspielhaus, Hamburg as assistant producer and put on several productions of her own. Spent three years in Göttingen and a further three years at the municipal theatres, Essen. During the war worked at the municipal theatres, Hanover (*Intendant:* Gustav Rudolf Sellner). 1945–7: at the Staatsoper, Munich; visiting appointments at the Städtische Oper, Berlin; 1950–75: Württemberg national theatres, Stuttgart; visiting appointments in Munich, Vienna, Salzburg, Zurich, Berlin.

Collaboration with the following producers: Günther Rennert, Boleslaw Barlog, Walter Jokisch, Ernst Poettgen, Karl-Heinz Stroux, Otto Schenk, Dietrich Haugk, Bohumil Herlischka, Hans Bauer.

Major productions: *Wozzeck, Blood Wedding, The Devils of Loudun, From the House of the Dead, Falstaff, Jenufa, Così fan tutte* (Salzburg and Stuttgart). In Berlin: *Schau heimwärts Engel, Elizabeth Queen of England, Joan of Arc at the Stake.*

WINFRIED BAUERNFEIND

Born in Bielefeld in 1935; in 1954 began to study at the Kassel Musikakademie; in 1957 continued at the Hochschule der Kunst, Berlin. 1959–61: assistant to Wolf Völker at the studio of the Städtische Oper, Berlin. 1961–4: assistant producer at the Deutsche Oper, Berlin; those he worked with included: Carl Ebert, Herbert von Karajan, Wieland Wagner, especially Gustav Rudolf Sellner in Berlin, Tokyo, Mexico and at the Salzburg Festival. 1964–8: head of the studio of the Deutsche Oper. Experimented with contemporary musical drama. 1968: first production at the Grosses Haus of the Deutsche Oper: *Mr. Brouček's Excursions* by Janáček. 1972: principal stage-manager at the Deutsche Oper, Berlin. In 1974 television production (ARD): *Preussisches Märchen* by Blacher.

Visiting producer in Kassel, Essen, Augsburg, Frankfurt, Wuppertal, the Schwetzinger Festival, Den Jydsken Operan in Aarhus, Théâtre des Nations in Paris, Théâtre Royal in Brussels.

Taught at the Mozarteum, Salzburg, and at the Hochschule der Kunst, Berlin.

HORST BONNET

Born in 1931. Trained as an actor. 1949: began his career as actor and assistant producer in Schwerin. 1950–2: assistant producer to Bertold Brecht (Berliner Ensemble); 1952–7: producer of plays in Schwerin and Erfurt; first musical mises-en-scène. 1957–9: assistant producer to Walter Felsenstein at the Komische Oper, Berlin. 1959–61: chief stage-manager for opera and operetta in Potsdam. Since 1961: producer in Berlin. Visiting producer: Metropoltheater, Staatsoper in Berlin, Komische Oper in Berlin, Volksoper in Berlin. Two feature films: 1964 'Salon Pitzelberger' after Offenbach, 1973 'Orpheus in the Under-

world' after Offenbach. In both films he was the script-writer and director.

JAN BRAZDA

Born in Rome in 1917; painter, architect; studied at the Academy of Fine Arts in Prague. His works are in public and private collections in Sweden and other countries. Important works: paintings, restoration of Wäxiö Cathedral, stained-glass windows of St. Andreas Cathedral in Malmö and of the town-hall in Örebro. Designed sets and costumes for the opera in Stockholm and for Covent Garden, London.

ROGER BUTLIN

English stage designer. Taught for eight years. Reader at Goldsmiths' College, University of London. Was awarded a prize by the Arts Council. Collaborated with the English National Opera; 1969: appointed principal stage designer at the Greenwich Theatre. Décor includes: *Forget-me-not Lane* (décor of the year), Brussels, High School, *Rosmersholm, Three Sisters.* Opera décor: *Billy Budd* (Welsh National Opera), *Idomeneo* (Glyndebourne), *Barber, Albert Herring* (both in Sydney). Now adviser to an art school in Dartington Hall, Devon, England.

TITO CAPOBIANCO

Born in Argentina. Début at the age of fifteen in *Tosca* in the part of the Cardinal. Later chief stage-manager, technical manager, assistant producer. First production at the age of twenty-two; *Aida* at La Plata University. Mises-en-scène in South America and Mexico included *Macbeth, The Mastersingers of Nuremberg, Otello, The Love for Three Oranges, The Rake's Progress, Duke*

Bluebeard's Castle, The Saint of Bleecker Street, Così fan tutte, Hamlet. In 1962 left the Teatro Colón in Buenos Aires and went to the USA. Artistic director of the Cincinnati Summer Opera; producer and *Intendant* of the Pittsburgh Opera Company, the Philadelphia Lyric Opera Company and the New Orleans Opera Company. US début in 1964 with *Carmen.* Visiting producer in Hamburg, Spoleto, San Francisco, Paris, Berlin, Australia, at the Holland Festival.

MARC CHAGALL

Born in Vitebsk, White Russia, in 1887. 1907–9: studied under Pen in Vitebsk, Academy of Arts in St. Petersburg. And later under Leon Bakst. 1910–4: in Paris; first one-man exhibition in Berlin. 1917–21: Commissar of Fine Arts in Moscow. 1922–3: dry point engravings for his autobiography *My Life in Berlin;* returned to Paris. 1924–39: line engravings for Vollard's editions of Gogol's *Dead Souls,* La Fontaine's *Fables* and the Bible. 1937: became a French citizen. 1941–7: exiled in New York. Lithographs for *Thousand and One Nights.* Stage sets for ballets: *Aleko* and *Firebird.* In 1948 his lithographs were printed by Fernand Mourlot. Since 1950 has lived in Vence. 1961: publication of *Daphne and Chloe;* 1967: *Circus.* 1968: coloured wood-cuts for *Poèmes.* 1970: vast exhibition of all his works in Paris.

PATRICE CHÉREAU

Born in Lézigné (Maine-et-Loire) in 1944. 1963: first mise-en-scène: *L'Intervention* by Victor Hugo, staged at the Louis-le-Grand lycée. Productions at the cultural festival of the National Student Union in Marseilles (1964), at the student theatre festival in Erlangen (1964) and at the university festival in Nancy (1965). 1966–9: head of the municipal theatre at Sartrouville. Visiting producer in Spoleto and Milan. 1971: with Roger Planchon artistic director at the Théâtre National Populaire. 1976: *The Ring of the Nibelungs* in Bayreuth.

JOHN COX

Born in Bristol in 1935. First engagement as producer in Oxford; collaboration with Professor Neville Coghill and Sir Jack Westrup. 1959: first appointment with the Glyndebourne Opera Company as assistant to Carl Ebert and Günther Rennert. A scholarship from the Munster Trust enabled him to study production at opera-houses in Düsseldorf, Frankfurt, Hamburg and Berlin. 1960: producer at the Royal Theatre, York. 1966: visiting producer at the University of Wisconsin, Milwaukee, USA. In 1968, in collaboration with the composer Alexander Goehr, he founded the Music Theatre Ensemble, which produced avant-garde works at festivals in Brighton, the City of London, Edinburgh, Perugia. 1972: stage-manager of the Glyndebourne Festival. Major mises-en-scène: *The Abduction from the Seraglio, Idomeneo, Capriccio, The Visit, The Rake's Progress, Intermezzo, Der Freischütz* (The Free Shooter). Visiting producer in Sydney, Washington, Houston, Amsterdam, New York and Santa Fé.

LUCIANO DAMIANI

Born in Bologna in 1923; studied at the Accademia di Belle Arti, Bologna. 1954: at the Piccolo Teatro di Milano was responsible for the décor for Strehler's mises-en-scène. Worked as an opera stage designer at the Teatro La Fenice, Venice, also in Vienna, Salzburg, at the Holland Festival and at the Maggio Musicale Fiorentino.

Major settings for: *Macbeth, Rise and Fall of the City of Mahagonny, Don Giovanni, The Abduction from the Seraglio, Wozzeck.*

PAUL-EMILE DEIBER

Born at La Broque, Alsace, in 1925. 1942–4: attended the music college in Paris; awarded first prize for tragedy and comedy. Entered the Comédie Française. His repertoire included all the classical authors: Molière, Racine, Corneille, Victor Hugo, Rostand, etc.; modern repertoire: Claudel, Giradoux, Montherlant, Achard, Grumberg. Mises-en-scène of operas: in New York (*Romeo and Juliet, Norma, Werther, Pelléas and Mélisande*), San Francisco, Dallas, Chicago, Vienna, Berlin, Paris (*The Barber of Seville, Medea, The Trojans, Benvenuto Cellini*), Geneva (*Carmina Burana, Antigone*). 1971: left the Comédie Française after twenty-seven years. 1970–2: deputy *Intendant* of the Opéra in Paris. Worked for television as actor and producer. Author of a one-act play about Molière, *La Troupe du Roy.*

PANTELIS DESSYLLAS

Born in Piraeus in 1936. After leaving school studied painting at the Academy of Fine Arts in Athens, and then attended the Akademie für angewandte Kunst in Vienna. 1959: diploma for stage and film design. Began his work with settings for television and films. 1965: engaged at the Staatsoper, Vienna. Since 1971 he has been head of the Zentrale Dekorationswerkstätten der österreichischen Bundestheater. Also produced décors for the Staatsoper and Volksoper in Vienna, the Teatro Comunale in Florence and the Theater an der Wien. Taught at the Akademie der bildenden Künste. Major sets for: *Per Aspera, Orpheus, Relazione fragili, The Prodigal Son, Zwei Herzen im Dreivierteltakt, Let's Dance.*

JÜRGEN DREIER

Born in Mannheim in 1927. Discontinued his studies at a secondary modern school; followed by national labour service and was in the armed forces. 1945–50: first appointment at the Kammerspiele in Heidelberg, as a messenger and 'telephone replacement'. Assistant producer to Gustav Hartung, A.M. Rabenalt and Karl-Heinz Stroux. Later became assistant stage designer at the municipal theatres in Heidelberg. Practised for two years as scene-painter. Was greatly influenced at first and initially helped by Wilhelm Reinking; calls himself a Reinking pupil. 1950: in charge of décor at the municipal theatre in Ulm. 1952–6: stage designer at theatres in Lübeck. 1956: worked for theatres in Wuppertal. Collaboration with Kurt Horres, A. Wüstenhöfer and with the stage designer Heinrich Wendel. 1961: appointment as chief stage designer to the Staatstheater in Darmstadt.

PETER EBERT

Born in Frankfurt in 1918; son of Carl Ebert. 1936: left Gordonstoun School, followed by a two-year course at a private London bank. 1938: worked for small film company that had just been founded and was a partner in setting up a theatre for children. 1945–6: producer and announcer at the BBC. 1947: assistant producer at the Glyndebourne and Edinburgh festivals. 1951: first operatic production: Boito's *Mefistofele*, in Glasgow. Visiting producer in Rome, Naples, Venice. 1954: returned to Germany; stage-manager in Hanover. 1956: chief stage-manager in Hanover. 1960–2: chief stage-manager at the Deutsche Oper am Rhein and at the same time director of the opera studio. 1962–8: free-lance work on operas, plays, musicals, films and television. 1967–8: director of the opera school at the University of Toronto. 1968: *Intendant* at the municipal theatres in Augsburg. Director of both this enterprise and the Freilichtbühne am Roten Tor. 1973–5: *Intendant* of the municipal theatres in Bielefeld. Since 1975 has been *Intendant* of the Hessisches Staatstheater in Wiesbaden. Visiting producer in Los Angeles, Toronto, Copenhagen, Amsterdam, Basle, Johannesburg and in various German towns.

GÜNTHER FLECKENSTEIN

Born in 1925. 1948: beginning of theatrical career. Actor, assistant producer and dramatic critic in Mainz. 1954: chief stage-manager of plays and operas in Ulm. First productions: *The Marriage of Figaro, The Rape of Lucretia*. 1955: held same position in Gelsenkirchen. 1956: stage-manager at the municipal theatres in Essen. 1957–9: chief dramatic stage-manager in Münster. 1959–

65: chief dramatic stage-manager at the Staatstheater, Hanover. Visiting producer at the Württemberg national theatres in Stuttgart, at the Residenztheater in Munich and at the Freie Volksbühne in Berlin, as well as at the festivals in Recklinghausen and Bad Hersfeld. In addition was television producer for the ARD and ZDF; screening his own adaptations of, for example, 'Der Grosstyrann und das Gericht'. Stage adaptations of Sartre's *L'engrenage* and *Les Jeux sont faits* as well as Aristophanes' *The Knights*. In 1966 succeeded Heinz Hilpert as director of the Deutsches Theater in Göttingen. From 1976 director of the Bad Hersfeld festival.

ACHIM FREYER

Born in Berlin in 1934; studied applied graphics and stage design; was a brilliant pupil of Bert Brecht at the Deutsche Akademie der Künste in Berlin. Produced many prize-winning cartoon films and designed theatrical posters. Helped to produce operas and plays; participates in one-man exhibitions of action paintings and three-dimensional objects: monument to Heinrich von Kleist. Painter and stage designer as well as professor at the Hochschule der Künste in Berlin.

GÖTZ FRIEDRICH

Born in Naumburg in 1930. 1949–53: studied drama at the Deutsches Theaterinstitut in Weimar; awarded diploma in drama. Appointed to the Komische Oper, Berlin. 1953–72: member of the Komische Oper, Berlin: first as dramatic critic and assistant producer; later as chief assistant producer and research assistant to the *Intendant*; from 1959 as producer; and from 1968 as principal stage-manager. Since 1973: principal stage-manager at the Staatsoper, Hamburg. Visiting producer at the Nationaltheater in Weimar, the Staatstheater in Kassel, the Theater der Freien Hansestadt Bremen, the Royal Theatre, Copenhagen, Den Norske Opera in Oslo, the Deutsches Theater in Berlin, the Holland Festival, the Bayreuth

Festival, the Castle theatre in Drottningholm and the Württemberg national theatres in Stuttgart. Various settings for films and television. 1970: professor at the Hochschule für Musik, Berlin. 1974: university professor, Hamburg. Various literary publications.

EZIO FRIGERIO

Born in Erba, Como in 1930. Studied architecture at the Polytechnic, Milan. First achieved fame as a painter: silver medal at the Triennale di Milano, 1954. Also in 1954: designed costumes for *As You Like It*. 1955–8: costume designer at the Piccolo Teatro, Milan; from 1958: also stage designer for productions by Giorgio Strehler. Later also costume designer for television and film productions.

HEINZ BRUNO GALLÉE

Born in Vienna in 1920. Studied architecture and stage design in Vienna. Produced several stage designs for theatres in Austria and elsewhere in Europe, including Vienna, Salzburg, Brussels, Paris, London, Milan, Rome and Naples. Head of the department of stage design, costume and scene-painting at the Mozarteum Hochschule and at the University of Salzburg. Chairman of the international organization for stage design, theatre architecture and stage technique; head of the international commission for artistic and technical matters in the theatre. Several publications, lectures and seminars.

JÚLIUS GYERMEK

Born in Dolné Hámry (central Slovakia) in 1931. Studied at the college of arts and music in Bratislava: first produced plays, then operas. 1958: completed his studies with *The Two Widows* by Smetana. 1954–9: assistant producer at the Slovak national theatre. 1959: début with production of Werner Egk's *The Government Inspector* (Czech première). Appointed operatic producer. Has to his credit so far thirty productions of operas at the Slovak national theatre; visiting producer on several occasions. Opera performances and ballet settings for television; four film shorts; translated libretti of operas and operettas.

HANS HARTLEB

Born in Kassel in 1910; studied German philology, music and art history; awarded a Ph.D. in Munich; studied also music (piano and singing). 1935: at the Volksoper, Berlin, with Carl Hagemann. First mise-en-scène in 1937: *Madame Butterfly*. 1947–55: principal stage-manager in Essen; held the same position in 1955–61 in Frankfurt and 1961–7 in Munich. Famous for his premières or world premières of modern operas. Has also adapted or retranslated operas; was producer at the world premières of Fortner's *Der Wald*, Reutter's *The Bridge of San Luis Rey* (both in Essen) and Steffens's *Eli* (Dortmund), Henze's *Il Re Cervo* (new version of *König Hirsch*) in Kassel, 1963; later also in Munich, 1964. Also has produced the German premières of several operas, including *Der Zaubertrank* and *Der Sturm* by Frank Martin, *Karl V* by Křenek, *Lulu* by Alban Berg and *Prigioniero* (The Prisoner) by Dallapiccola.

Mises-en-scène: Berlin, Dortmund, Düsseldorf, Duisburg, Essen, Frankfurt, Karlsruhe, Kassel, Kiel, Cologne, Leipzig, Munich, Wuppertal. Was also producer in: Argentina (Buenos Aires), Belgium (Antwerp), England (London), France (Paris), Holland (Amsterdam, The Hague), Iran (Teheran), Japan (Tokyo), Switzerland (Basle, Berne, Geneva, Lausanne, Zurich), USA (Chicago). Presently at work on the Swedish première of *Lulu* in Stockholm.

RUDOLF HARTMANN

Born in Ingolstadt in 1900. After his father's death in 1911 he left for Munich, where he went to school, and decided to become an opera producer. First worked at Bamberg where, in the old E.T.H. Hoffmann Theat-er, he produced *Tosca, Manon Lescaut* and *Julius Caesar*. Went to the Staatsoper, Berlin as chief producer by way of Altenburg/Thuringia, Gera, Nuremberg. Collaborated with Erich Kleiber, Leo Blech and Clemens Krauss. Returned to Munich as director of the opera; co-producer with Clemens Krauss until 1945. After the war visiting engagements in Austria, Italy, France and Switzerland. 1951: reopening of the Bayreuth festival with *The Mastersingers*. 1952: *Staatsintendant* of the Bayerische Staatsoper; reconstruction of the Cuvilliés theatre and of the Nationaltheater. Ended his fifteen-year career as *Intendant* in 1967, and then engaged in free-lance artistic activity.

DESMOND HEELEY

English stage designer. Born in London. Worked at the National Theatre with Sir Laurence Olivier; also in Stratford/Ontario and in New York. Major mises-en-scène: *Rosencrantz and Guildenstern Are Dead, Pelléas and Mélisande, Faust* (Gounod), *Norma*.

RUDOLF HEINRICH

Born in Halle in 1926; education at the art school in Burg Giebichstein (classes in painting). Worked in the drama workshops in Halle. 1948: assistant at the municipal theatres in Leipzig. 1950–4: stage designer at the Halle theatre. 1952: taught stage design at the Halle Hochschule für Theater und Musik, 1954–63: in charge of décor at the Komische Oper, Berlin. Study trips to Italy, France, Finland, Slovakia, Albania. Accompanied the ensemble on tour to Paris, Moscow and Prague; personal visiting engagements in Sweden and Milan. 1959–60: in charge of courses on stage design for the Bayreuth Festival Meisterklasse. 1964: appointment to the Akademie der bildenden Künste in Munich. Visiting producer in Munich, Zurich, Frankfurt, Hamburg, Cologne, Vienna, London, Milan, Boston, Montreal, Halle, New York, Santa Fé and Salzburg. After completing the model for the Leipzig *Götterdämmerung* died in 1976.

BOHUMIL HERLISCHKA

Born in Čáslav, Czechoslovakia, in 1919; studied at the national conservatoire in Prague. 1946–50: producer at the National Theatre in Ostrava; from then until 1957: chief stage-manager at the National Theatre, Prague. Thereafter free-lance producer in Germany, Austria and Italy. Important mises-en-scène: *William Tell* (Vienna), *The Bartered Bride* (Milan), *Der Freischütz, Lady Macbeth of Mtsensk District, The Tales of Hoffmann* (all these operas performed in Düsseldorf), *Carmen, The Queen of Spades, The Nose* (all these operas performed in Frankfurt), *The Distant Sound* (Kassel), *The Prophet* (Berlin), *The Queen of Spades* (Munich), *Jenufa* (German television).

JOACHIM HERZ

Born in Dresden in 1924; studied music in Dresden; awarded music teaching diploma. Course in conducting and opera production at the college of music. During his studies *répétiteur* at the opera school. 1945–51: studied music at the Humboldt University, Berlin. Assistant to Heinz Arnold in Dresden. First production: *Bremer Stadtmusikanten* (Mohaupt) in the Kleines Haus of the Staatstheater in Dresden. 1951–3: producer at the Landesoper, Dresden-Radebeul; reader at the college of music. 1953–6: producer at the Komische Oper, Berlin and taught at the Humboldt University; assistant to Walter Felsenstein; visiting producer in Dresden (Staatsoper and Landesoper). 1956–7: producer in Cologne and reader at the college of music. 1957: appointment in Leipzig as chief stage-manager; since 1959: director of the opera. 1960: opening of the new opera-house with *The Mastersingers*. Visiting producer in Berlin, Moscow, Buenos Aires, Vienna, Belgrade, Hamburg, Frankfurt, London, and also worked for Danish television. Made a film of Wagner's *Flying Dutchman*. Co-operation with the National Theatre in Havana. Went on tour with the Komische Oper to Paris, Moscow and Budapest; and with the Leipzig Opera to Dresden, Berlin, Wiesbaden, Ljubljana,

Lódź, Bratislava, Brno, Prague, Ghent, Brussels and Genoa.

KURT HORRES

Born in Düsseldorf in 1932; studied drama, German philology and art history at the University of Cologne. Assistant producer at theatres in Cologne and at Komische Oper, Berlin. Producer at the municipal theatre, Bonn. 1960–4: chief stage-manager of opera at the municipal theatres, Lübeck. 1964–75: director of opera at the theatres in Wuppertal. Professor at the Staatliche Hochschule für Musik in Cologne. 1976: *Intendant* at the Staatstheater in Darmstadt.

HELMUT JÜRGENS

Born in Höxter on the Weser in 1902; went to high school in Höxter and Warburg (Westphalia). Trained with church and scene-painters in Lippspringe near Paderborn; five semesters at the polytechnic in Kassel, followed by five semesters at the Kunstakademie in Düsseldorf (attended drama classes of Professor von Wecus). At the same time worked as scene-painter and stage technician at the municipal theatres there. 1926–30: chief stage designer in Krefeld, Mönchengladbach and Aachen. 1930–8: in charge of décor at the municipal theatres in Frankfurt. Tours abroad to Budapest, Prague and Barcelona. Since 1948: chief designer of the Bayerische Staatsoper, Munich. Tours to Hamburg, Düsseldorf, Rome, London, Naples, Athens and Salzburg. 1953: taught a class on stage design at the Staatliche Kunstakademie in Munich. 1963: after completing stage designs for the opening of the Nationaltheater, Munich, died unexpectedly of heart disease before the performance. World premières: *Columbus, Chinesische Nachtigall, Danza* (all by Egk); *Die Kluge, Astutuli, Entrata* (all by Orff); *Odysseus* (Reutter), *Harmonie der Welt* (Hindemith), *La Buffonata* (Killmayer), *Elegie für junge Liebende* (Elegy for Young Lovers) (Henze), *Le Mystère de la*

Nativité (Martin). German premières: *Raskolnikoff* (Sutermeister), *A Midsummer Night's Dream* (Britten).

HERBERT VON KARAJAN

Born in Salzburg in 1908. At the age of six first public appearance as pianist. On the advice of Bernhard Paumgartner trained as conductor. 1927: début as conductor: *Fidelio,* in Salzburg. 1927–9: studied at Hochschule für Musik, Vienna; course on conducting. 1929–34: opera conductor in Ulm. 1930–4: teacher at international courses on conducting during the Salzburg Festival. Guest conductor of the Vienna Symphony Orchestra. 1935: director-general of music in Aachen. 1937: first appearance as conductor at the Staatsoper, Vienna. 1938: attains international fame with *Tristan* at the Staatsoper, Berlin. 1941: State conductor at the Staatsoper, Berlin. 1946: first concert with the Vienna Philharmonic Orchestra. From 1948: builds up the London Philharmonic Orchestra. 1950: appointed for life conductor of the London Philharmonic Orchestra. From 1950: several visiting engagements in Europe and overseas; artistic director at La Scala, Milan and the Lucerne Festival. From 1951: Salzburg Festival. 1951–2: Bayreuth Festival. From 1955: appointment for life as conductor in chief of the Berlin Philharmonic Orchestra. 1957–64: in charge of artistic matters at the Staatsoper, Vienna. From 1965: musical films taken from concerts and operas. Producer and conductor. 1966: founds the Salzburg Easter Festival, opened with Wagner's *Valkyrie.* 1969–71: artistic adviser to the Orchestre de Paris. 1973: founds the Salzburg Whitsun concerts. Tours, in particular with the Berlin Philharmonic Orchestra and the Singverein, Vienna, to all the musical centres of the world.

NIKOLAUS LEHNHOFF

Born in Hanover; studied philosophy, drama and music at the Universities of Vienna and Munich. Ph.D. 1963–6: assistant pro-

ducer at the Deutsche Oper, Berlin and at the Bayreuth Festivals (Wieland Wagner). 1966–71: stage-manager at the Metropolitan Opera, New York. Collaboration with Karl Böhm, Franco Zeffirelli, Herbert von Karajan. First staging of *Die Frau ohne Schatten* with Jörg Zimmermann and Karl Böhm at the Opéra, Paris, in 1972. Further mises-en-scène: *Tristan* with Karl Böhm and the lighting expert Heinz Mack at the Orange Festival; *Fidelio* in Bremen with Günter Uecker with textual inserts adapted by Hans Magnus Enzensberger; *Salome* in San Francisco with Karl Böhm and Jörg Zimmermann; *Blood Wedding* with Michel Raffaelli in Nuremberg; *Tristan* with Christoph von Dohnanyi in Frankfurt, lighting effects by Adolf Luther.

MARTIN MARKUN

Born in 1942; studied music (bassoon and piano) at the Musikakademie, Zurich, then studied opera in Zurich (course for producers). 1963–6: stage-manager and assistant producer at the Opernhaus, Zurich. 1967: stage-manager in Heidelberg. 1968: stage-manager at the Opernhaus, Zurich. 1970: chief stage-manager at the same opera-house. 1972: chief stage-manager at the Stadttheater, Basle.

Touring performances at the Volksoper, Vienna and Staatsoper, Brunswick as well as at Freiburg, Heidelberg and Zurich.

ULRICH MELCHINGER

Born in Frankfurt in 1937; grew up in Vienna. 1957: finished school in Stuttgart. Until 1959: assistant producer at the Staatsoper, Vienna, with Herbert von Karajan. 1959–64: assistant producer and resident stage-manager at the Staatsoper, Hamburg under Liebermann. 1964–6: chief stage-manager at the opera in Lübeck. 1966–77: chief stage-manager at the opera in Kassel. From 1977: responsible for producing operas at the Stadttheater, Freiburg.

GIAN-CARLO MENOTTI

Born in Cadegliano (near Varese, Lombardy) in 1911. Composer; since *The Medium* (1946) he himself has staged all the world premières of his operas, especially at the Festival dei due mondi in Spoleto; now also producer of operas by other composers, for example, *La Bohème*, *Pelléas and Mélisande*, *Tristan and Isolde* and *Don Giovanni*. His works include: *Amelia al ballo* (Amelia Goes to the Ball), *Amahl and the Night Visitors*, *Sebastian*, *Le dernier sauvage* (The Last Savage); *Labyrinth* (television opera); *Martin's Lie* (one-act religious opera); *Help! Help! The Globolinks!*, *The Most Important Man* (children's operas); *Tamu-Tamu* (chamber opera, based on an Indonesian theme); music for Cocteau's *Le Poète et sa muse*, *Romeo and Juliet*; *Triplo concerto a tre*; *The Death of the Bishop of Brindisi* (cantata); *Canti della lontananza* (cycle of songs). Wrote libretti for Samuel Barber's *A Hand of Bridge* and for Lukas Foss's *Introductions and Goodbyes*. Furthermore, wrote short stories, plays and scripts.

NATHANIEL MERRILL

American producer. 1974: after twenty years' experience as producer at the Metropolitan Opera, New York (with visiting performances at most of the leading opera-houses in the USA, Canada, Europe and South America) appointed resident producer and technical director at the opera in Strasbourg, where his work includes planning and administration. Mises-en-scène: *Carmen*, *Don Carlos*, *Salome*, *The Mastersingers*, *Boris Godunov* and *Der Rosenkavalier*; in New York revivals of *Turandot*, *The Mastersingers*, *Der Rosenkavalier*, *Il Trovatore* (The Troubadour).

HANS NEUGEBAUER

Studied stage design, costume and singing at the academy; appeared as baritone in Frankfurt in the Solti era; finally decided to become a producer. Since 1964: chief producer at the opera in Cologne; three mises-en-scène per season. Most striking production *Die Soldaten* (The Soldiers) by Bernd Alois Zimmermann. Visiting producer at the Chicago Lyric Opera, as well as in Tokyo, Trieste, Frankfurt, Düsseldorf, Geneva and Copenhagen. Engagements at the festivals in Glyndebourne, Wiesbaden and Schwetzingen. Latest mises-en-scène: *Eugene Onegin*, *Pelléas and Mélisande*, *Wozzeck*.

RUDOLF NOELTE

Born in Berlin in 1921; after leaving school studied German philology and philosophy at the University of Berlin. Since 1947: producer in Berlin (plays, operas, films, radio, television). 1960: awarded 'Kunstpreis' by the municipality of Berlin. 1975: awarded Bundesverdienstkreuz, 1st class.

ROBERT RAYMOND O'HEARN

Born in Elkhart, Indiana in 1921. 1943–5: member of the Art Students League. 1948–52: stage designer at the Brattle Theatre, Cambridge, Mass. Stage designer for Broadway shows: *The Relapse*, *Love's Labour Lost*, *Othello*, *The Apple Cart* and *Child of Fortune*. Assisted in the production of *Kismet*, *Pajama Game*, *My Fair Lady*, *West Side Story*. Designs for the film 'A Clerical Error.' 1959–63: stage designer at the Central City Opera House. 1958–61: stage designer to the Opera Society, Washington. Visiting producer: Metropolitan Opera House (*The Elixir of Love*, *The Mastersingers*, *Aida*, *Queen of Spades*, *Rosenkavalier*, *Parsifal*, *The Marriage of Figaro*); Los Angeles Civic Light Opera (*Kiss me Kate*, *Rosalinde*, *The Mind with the Dirty Man*); Central City Opera House (*Falstaff*, *Gianni Schicci*, *The Barber of Seville*, *A Midsummer Night's Dream*, *Scipio Africanus*); Miami Opera, Volksoper in Vienna, Karlsruhe, Kennedy Center, Bregenz Festival, Boston Opera, Santa Fé Opera, San Francisco Opera, Staatsoper in Hamburg, Strasbourg.

TEO OTTO

Born in Remscheid (Ruhr) in 1904; first studied engineering, then trained as a painter at the Kunstakademie, Kassel. Assistant at the Bauhaus in Weimar. After a spell in Paris turned to the theatre; appointed by Otto Klemperer at the Kroll opera as stage designer. 1931: in charge of décor at the Staatstheater in Berlin. 1933: emigrated to Zurich; on the advice and at the request of Leopold Lindtberg, became stage designer at Rieser's Pfauenbühne. After the war engagements in Berlin, Düsseldorf, Frankfurt, Hamburg, Munich, Volkstheater in Vienna, Piccolo Teatro di Milano, Teatro alla Scala, Royal Court Theatre in London, Metropolitan Opera House in New York.

Worked with the following producers: Peter Brook, Harry Buckwitz, Herbert Graf, Gustav Gründgens, Heinz Hilpert, Kurt Horwitz, Leopold Jessner, Leopold Lindtberg, Günther Rennert, Oscar Fritz Schuh. Died on 8 June 1968.

RICHARD PEDUZZI

Born in Argentan (Orne) in 1943; studied painting at the Académie de Dessins de la Rue Malebranche in Paris under Charles Auffret. In January 1969 meeting with Patrice Chéreau, assisted in the production of *Don Juan*. Since: designer of all Patrice Chéreau's productions.

ERNST POETTGEN

Studied history of music, drama and German philology in Berlin, Hamburg and Munich. 1951–2: assistant producer at the Bayerische Staatsoper, Munich. 1952–5: assistant producer at the municipal theatres, Frankfurt. 1955–8: assistant producer, later producer, at the Staatsoper, Hamburg. 1958–61: chief stage-manager at the Nationaltheater, Mannheim. Since 1961: chief stage-manager at the Württemberg Staatstheater, Stuttgart. Fourteen seasons at the Teatro Colón, Buenos Aires.

Festivals: Maggio musicale in Florence,

Schwetzingen, Salzburg, Edinburgh. Since 1968: regular engagements at the Théâtre de la Monnaie. Also visiting producer in Munich, Berlin, Düsseldorf, Zurich, Geneva, Vienna and Athens.

JEAN-PIERRE PONNELLE

Born in Paris; studied painting, art history and philosophy at the Sorbonne. During his studies produced the décor for the première of Henze's *Boulevard Solitude* in Hanover. Subsequently moved to and fro between the Sorbonne and Germany. After his return from serving in the army in Algeria began his career as producer, starting with Camus's *Caligula* in Düsseldorf (1961), followed by *Tristan* at the opera there. Also growing interest in the cinema. Contrary to the practice of filming stage sets for television, and thus simply reproducing them, made his own films specially designed, starting with Rossini's *The Barber of Seville,* followed by Orff's *Carmina burana,* Puccini's *Madame Butterfly* and Mozart's *The Marriage of Figaro.*

GEORG REINHARDT

Born in 1911; studied at the Philosophische Hochschule in Augsburg as well as at the Universities of Berlin and Munich. Subsequently assistant to Walter Felsenstein, Oskar Wälterlin and Hans Pfitzner. Producer, later chief producer in Frankfurt, Aachen, Lübeck, Berlin, Wiesbaden and Zurich. Director of the Opera in Wuppertal. Since 1964: director of the Deutsche Oper am Rhein (Düsseldorf/Duisburg). Visiting producer in Stuttgart, Hanover, Vienna, Paris, Nice, Brussels, Ghent (Flanders Festival), Milan, Naples, Zagreb, Stockholm, Helsinki, Edinburgh, Buenos Aires, Ankara and at the Holland Festival. Co-founder of the first Monteverdi Festival in Wuppertal in 1962. Television transmissions of productions in Munich, Hamburg, Salzburg, Naples, Brussels and Ghent. Was reader in drama at the Staatliche Hochschule für Musik, Cologne,

and at the Mozarteum in Salzburg. Now director of the opera studio of the Deutsche Oper am Rhein.

GÜNTHER RENNERT

Born in Essen in 1911; spent his childhood in Argentina; studied law and drama in Munich, Berlin and Halle. Mises-en-scène in Frankfurt as early as 1936–7; by way of Wuppertal and Mainz made his way to Berlin in 1942 and was chief stage-manager there until 1945. After the war mises-en-scène in Munich; 1946–56: *Intendant* at the Staatsoper, Hamburg. Also put on operas and plays in Vienna, Salzburg, London, Edinburgh, Milan, Naples, New York, San Francisco, Vancouver, Buenos Aires, Stockholm, Amsterdam, Florence, Athens, Berlin, Stuttgart, Munich, Frankfurt, Düsseldorf and Cologne. 1959–67: Artistic Counsellor and Chief of Production at the Glyndebourne Opera. 1967: *Intendant* of the Bayerische Staatsoper, Munich. Besides mises-en-scène adapted works by Handel, Gluck, Rossini, Prokofiev and Puccini. Since the winter semester of 1973–4: professor at the Staatliche Hochschule für Musik, Munich.

THOMAS RICHTER-FORGÁCH

Born in Komárom (Hungary) in 1940; came to Germany in 1956. 1958: Staatliche Kunstakademie, Düsseldorf; attended courses on drama by Teo Otto. 1960: assistant to Teo Otto; worked at theatres in Salzburg, Vienna, Munich and Amsterdam. 1962: chief of décor at the Kammerspiele, Düsseldorf. 1963–6: chief of décor at the municipal theatres, Ulm. 1964–6: taught drama at the Staatliche Kunstakademie, Düsseldorf. 1966–72: chief stage designer at the Staatstheater, Kassel. 1972–6: chief stage designer at the Düsseldorf Schauspielhaus.

Visiting engagements to Vienna, Basle, Amsterdam, Berlin, Munich, Stuttgart, Hamburg, Graz, Antwerp and Karlsruhe.

JÜRGEN ROSE

Born in Bernburg on the Saale in 1937. After leaving the Odenwaldschule worked as assistant at the Landestheater, Darmstadt with Gustav Rudolf Sellner and F. Mertz. 1958–60: studied at the Akademie der bildenden Künste, Berlin and at the M. Ludwig School of Drama, Berlin. 1959–61: appointment at the municipal theatres, Ulm as stage designer and actor. 1961–7: worked at the Munich Kammerspiele as stage designer. 1963: awarded 'Bundesfilm in Gold' for the décor of the film 'Das schwarz-weiss-rote Himmelbett'. 1962–73: worked closely with the choreographer John Cranko in Stuttgart, Munich, New York and London. 1965–9: mostly worked on décor for plays produced by Rudolf Noelte and H. Lietzau. Since 1970: décors for operas on international stages: *Salome, Don Carlos, The Mastersingers* (Staatsoper, Vienna), *Der Rosenkavalier, Don Giovanni, La Traviata, Così fan tutte* (Deutsche Oper, Berlin), *Masked Ball* (London), *Salome, Der Rosenkavalier* (Scala, Milan), *Tannhäuser* (Bayreuth), *Wozzeck* (Salzburg). Since 1972: collaborated on many occasions with the choreographer John Neumeier. 1973: professor at the Staatliche Akademie der bildenden Künste, Stuttgart; holds the Chair of Drama and Art.

OTTO SCHENK

Born in Vienna in 1930; studied at the Reinhardtseminar in Vienna; in addition to this passed his first law examination at the University of Vienna. Acted at the Volkstheater and the Theater in der Josefstadt. Made a name for himself as an opera producer. Mises-en-scène: in Frankfurt, Stuttgart, Berlin, Munich, Zurich, New York, Salzburg, etc.; also for television. Since 1966: permanent appointment as producer at the Staatsoper, Vienna. Major works in Vienna: *Lulu* (1962, 1968), *Der Rosenkavalier* (1968) and *Fidelio.*

HANS ULRICH SCHMÜCKLE

Born in Ulm in 1916; 1932–5: voluntary

work at the Staatstheater, Stuttgart. Pupil of the painter Adolf Hölzel. 1935–7: studied at the Akademie der bildenden Künste, Munich under Karl Caspar; also with the art historian Hans Hildebrand in Stuttgart. 1946–9: stage designer at the Schauspielhaus and at the Kammerspiele, Stuttgart. Began to work with the costume designer Sylta Busse. 1950–2: visiting stage designer at the Württemberg national theatres, Stuttgart. 1954: in charge of décor at the municipal theatres, Augsburg. Décors in Berlin, Salzburg, Naples, Florence, Brussels, Tel Aviv, Leipzig, Glasgow, Zurich; also for the première of Peter Weiss's *Die Ermittlung,* Heinar Kipphardt's *In der Sache J. Robert Oppenheimer* and Rolf Hochhuth's *Die Hebamme.*

GÜNTHER SCHNEIDER-SIEMSSEN

Born in Augsburg in 1926. 1941–6: studied at the Akademie für angewandte Kunst and at the Akademie der bildenden Künste, Munich, under Ludwig Sievert and Emil Preetorius, also drama under Artur Kutscher and opera under Rudolf Hartmann. 1947–9: director of the Junges Theater, Munich. First appointment at the Lustspielhaus, Munich-Schwabing; Staatsoperette, Munich. 1949–51: built film sets in Munich-Geiselgasteig and Berlin-Tempelhof: seven feature films. 1951–4: engagement at the Landestheater, Salzburg. 1954–62: chief of décor at the Staatstheater, Bremen. 1952–72: permanently associated with the 'Salzburger Marionetten'. 1960: first mise-en-scène with Herbert von Karajan. Since 1962: chief stage designer at the Staatsoper, Vienna with simultaneous engagement at the Burgtheater and the Volksoper. 1962–4: personal adviser to Herbert von Karajan on matters of décor. Since 1969: chief instructor of stage design at the Internationale Sommerakademie für bildende Kunst, Salzburg.

Engagements in Stuttgart, Cologne, Frankfurt, Nuremberg, Düsseldorf, Zurich, Geneva, Sofia, London, Buenos Aires and Chicago. Visiting producer in New York, Munich, Hamburg and Moscow.

Major mises-en-scène: *Fidelio* (with Karajan, 1962; Schenk, 1970), *Rosenkavalier, Faust, Ring* (with Karajan, New York, 1967), *Fledermaus* (Bat), *Parsifal, Moses and Aron.* World première of Orff's *De Temporum Fine Comoedia* with August Everding at the Salzburg Festival.

OSCAR FRITZ SCHUH

Born in Munich in 1904. Studied art history, philosophy and German philology at the University of Munich. 1924: assistant drama adviser at the Bayerische Landesbühne, Munich, where his talents as a producer were discovered; later worked in Oldenburg, Osnabrück and Darmstadt. 1928–31: engagement at Gera. 1931–2: season at Prague. 1932–40: appointment at the Staatsoper, Hamburg, as producer, drama adviser and head of art department. 1940–1: chief stage-manager at the Staatsoper, Vienna. 1947–66: Salzburg Festival: premières of operas and of works by O'Neill. 1953–8: head of the Theater am Kurfürstendamm, Berlin. 1960–3: *Intendant* at the Opera, Cologne. 1963–8: *Intendant* at the Schauspielhaus, Hamburg. Visiting producer in Salzburg, Milan, Rome, London, Naples and Zurich.

WERNER SCHULZ

Born at Spremberg (now in the DDR) in 1929. After leaving school, studied at the Meisterschule für Kunsthandwerk, Berlin. First appointment at the Hans-Otto-Theater, Potsdam. Since 1962: chief stage designer at the Metropoltheater, Berlin. Visiting stage designer at the Deutsche Staatsoper, Berlin, as well as in Prague and Leningrad. Was also involved in making the film version of *Orpheus in the Underworld.*

GUSTAV RUDOLF SELLNER

Born at Traunstein (Upper Bavaria) in 1905. Already as a schoolboy in Munich came into close contact with the theatre and opera.

Studied drama under Arnold Marlé, of the Kammerspiele in Munich, for two semesters. First engagements at the Bayerische Landesbühne, Munich, the Nationaltheater in Mannheim, and the Landestheater in Oldenburg; at the latter secured his first contract as deputy drama adviser and assistant producer. In 1927 went to Gotha as drama adviser and chief stage-manager, where he put on his own adaptations of the classics (*Die Räuber:* without Amalia) and a lot of Brecht. In 1929 went to the Landestheater at Coburg and in 1932 returned to Oldenburg, first in the same job but later as artistic director and deputy to the chief *Intendant.* First became *Intendant* in his own right in 1940 in Göttingen, from where he went to the Deutsche Theater, Hanover, until it was closed down. Called up for military service at the end of 1943. In 1948 head of drama and operatic producer in Kiel. Visiting producer at the Schauspielhaus, Hamburg, and in Essen, where he was head of drama. 1951–61: *Intendant* at Darmstadt. Visiting stage designer at Munich, Hamburg, Recklinghausen, Vienna and Brussels; also made a tour of Scandinavia. In 1959: German première of Schönberg's *Moses and Aron* at the Städtische Oper, Berlin; after this he was appointed to this house. 1961–72: *Generalintendant* at the Deutsche Oper, Berlin. Formed an ensemble in close collaboration with Ferenc Fricsay, Lorin Maazel, and (after Fricsay's death) above all with Karl Böhm and Egon Seefehlner. In addition to his own guest performances, took the ensemble to Paris, Vienna, Milan, Rome, Brussels, Helsinki, Edinburgh, Zagreb, Belgrade, Mexico, Korea, Tokyo and Osaka.

HERMANN SOHERR

Born in Mannheim in 1924. After leaving school in 1943, studied at the Kunstakademie and the Staatsoper in Munich under Emil Preetorius and Ludwig Sievert. First engagement in 1946. Until 1956 worked at the municipal theatres, Frankfurt; from 1957–61: chief of décor in Mainz. 1962–3: worked at Oberhausen, Nuremberg and Wuppertal. From 1964: at the Deutsche

Oper am Rhein, Düsseldorf. Guest appearances in Amsterdam, Berlin, Buenos Aires, Dortmund, Mannheim, Munich, Schwetzingen and Vienna. From 1954: worked for television in Baden-Baden, Frankfurt and Munich.

GIORGIO STREHLER

Born at Barcola (Trieste) in 1921. Studied at the Accademia Filodrammatici, Milan, and became an actor with a travelling company. 1947: founded the Piccolo Teatro di Milano with Paolo Grassi. Major operatic mises-en-scène: *Ariadne on Naxos, Lulu, Giuditta, Il Matrimonio Segreto* (The Secret Marriage), *The Abduction from the Seraglio, The Fiery Angel, The Soldier's Tale, Rise and Fall of the City of Mahagonny, Simone Boccanegra.* D.Litt. and Ph.D. h.c. of the University of Rome. Awarded the Hansische Goethepreis and the Max Reinhard sceptre; and is member of the Grand Order of Chivalry for services to the Republic of Italy.

LADISLAV ŠTROS

Born at Hušinec near Prague in 1926. Went to school in Prague and later studied art history there. Was attracted for some years to sculpture, but eventually decided on a stage career. First theatrical appointment in 1945. From 1959: chief stage-manager at the National Theatre, Prague. Taught at the Conservatory (drama classes for opera-singers). Visiting stage designer in the USSR, Poland, Bulgaria, Austria, Germany, England, Switzerland, Belgium, Netherlands, France and Italy. Has also designed the sets for works he has produced himself.

VLADIMÍR SUCHÁNEK

Born in 1934. Trained at a craft school and at the College of Music and Drama. 1962: appointment at the Slovak National Theatre, Bratislava. Major mises-en-scène: *Who's Afraid of Virginia Woolf, The Witches of*

Salem, The Idiot, Cyrano de Bergerac, King John, King Lear.

JOSEPH SVOBODA

Born at Čáslav in 1920. 1945–51: studied at the Academy of Arts, Prague. 1945–8: chief of décor at the Grand Opera of 5th May, Prague. 1948–51: stage designer at the National Theatre, Prague. From 1951: chief of décor and artistic and technical director at the National Theatre, Prague. 1958: honorary member of the National Theatre. Awarded Grand Prix of Expo '58, Brussels for his laterna magica; honorary diploma for the 'antennae transformer'; gold medal for the exhibition 'Histoire des Glaces'. 1961–70: exhibition of all his works in all great theatrical centres of Europe. 1967: British critics' prize for best décor of the season. 1969: Nederlandse Sikkenprijs. Honorary doctorate from the Royal College of Art, London. Professor of architecture at the Academy of Arts, Prague.

ROUBEN TER-ARUTUNIAN

Born in Tiflis (USSR) in 1920, to an Armenian family. Went to school in Berlin, where he trained to become a concert pianist. 1939–41: studied at the Reimann art school. 1941–2: College of Music: took course on film music. 1941–5: studied art history, drama, literature and philosophy in Berlin and Vienna. 1945–7: stage and costume designer for the American Third Army Special Services in Western Germany; also decorated club-houses for them. 1947–50: Ecole des Beaux-Arts, Atelier Souverbie: took courses in painting and sculpture. Académie Julian, Académie de la Grande Chaumière. From 1951: in the United States. Décor for premières of works by Edward Albee, Samuel Barber, Lukas Foss, Hans Werner Henze, Peggy Glanville-Hicks, Lee Hoiby, Noeman dello Joio, Gian-Carlo Menotti and Igor Stravinsky.

Major works: Broadway production of Brecht's *Arturo Ui,* Debussy's *Pelléas and*

Mélisande, The Nutcracker Suite, Die sieben Todsünden, Laborintus.

GÜNTHER UECKER

Born in Mecklenburg in 1930; studied at Wismar and at the colleges of Berlin-Weissensee and Düsseldorf. 1955–6: executed a number of paintings in which colour was treated as a source of energy; structured paint to convey a sense of vibration and to excite the viewer erotically. Also horizontal and structured images. 1957: first used three-dimensional volumes and prefabricated elements as vehicles for paint; also made first 'nail pictures'; first white structured objects to reflect colour values. 1960: first revolving structured discs, exhibited at the Festival d'art avant-garde, Paris. 1961: first demonstration of a nail object shown horizontally and encircled by light. 1962: with Mack and Piene, inaugurated a Salon de lumière at the Stedelijk Museum, Amsterdam. 1964: awarded a prize by province of North Rhine Westphalia. With Mack and Piene, first Zero exhibition in New York, later also in Philadelphia and Washington. Exhibitions of kinetic work in Montreal, Ulm, Düsseldorf, Baden-Baden, Dortmund, Berne, New York, Paris, Venice, Ithaca, Osaka, Boston, Brussels, Berlin, Basle, Milan, Stockholm, Cracow, St. Gallen, Nuremberg and Bochum. 1974: stage designs for *Fidelio* in Bremen; and in 1976 for *Parsifal* in Stuttgart.

JOSÉ VARONA

Born in Argentina in 1930; in 1951 began his career as costume and stage designer for the Ballet Nacional de Cuyo. During the next ten years worked in Buenos Aires as stage and costume designer for opera, ballet, drama, television and cinema. Participated in numerous ensembles, *inter alia* for the New York Shakespeare Festival, the opera-houses of San Francisco and Vancouver, and notably the New York City Opera, where on numerous occasions he collaborated with Tito Capobianco as producer. In

Europe designed sets for *Julius Caesar* (Hamburg), *Attila* and *Aida* (Berlin Opera), *Rodelinda* (Amsterdam) and *The Troubadour* (Paris).

WIELAND WAGNER

Born in Bayreuth in 1917; designed stage sets at an early age; in 1938 studied painting under Ferdinand Staeger in Munich. 1940: studied music intensively under Kurt Overhoff. 1942: stage design for *The Flying Dutchman* in Nuremberg; decided that henceforth he would create sets in operas of which he was also the producer. 1943: went to Altenburg as chief stage-manager. 1948: returned to Bayreuth; first negotiations concerning the resumption of the Bayreuth Festival. 1949: Wieland and Wolfgang Wagner took charge of the festival, which was reinaugurated in 1951. Also did many guest productions. Died in 1966.

WOLFGANG WAGNER

Born in Bayreuth in 1919. 1940: worked directly for the Bayreuth Festival as *Inspizient*. Assistant at the Preussische Staatsoper, Berlin; simultaneously studied music privately and was concerned with all theoretical and practical problems relating to operas and the like. 1944: first independent mise-en-scène: *Andreasnacht* at the Staatsoper, Berlin. 1949: together with Wieland Wagner, in charge of the Bayreuth Festival. 1952: led a tour of the Bayreuth ensemble to Naples, also with Wieland Wagner. 1953:

first new production of *Lohengrin* in Bayreuth. Guest productions in Brunswick, Rome, Venice, Bologna, Osaka. From 1966: solely responsible for the Bayreuth Festival. Has directed no less than 240 performances at the festivals from 1953 to 1975.

HEINRICH WENDEL

Born in Bremen in 1915 as the son of Ernst Wendel, director-general of music; went to secondary school; from the age of nine intensive interest in painting. 1929: accompanied his father on concert tours; in Florence copied old masters, using their original techniques. 1930: worked privately with models of stage designs (studied drama, photography, optics, history of philosophy and astronomy). 1931–5: training as stage designer, went to art school in Bremen; Akademie am Steinplatz, Berlin; Theaterkunststätten, Berlin; Staatliches Schauspielhaus und Kunstakademie, Hamburg. 1935–43: stage designer in Stendal and Halberstadt, later in charge of décor in Wuppertal and Nuremberg. 1945–7: chief of décor at the Wurttemberg national theatres in Stuttgart. 1947–50: free-lance painter and stage designer at several German theatres, regular engagement at the Staatstheater, Stuttgart as well as at Wiesbaden and the Deutsches Theater, Göttingen. 1950–64: in charge of décor at the theatres in Wuppertal. From 1964 in charge of décor at the Deutsche Oper am Rhein, Düsseldorf.

Visiting engagements in Salzburg, Berlin,

Vienna and Milan. Archaeological expeditions and publications.

FRANCO ZEFFIRELLI

Born in Florence in 1923, studied architecture in Florence and worked with Visconti as assistant producer and actor. As producer of operas attained international fame with Rossini's *La Cenerentola* (Milan, 1953). Usually also designed the sets and costumes. Major mises-en-scène: *The Elixir of Love, Falstaff, Rigoletto, Don Giovanni, Orfeo, Euridice, La Bohème*. As producer of plays won special merit through his Shakespeare productions (also in film versions).

JÖRG ZIMMERMANN

Born in Zurich in 1933. Studied stage design at the craft school in Zurich. 1950: Schauspielhaus, Zurich; assistant to Teo Otto. 1952: stage designer at the Schauspielhaus, Hamburg. During the first years of his career mainly put on plays, later also operas: Staatsoper in Vienna, Nationaltheater in Munich, Opernhaus in Zurich, l'Opéra in Paris, Teatro alla Scala in Milan, Berlin and Stockholm. Festivals: Salzburg, Bayreuth, Berlin, Vienna, Edinburgh, Holland Festival, Aix-en-Provence. Collaborated with: Fritz Kortner, Günther Rennert, Gustav Rudolf Sellner, August Everding, Karl Böhm, Rafael Kubelik, Eugen Jochum and Wolfgang Sawallisch.

Bibliography

For: Stage Design in the History of the European Theatre

Alewyn, R. and Sälzle, K.: *Das grosse Welttheater.* Hamburg, 1959 — Appia, A.: *Die Musik und die Inszenierung.* Munich, 1899 — Bayer, H., Gropius, W. and Gropius, I. (eds.): *Bauhaus 1919–1928.* 3rd enlarged edition, Stuttgart, 1955. (English ed.: Bayer, H. *et al.: Bauhaus 1919–1928.* London 1976) — Borcherdt, H.H.: *Das europäische Theater im Mittelalter und in der Renaissance.* Hamburg, 1969. — Burchartz, M.: *Gleichnis der Harmonie.* Munich, 1949 — Freedley, G. and Reevers J.A.: *A History of the Theatre.* New York, 1941 — Frey, D.: *Kunstwissenschaftliche Grundfragen.* Vienna, 1946 — Gaehde, C.: *Das Theater,* Leipzig, 1921 — Gollwitzer, G.: *Die Kunst als Zeichen.* Munich, 1958 — Hauser, A.: *Sozialgeschichte der Kunst und der Literatur.* 2 vols. Munich, 1953. (English version: *The social history of art,* trsl. S. Godman. 4 vols. London, 1969) — Kindermann, H.: *Theatergeschichte Europas.* 9 vols. Salzburg, 1957–70 — Kindermann, H.: *Bühne und Zuschauerraum.* Austrian Academy of Science (Phil. Hist. 245/1), Vienna, 1964 — Klee, P.: *Das bildnerische Denken.* Basle, 1956. (Engl. ed.: *The Thinking Eye,* ed. J. Spiller, trsl. R. Manheim. London, 1961) — Laban, R. von: *Die Welt des Tanzes.* Stuttgart, 1920. (Engl. ed.: *A Life for Dance; Reminiscenes,* trsl. and annot. L. Ullmann. London, 1975) — Mello, B.: *Trattato di scenotecnica.* Milan, 1962 — Merloo, J.A.M.: *Rhythmus und Ekstase.* Vienna, 1959 — Melchinger, S.: *Theater der Gegenwart.* Frankfurt, 1956 — Melchinger, S.: *Atlantisbuch des Theaters.* Zurich, 1966 — Parker, W.O. and Smith, H.K.: *Scene Design and Stage Lighting.* New York, 1968 — Pignarre, R.: *Geschichte des Theaters.* Hamburg, 1960 — Pörtner, P.: *Experiment Theater.* Zurich, 1960 — Ronge, H. (ed.): *Kunst und Kybernetik.* (Report on three art education sessions held in 1965, 1966 and 1967). Cologne, 1968 — Schöne, G: *Tausend Jahre deutsches Theater.* Munich, 1962 — Schuberth, O.: *Das Bühnenbild.* Munich, 1955 — Sellner, G.R.: *Theatralische Landschaft.* Bremen, 1962.

For: The stage as cosmic space

Becsi, K. (ed.): *Die Bühne als kosmischer Raum. Zum Bühnenbildschaffen von Günther Schneider-Siemssen.* Vienna, 1976.

The publishers wish to acknowledge gratefully permission to reproduce passages from the following books: Dent, E.J.: *The Barber of Seville,* trsl., O.U.P., London, 1940 — Dent, E.J.: *Don Giovanni,* trsl., O.U.P., London, 1965 — Dent, E.J.: *Don Pasquale,* trsl., O.U.P., London, 1946 — Dent, E.J.: *Fidelio,* trsl., Boosey & Hawkes, London, n.d. — Dent, E.J.: *The Magic Flute,* trsl., O.U.P., London 1937 — Giovaninetti, R. and Ponnelle, J.P.: Programme of the Bavarian State Opera, Munich, for *Pelléas and Mélisande,* 1973 — Grosse, H.: 'Thomas Richter-Forgách. Szenische Entwürfe zu Richard Wagners Musikdramen'. Programme for an exhibition of the Institute of Theatrical Science, University of Cologne, on behalf of Deutsche Bank, Bayreuth. 26th July–28th August, 1976 — Jameson, F.: *Götterdämmerung,* trsl., G. Schirmer, New York, n.d. — Jameson, F.: *Die Meistersinger von Nürnberg,* trsl., London Coliseum, 1968 — Noelte, R.: 'Eine Nacht im Leben und Sterben des Don Giovanni', in *Opernwelt,* Erhard Friedrich Verlag, Seelze, 1974, pp. 7–11 — Rennert, G.: *Opernarbeit. Inszenierungen 1963–1973.* Deutscher Taschenbuch Verlag, Munich, 1974 — Rennert, G. and Schneider-Siemssen, G.: 'Anmerkungen zur Inszenierung der *Frau ohne Schatten*' in *Opernwelt,* Erhard Friedrich Verlag, Seelze, 1974 — Schaefer, H.J.: 'Stimmung ist nichts, Kenntnis alles!' A conversation with Ulrich Melchinger in Kassel Staatstheater Programme Notes for 1973–1974 — Strehler, G.: *Für ein menschliches Theater,* Suhrkamp, Frankfurt, 1975 — Uecker, G.: 'Eine Arbeits-Chronik' in Programme Notes, Bremen 1974 — Wagner, W.: (No title) in *Opernwelt,* Erhard Friedrich Verlag, Seelze, 1963, p. 19.

The technical data have been kindly provided by the various operahouses. In part they coincide with the data published in the *Deutsches Bühnenjahrbuch 1977.*

TRANSLATOR'S NOTE

For the English edition, the translator has consulted the following libretti or vocal scores: — *Don Giovanni,* E.J. Dent's translation, Oxford University Press, London, 1965 — *The Magic Flute.* E.J. Dent's translation, Oxford University Press, London, 1937 — *Fidelio,* E.J. Dent's translation, Boosey & Hawkes (Royal ed.) London, n.d. — *The Barber of Seville,* E.J. Dent's translation, Oxford University Press, London, 1940 — *Don Pasquale,* E.J. Dent's translation, Oxford University Press, London, 1946 — *Die Meistersinger von Nürnberg,* F. Jameson's translation, London Coliseum, 1968 — *Götterdämmerung,* F. Jameson's translation, G. Schirmer, New York, n.d. — *The Tales of Hoffmann,* R. & T. Martin's translation, G. Schirmer, New York, 1967 — For *Don Carlos, Pelléas and Mélisande,* and *Die Frau ohne Schatten,* the translator has consulted directly the original scores.
A.J.P.

Picture credits

Illustrations of sets and workshops have been kindly contributed by:

Archives of the Salzburg Festspiele: *The Magic Flute* 1967 (7 sets); *Don Giovanni* 1968 (6 sets); *Fidelio* 1968 (4 sets); *Barber of Seville* 1968 (3 sets); *Don Pasquale* 1971 (7 sets); *Die Frau ohne Schatten* 1974 (6 sets); *Don Carlos* 1975 (5 sets) — Archives of the Technical Administration of the Vienna State Opera: *Don Giovanni* 1972 (6 sets); *The Mastersingers* 1975 (pp. 175, 178) — Foto-Sepp Bär, Kassel: *Götterdämmerung* 1974 (4 sets) — Festspiel Administration, Bayreuth: *The Mastersingers* 1963 (p. 174); *Götterdämmerung* 1965 (p. 193); *The Mastersingers* 1968 (pp. 167, 172, 176, 178); *Götterdämmerung* 1976 (5 sets) — Beth Bergmann ©, New York: *Pelléas and Mélisande* 1972 (3 sets) — Rudolf Betz, Munich: (p. 67) — Ilse Buhs, Berlin: *Die Frau ohne Schatten* 1964 (5 sets); *Don Giovanni* 1973 (5 sets) — Pantelis Dessyllas, Vienna: (9 workshop illustrations, pp. 33–4) — Rudolf Eimke, Düsseldorf: (pp. 45–7, 2 sets each; p. 48 below): *The Tales of Hoffmann* 1969 (4 sets); *Fidelio* 1971 (4 sets); *Don Carlos* 1972 (6 sets) — Photo Fayer, Vienna: *Fidelio* 1970 (3 sets); *Don Carlos* 1970 (6 sets); *The Magic Flute* 1974 (pp. 98, 100, 104: one set each); *The Mastersingers* 1975 (pp. 172, 176) — Teatro Comunale Firenze (Foto Marchiori): *Fidelio* 1969 (4 sets) — Heinrich Fürtinger and Hans Ulrich Schmückle, Augsburg: *Don Giovanni* 1972 Augsburg (6 sets) — Foto Hausmann, Vienna: *Götterdämmerung* 1970 (p. 182) — Ulrich Horn: (p. 45) — Martin Hürlimann, Zürich: (p. 22) — Anne Kirchbach, Söcking–Starnberg: *The Magic Flute* 1970 (6 sets); *Götterdämmerung* 1976 Munich (4 sets) — Fred Kliché, Düsseldorf: (p. 48, top) — Siegfried Lauterwasser, Überlingen: (p. 54: lowermost sets); *The Mastersingers* 1963 (pp. 166, 173, 177, 178): *The Mastersingers* 1968 (p. 174); *The Mastersingers* 1974 (4 sets); *Götterdämmerung* 1965 (pp. 181, 197, 199); *Götterdämmerung* 1970 (pp. 193, 195, 197, 199) — Metropolitan Opera Ass. Inc. Press Dept. © by ADAGP, Paris and COSMOPRESS, Geneva: *The Magic Flute* 1967 (p. 102: 1 set) — Werner Neumeister, Munich: *The Magic Flute* 1970 (p. 104: 1 set) — Robert O'Hearn/Nathaniel Merrill, New York: *Die Frau ohne Schatten* 1966 (pp. 240, 247, 248) — Stefan Odry, Cologne: *Don Giovanni* 1971 (5 sets); *Pelléas and Mélisande* 1974 (3 sets) — Paris, L'Opéra: *The Tales of Hoffmann* 1974 (5 sets) — Erio Piccagliani, Milan: *Don Carlos* 1968 (6 sets); *Pelléas and Mélisande* 1972 (5 sets); *Fidelio* 1974 Milan (4 sets) — Günther Rennert, Munich © by ADAGP, Paris and COSMOPRESS, Geneva: *The Magic Flute* 1967 (p. 109–10: 1 set each) — E.M. Rydberg, Stockholm: *Die Frau ohne Schatten* 1975 (6 sets) — Foto Studio Santvoort, Wuppertal: *The Tales of Hoffmann* 1973 (5 sets) — Werner Schloske, Stuttgart: *Die Frau ohne Schatten* 1970 (4 sets); *Don Pasquale* 1972 (2 sets) — Marion Schöne, Berlin (DDR): *Don Pasquale* 1974 (4 sets) — Charles Sorlier, Paris © by ADAGP, Paris and COSMOPRESS, Geneva: *The Magic Flute* 1967 (p. 93: 1 set; p. 105: 1 set) — Eduard Straub, Meerbusch: *The Magic Flute* 1972 (7 sets); *Pelléas and Mélisande* 1973 (5 sets) — Hildegard Steinmetz, Gräfelfing (4 sets: p. 54) — Peter Stöckli, Basle: *The Barber of Seville* 1973 (3 sets) — Joseph Svoboda, Prague: *Götterdämmerung* 1976 London (5 sets) — Jaromir Svoboda, Prague: *The Tales of Hoffmann* 1971 (4 sets) — Sydney Opera House: *The Barber of Seville* 1974 (3 sets); *The Tales of Hoffmann* 1974 (5 sets) — Theatermuseum, Munich (formerly Clara-Ziegler Stiftung) (Photo: Rudolf Betz): *The Mastersingers* 1963 (5 sets) — Sabine Toeppfer, Munich: (p. 68: 2 sets) — Kamil Vyskočil, Bratislava: *Don Pasquale* 1973 (4 sets) — Helga Wallmüller, Leipzig: *The Magic Flute* 1975 (pp. 108, 110; 1 set each); *Götterdämmerung* 1976 (5 sets) — Foto Wolleh, Düsseldorf: *Fidelio* 1974 Bremen (7 sets).

Sets, costume designs and sketches:

Archives of the Vienna State Opera: *Don Giovanni* 1972 (2 designs, p. 76); *The Magic Flute* 1974 (2 costume designs) — Inge Diettrich, Düsseldorf: *Don Carlos* 1972 (2 costume designs, p. 151) — Liselotte Erler, Düsseldorf: *Fidelio* 1971 (costume designs, p. 117) — Günther Fleckenstein, Göttingen: *Don Pasquale* 1972 (2 designs, pp. 137, 145) — Achim Freyer, Berlin: *Pelléas and Mélisande* 1974 (design, p. 218) — Heinrich Fürtinger and Hans Ulrich Schmückle, Augsburg: *Don Giovanni* 1972 (p. 78–9) — Sylta Busse, Augsburg: *Don Giovanni,* 1972 (4 costume designs, pp. 78–9) — Heinz Bruno Gallée, Linz: original drawings (pp. 15, 16, 21) — Pet Halmen: *The Tales of Hoffmann* 1969 (4 costume designs, p. 201) — Rudolf Heinrich, Munich: *The Magic Flute* 1974 (1 costume design each on pp. 97, 101, 102) — Institut für Theaterwissenschaft, Cologne University: *Götterdämmerung* 1974 (p. 183) — Cläre Jürgens, Munich: *The Mastersingers* 1963 (design, p. 165) — Robert O'Hearn and Nathaniel Merrill, New York: *Die Frau ohne Schatten* 1966 (design, p. 233, 3 costume designs, pp. 244 [2], 247 [1]) — Metropolitan Opera Ass. Inc. Press Dept.: *Die Frau ohne Schatten* 1966 (2 costume designs, p. 244) — Jean-Pierre Ponnelle, Munich: *Pelléas and Mélisande* 1973 (design, p. 217) — Jürgen Rose, Munich: design (p. 79), 3 costume designs (p. 84); *Don Carlos* 1970, 2 costume designs (p. 151); *The Mastersingers* 1975 (design p. 169), costume designs (p. 170) — Günther Schneider-Siemssen, Vienna: designs (pp. 39, 40 [2], 53 [3]), *Pelléas and Mélisande* 1962 (6 designs); *Fidelio* 1970 (4 designs, p. 115); *Don Carlos* 1975 (1 design, p. 152); *The Mastersingers* 1974 (1 design, p. 168); *Die Frau ohne Schatten* (1 design, p. 238) — Werner Schulz, Berlin (DDR): *Don Pasquale* 1974 (1 costume design, p. 139) — Georges Wakhevitch: *Pelléas and Mélisande* 1962 (1 costume design, p. 228) — Heinrich Wendel, Düsseldorf: 4 original sketches (p. 44).

Our thanks to all the artists, archives of the various opera-houses and photographers who have been kind enough to let us have original designs, photographs and transparencies.

Acknowledgments

The editor and publisher are most grateful to all those who have contributed to the success of this book with interviews, articles and photographs. In addition to the producers, stage designers and photographers directly involved in the making of this book, we would also express our thanks to Dr. Oswald Georg Bauer, Bayreuth; David Colville, Sydney; Kveta Dibarborová, Bratislava; Doris Hauns, Berlin; Dr. Klaus-Peter Kehr, Cologne; Dr. Lothar Knessl, Vienna; Helga Kostens, New York; Dr. Ilka Kügler, Düsseldorf; Jane Lambert, London; Erna Neunteufel, Salzburg; Dr. Hans Joachim Schaefer, Kassel; Othmar Schwarz, Salzburg; Dr. Hans Widrich, Salzburg, and Eva Maria von Wildemann, Munich.

This book was printed in July 1977 by Imprimerie Paul Attinger SA, Neuchâtel
Setting: Filmsatz Stauffer + Cie, Basle
Photolithos: Schwitter AG, Basle
Binding: Mayer & Soutter SA, Renens
Production and Lay-out: Franz Stadelmann

Printed and bound in Switzerland